ATTENTION

DEFICIT

DISORDERS

ASSESSMENT AND TEACHING

Attention

Deficit

Disorders

Assessment
and Teaching

Janet W. Lerner
Northeastern Illinois University

Barbara Lowenthal
Northeastern Illinois University

Sue R. Lerner

Brooks/Cole Publishing Company

I(T)P™ An International Thomson Publishing Company

Pacific Grove • Albany • Bonn • Boston • Cincinnati • Detroit • London • Madrid • Melbourne
Mexico City • New York • Paris • San Francisco • Singapore • Tokyo • Toronto • Washington

Sponsoring Editor: *Vicki Knight*
Marketing Representative: *Elizabeth Covello*
Marketing Team: *Frank Barnett and*
  Roxane Buck Ezcurra
Editorial Associate: *Lauri Banks Ataide*
Production Editor: *Laurel Jackson*
Production Assistant: *Tessa A. McGlasson*
Manuscript Editor: *Lynne Y. Fletcher*

Permissions Editor: *Elaine Jones*
Interior and Cover Design: *Susan H. Horovitz*
Cover Photo: *Elizabeth Crews*
Interior Illlustration: *Susan H. Horovitz*
Photo Editor: *Kathleen Olson*
Typesetting: *Bookends Typesetting*
Printing and Binding: *Malloy Lithographing,*
  Inc.

For more information, contact:

BROOKS/COLE PUBLISHING COMPANY
511 Forest Lodge Road
Pacific Grove, CA 93950
USA

International Thomson Publishing Europe
Berkshire House 168–173
High Holborn
London WC1V 7AA
England

Thomas Nelson Australia
102 Dodds Street
South Melbourne, 3205
Victoria, Australia

Nelson Canada
1120 Birchmount Road
Scarborough, Ontario
Canada M1K 5G4

International Thomson Editores
Campos Eliseos 385, Piso 7
Col. Polanco
11560 México D. F. México

International Thomson Publishing GmbH
Königswinterer Strasse 418
53227 Bonn
Germany

International Thomson Publishing Asia
221 Henderson Road
#05–10 Henderson Building
Singapore 0315

International Thomson Publishing Japan
Hirakawacho Kyowa Building, 3F
2-2-1 Hirakawacho
Chiyoda-ku, Tokyo 102
Japan

Printed in the United States of America.

10 9 8 7 6 5 4 3 2 1

Library of Congress Cataloging-in-Publication Data

Lerner, Janet W.
  Attention deficit disorders : assessment and teaching / by Janet
W. Lerner, Barbara Lowenthal, Sue R. Lerner.
    p. cm. — (Brooks/Cole special education series)
  Includes bibliographical references and index.
  ISBN 0-534-25044-0
  1. Attention-deficit disordered children—Education—United
States. 2. Attention-deficit hyperactivity disorder—Diagnosis.
I. Lowenthal, Barbara, [date] . II. Lerner, Sue R., [date]
LC4713.4.L47 1994
371.93—dc20
                                              94-20274
                                              CIP

To the parents of children with attention deficit disorders for their commitment, dedication, and steadfast efforts as advocates for their children.

BRIEF CONTENTS

CONTENTS

CHAPTER 5
TEACHING STUDENTS
WITH ADD
IN THE REGULAR
CLASSROOM   88

CHAPTER 6
SPECIAL EDUCATION
INTERVENTIONS   122

CHAPTER 7
THE FAMILY SYSTEM: PARENT TRAINING TRAINING, COUNSELING, AND HOME MANAGEMENT 152

This book is written for regular classroom teachers, special education teachers, other school personnel (such as school psychologists, counselors, social workers, administrators, and so on), parents, and prospective teachers. It provides basic information about attention deficit disorders (ADD) and will prepare current and prospective teachers and other school personnel to teach and work with students with ADD in the schools. Designed to be a practical guide for teachers and parents in dealing with children with ADD, this book can be used for preservice or inservice courses or for a workshop for parents. The useful material can comprise an entire course on ADD, or it can serve as part of a course in a related area.

The persistent efforts of parents of children with attention deficit disorders and the endeavors of parent support organizations, such as CH.A.D.D. (Children and Adults with Attention Deficit Disorders), alerted legislators and professionals in several disciplines to the plight of children with ADD. These children were not being recognized or appropriately served by the schools; instead, they were misdiagnosed, denied appropriate school services, or simply neglected.

In 1991, the U.S. Department of Education issued a memorandum entitled *Clarification of Policy to Address the Needs of Children with Attention Deficit Disorders within General and/or Special Education*. This memorandum clearly established schools' responsibility to serve children with ADD. The memorandum also emphasized the need to provide training for regular and special education teachers about ADD and information about ways to serve students with ADD. Now the situation is beginning to change. Finally, schools are starting to identify children and adolescents with attention deficit disorders, and teachers are recognizing the need to learn ways of serving these students.

ORGANIZATION

This book is divided into three parts. Part I is an overview of attention deficit disorders. Chapter 1, "Attention Deficit Disorders: An Overview," introduces the field and reviews characteristics of ADD, symptoms at different stages of life, and coexisting conditions. Chapter 2, "A History of Attention Deficit

Disorders," contains a brief history of the field, including the contributions of the *Diagnostic and Statistical Manual of Mental Disorders, Fourth Edition* (DSM-IV). Chapter 3, "ADD and the Law," discusses legislation and the important role it plays in the schools.

Part II includes assessment, teaching methods, and parenting. Chapter 4, "Assessment," reviews assessment methods, the diagnostic process, and testing instruments. Chapter 5, "Teaching Students with ADD in the Regular Classroom," describes methods that regular teachers can use in the classroom. Chapter 6, "Special Education Interventions," describes methods used by special educators. Chapter 7, "The Family System: Parent Training, Counseling, and Home Management," discusses the challenges faced by a parent of a child with ADD, methods of counseling, and home management for parents.

Part III covers medication and the neurobiology of ADD. Chapter 8, "Medical Treatment of ADD," reviews the kinds of medications that are administered to many children with ADD and examines the issues involved in using medications. Chapter 9, "Biological Bases of ADD," focuses on the neurobiology that underlies attention deficit disorders, neurobiological theories, and current research.

The appendices contain useful information for teachers and parents. Appendix A is the U.S. Department of Education memorandum entitled *Clarification of Policy to Address the Needs of Children with Attention Deficit Disorders within General and/or Special Education.* Appendix B lists organizations that support the field of attention deficit disorders, and Appendix C provides useful resources for teachers and parents.

To make this text easy to study and appealing to use, the following features are included in each chapter:

- *Chapter outline:* A detailed overview of the chapter's contents
- *Snapshot:* A brief case vignette
- *Summary:* A section that summarizes important points covered in the chapter
- *Discussion questions:* A section that provides opportunities to synthesize and elaborate on the key ideas in the chapter

ACKNOWLEDGMENTS

According to a Chinese proverb, it takes an entire village to raise a child. Raising a child with attention deficit disorders requires an entire nationwide community—dedicated parents, caring teachers, knowledgeable psychologists, understanding medical specialists, empathic legislators, committed researchers, and many others.

As authors of *Attention Deficit Disorders: Assessment and Teaching*, we are indebted to all of these people. Our combined experience as teachers in the schools gave us firsthand experience with children with attention deficit disorders and their distraught parents and families. As college instructors, we learned much from current and prospective teachers in our classes. Our work as practitioners with children with ADD and their families enhanced our perspective in individual assessment and therapy. As professionals in the scholarly community, we learned much from the writings, research, and presentations of leaders in this field. We wish to thank the reviewers of earlier drafts of this manuscript, including Bonnie Fell and Cathy D. Kea (North Carolina Agricultural and Technical State University), for their valuable insights and critiques.

Children with ADD need all the help they can get. We hope this book offers teachers and parents the necessary information and guidelines to furnish appropriate, beneficial services for children and adolescents with ADD.

Janet W. Lerner
Barbara Lowenthal
Sue R. Lerner

PART I

An Overview
of Attention
Deficit
Disorders

CHAPTER ONE

ATTENTION DEFICIT DISORDERS: AN OVERVIEW

Snapshot

Background

Primary Characteristics of Attention Deficit Disorders
Inattention
Impulsivity
Hyperactivity
Poor Delay of Response: A New Theory

ADD at Different Life Stages
Young Children with ADD
Elementary-Age Children with ADD
Adolescents with ADD
Adults with ADD

Recognizing ADD in Schools under the Law

Coexisting Conditions
Learning Disabilities
Emotional and Behavioral Disorders
Social Problems
Gifted Children with ADD

The Influence of Parents and Parent Advocacy Groups

Causes of ADD

I always knew my daughter was special. Every mother "thinks" her child is special but I *knew*. So special that the supermarket manager would open another register just to get us through. So special that the nurses in the baby clinic would crowd around to see her shining eyes. So special that she stayed awake all day and most of the night in order to observe the world. . . . My child could get a roomful of people to notice her.

My daughter has brought me to the realization that I am a great mother. . . . Even when she was tossing furniture against the wall and screaming that she hated me, I controlled

my anger. I even learned to lock myself in the bathroom so that I would not hit her. . . .

She helped me overcome my inhibition about being a public spectacle by throwing outrageous temper tantrums. She helped me become better acquainted with her preschool teachers by challenging all of the educational theories and systems ever created. . . .

Though upset at having the most difficult child ever created, I felt pride. Pride that this daughter of mine who

Source: Schmidt, 1992.

routinely reversed letters and numbers and couldn't sit still if her life depended on it could actually be considered more intelligent and creative than the average child.

The opening snapshot is from a perplexed and frustrated mother describing a daughter with the baffling problem of an attention deficit disorder (ADD). The parent of a child with ADD may feel overwhelmed. He or she may experience a whirlwind of emotions—intense joy when the child succeeds and intense frustration, disappointment, even guilt, when the child fails. These parents are often tired. Life for the parent of a child with an attention deficit disorder is a struggle, but there is hope in that children with ADD can succeed (CH.A.D.D., 1993b).

In this overview chapter, we provide background information, look at the primary traits of ADD, examine the consequences of ADD at different stages of life, review coexisting disorders, look at parent advocacy groups, and review the causes of ADD.

BACKGROUND

Attention deficit disorders (ADD) constitute a chronic neurobiological condition characterized by developmentally inappropriate attention skills, impulsivity, and, in some cases, hyperactivity. In the professional literature, two terms are used to describe this condition: *ADD* (attention deficit disorders) and *ADHD* (attention deficit hyperactivity disorders). Though we recognize that the disorders of ADD and ADHD differ, we will follow the precedent of the U.S. Department of Education (1991) in its policy memorandum on ADD and use the term *ADD* to encompass both disorders.

A conservative estimate is that 3–5% of our school population, or approximately 2 million children and adolescents, are affected by ADD. Further, it is now recognized that many adults have ADD. In fact, studies show that approximately 50% of children with ADD grow up to become adults with ADD (CH.A.D.D., 1992).

Attention deficit disorders affect children in all areas of their lives. Characteristics of ADD are evident on a daily basis in all of their environments—at home, in school, and with peers. At home, parents often report that their children have difficulty accommodating to home routines and parental expectations. Children with ADD may resist going to bed, refuse to eat, or break toys during play. At school, they may be extremely restless and easily distracted. They have trouble completing work in class, often missing valuable information because of their underdeveloped attention capacity. They speak aloud out of turn and find themselves in trouble for their behavior. Their inattention, impulsivity, and hyperactivity can also be detrimental to their social lives, hampering their ability to make and keep friends. Thus, ADD interferes significantly with all major life activities, disrupting the child's home life, education, behavior, and social adjustments.

The challenges of treating children and youth with attention deficit disorders and serving them appropriately in schools increasingly are recognized by all who touch these children's lives—parents, family members, classroom teachers, special education teachers, psychologists, and medical specialists (including family physicians, pediatricians, neurologists, and child psychiatrists). Teaching students with ADD may be difficult because they do not respond to instruction in the same way as other students.

ADD affects individuals in distinctive ways at different age levels, with different symptoms and behaviors seen at the preschool, elementary, and secondary levels, and in adults. Adding to the complexity are other variations: Some children have only attentional problems with no academic difficulties; some have coexisting learning disabilities; for others, emotional or behavioral disabilities may accompany the ADD.

Though parents initially tend to accept with relief a diagnosis of ADD for their child because it is a recognized medical diagnosis, their relief is soon replaced by anxiety and frustration as physicians, psychologists, and educators try to clarify the implications of the diagnosis and steer the parents to the most appropriate and effective treatments (Schiller & Hauser, 1992).

PRIMARY CHARACTERISTICS
OF ATTENTION DEFICIT DISORDERS

Attention deficit disorders are among the most frequent causes for referrals of children to mental health clinics in the United States, accounting for as many as 50% of all referrals to outpatient mental health clinics. As noted earlier, a conservative estimate of the prevalence of ADD from authoritative

"BY THE TIME I THINK ABOUT
WHAT I AM GONNA DO...
I ALREADY DID IT!"

Source: Reprinted by permission,
Hank Ketcham Enterprises.

sources is approximately 3% (Schiller & Hauser, 1992). Less-conservative estimates range from 5% to 20%. Individuals with ADD have difficulty focusing their attention and concentrating on tasks. Described as rash, unpredictable, driven, easily distracted, they tend to race from one idea or interest to another. Hyperactivity accompanies the attention problem for some children, but not all.

The three primary characteristics of ADD are:

- inattention
- impulsivity
- hyperactivity

INATTENTION

The major focus in identifying ADD is an inability to attend to and concentrate on a target task. In the school environment, because of their inattention, children with ADD may not understand assignments or may drift off and forget what they are doing. Often these children are distracted by other stimuli or by their own thoughts, and they begin more activities than they complete. Paradoxically, even though children with ADD do not attend to routine school tasks, they may be extremely attentive for long periods while engaged in highly enjoyable activities, such as favored hobbies or playing video games, or in novel or new situations (Parker, 1992).

IMPULSIVITY

Children with ADD act impulsively, without thinking through the consequences of their behavior. Impulsive students get into trouble, because they come to decisions and act too quickly, without sufficient time between the stimulus and the response. They answer questions before hearing or reading the whole problem. They shout out remarks in school, without waiting their turns or raising their hands before speaking. They interrupt others without realizing the social consequences.

HYPERACTIVITY

Hyperactive behavior is the most readily observable characteristic of ADD. However, not all children with ADD are hyperactive. Some manifest normal activity levels, and some may even be less active than children without ADD. Hyperactivity is a trait that cannot be missed. Hyperactive children are always in motion, moving about the room, touching things and often breaking them. They continually talk, make noise, fall off chairs, and touch and fight with others. They are often disruptive in school and need constant supervision at home.

POOR DELAY OF RESPONSE: A NEW THEORY

A new theory of the characteristics of ADD has been proposed by Barkley (1993), who suggests that the primary characteristic of ADD is *disinhibition,* or *poor delay of response,* rather than inattention per se. Noting that the most consistent observation of individuals with ADD is a primary deficit in behavioral or response inhibitions, Barkley theorizes that individuals with ADD lack the ability to delay their responses; they have little tolerance for delay intervals within tasks.

Barkley's theory is based on the work of Bronowski (1967, 1977). This work suggests that as human language and communication evolved, human beings developed a capacity to delay their response to a signal, message, or event. This essential capacity to inhibit initial reactions to events arose from an evolutionary expansion of the frontal lobes, which allowed for four functions: separation of affect, prolongation, internalization, and reconstitution.

Applying this theory to individuals with ADD, Barkley hypothesizes that the primary deficit of ADD is one of poor delay of responses. This explanation sheds light on the pervasive impact of the disorder on daily life. Moreover, it offers a guide for understanding the disorder and new views on treatment.

ADD AT DIFFERENT LIFE STAGES

Symptoms of ADD change over time, and distinctive behaviors are evident at various stages of life. Young children, elementary-age youngsters, adolescents, and adults all display different traits.

YOUNG CHILDREN WITH ADD

Young children with ADD, ages 2 to 6, are often hyperactive, exhibiting excessive gross motor activity, such as running or climbing. They are described as being on the go, "running like a motor," and having difficulty sitting still. Often, they can sit for only a few minutes at a time and then wriggle excessively.

Parents of preschoolers with ADD report that public places are particularly trying. For example, in supermarkets, these children become unmanageable, running about and pulling things off shelves. Aggression sometimes characterizes ADD at this age. Some parents report sequestering themselves in their homes, never inviting friends over or venturing into places where their child's behavior would annoy other people. Hunsucker (1993) believes that preschoolers with ADD can tolerate more pain than other children and, consequently, may play rougher, often hurting other children. Other children may refuse to play with them because of their aggressiveness.

Preschoolers with ADD tend to be very inquisitive and may take toys apart, wanting to see how they work. Unfortunately, they may be unable to put things back together and may end up destroying them.

ELEMENTARY-AGE CHILDREN WITH ADD

Elementary school students with ADD are generally extremely restless and fidgety. Their behavior tends to be haphazard and poorly organized. They often talk too much in class, and they constantly fight with friends, siblings, and classmates. What distinguishes this disorder from ordinary overactivity is the quality of the motor behavior (DuPaul, Barkley, & McMurray, 1991; Frick & Lahey, 1991).

It is during the elementary years that parents may begin hearing from school staff, particularly if their child is also hyperactive. Often, parents are blamed for the child's behavior problems. Children with ADD are sometimes loners, with few or no friends. Their inappropriate behavior may irritate other children.

Attention deficit disorders may become more noticeable during the first or second grade, especially if the child encoun-

CASE EXAMPLE
A PRESCHOOLER WITH ADD

Joshua is a bright, active 4-year-old in Mrs. Shaeffer's preschool class. Over the past six months, Mrs. Shaeffer has found working with Joshua a frustrating experience. Recently she has been losing her patience, even over trivial matters. She describes Joshua as a child whose body is constantly "on the go." Mrs. Shaeffer feels Joshua has difficulty sustaining attention on a task. He often darts from one activity to another, rarely completing activities he has started, and seeming to destroy more than he accomplishes. Throughout the day Joshua interrupts other children as they seek her attention, and he seems to dominate daily group conversations. Mrs. Shaeffer reports [that] he often appears not to hear and does not follow directions well. To her, Joshua seems plagued or driven by boundless energy. Mrs. Shaeffer knows she is losing control of the situation and is looking for ways to help Joshua.

Source: Jones, 1993, p. 13.

ters problems in learning to read. If the child is above average in intelligence, the problem may not be noticeable at first, because with some extra effort he or she can achieve academically.

Children who have ADD with hyperactivity will be more conspicuous than those who are not hyperactive. In fact, because children with ADD without hyperactivity appear compliant, teachers and school staff members may not immediately notice their problems. However, their inability to concentrate and pay attention often will lead to school problems.

ADOLESCENTS WITH ADD

When ADD was first recognized as a condition, the focus was on young children. Many practitioners assumed that children would outgrow the symptoms by adolescence. For some children, hyperactivity tends to increase until age 3 but then diminishes, and by adolescence it may no longer be present. Parents were advised to be patient, because their child's problems would improve by the time he or she reached adolescence. Today, it is apparent that this assumption was overly optimistic and that hyperactivity and other behavioral problems do continue into adolescence. In fact, the attentional and

CASE EXAMPLE
ELEMENTARY-AGE CHILD

An 11-year-old left the following note of explanation for his mother. It reflects the impulsive behavior of this ADD boy.

I am sorry for using the baseball bats the wrong way   next time I'll use a flyswatter (which I was until . . . the flyswatter wasn't strong enough so I used a bat when the fly landed on the window I didn't even think first not to hit the fly there   I just hit it as a result the window smashed down on the ground!

I am definitely sorry . . .

Source: CH.A.D.D.er Box, October 1992, p. 7.

hyperactivity problems of the adolescent contribute to myriad adjustments. Almost as many adolescents as younger children experience skill deficits and performance problems due to attention deficit disorders (Goldstein, 1993).

Problems caused by deficiencies in academic skills intensify with age. Many adolescents have coexisting disabilities. In addition to ADD, they may have other neurobiological problems, learning disabilities, or behavioral or social difficulties. The coexistence of ADD and behavioral problems may lead to antisocial conduct and substance abuse problems in adolescence (Goldstein, 1993).

Although adolescents with ADD may appear less hyperactive during their teen years, they may develop other symptoms, such as behavioral disorders, low self-esteem, inattentiveness, or even depression (Shaywitz & Shaywitz, 1988).

ADULTS WITH ADD

At one time, experts in attention deficit disorders considered ADD a condition of childhood and believed that individuals outgrew their ADD symptoms as they reached adulthood. Now, clinicians recognize that for many adults, problems related to ADD, and the symptoms of impulsiveness, restlessness, hyperactivity, and short attention span, may continue throughout the individual's life span.

Sometimes adults are diagnosed with ADD when their children are evaluated. Then parents may recognize in themselves the same characteristics their children have.

With adults, ADD often is a "hidden disorder," with its symptoms obscured by problems with relationships, staying organized, and holding a steady job. Many adults who are diagnosed as having ADD are first recognized as having problems with substance abuse or impulse control. In addition, ADD in adults may not be recognized because many mental health practitioners lack training in childhood disorders or were taught that children with ADD grow out of their symptoms (CH.A.D.D. National Board of Directors, 1993).

Effective treatments for adults with ADD include therapy, medication, and counseling. According to Barkley (1990), the success rate for medical treatment is lower for adults than for children—about 50% for adults compared to about 70% for children. A recent longitudinal study showed that when children with ADD reach adulthood, they are disproportionately undereducated, underemployed, and plagued by mental problems. About 25% of these adults drop out of high school (compared with 2% in the control group), only 12% earn a B.A. degree (compared with 50% of the control group), and only 4% hold a professional position (compared with 21% of the control group). However, more adults with ADD owned a small business (18% compared with 5% of the control group) (Mannuzza, Klein, & Bessler, 1993).

CASE EXAMPLE
AN ADULT WITH ADD

The case of Gary Roy is an example of an adult with attention deficit hyperactivity disorder (Cowley & Ramo, 1993). His problem was not recognized until age 38, when he was diagnosed as having ADD by the Massachusetts Medical Center in Worcester, Massachusetts. Gary was employed as a security guard, had a respectable IQ, and displayed boundless energy. Until his diagnosis, he had never been able to finish even simple tasks, such as taking out the trash, without getting sidetracked. During his school years he was in constant trouble with both teachers and parents. Because of his trouble keeping a job, he had held over 128 positions. He was never able to complete his college degree even though he had attended college for over 13 years. Gary had been treated for manic depression, but the lithium the doctors prescribed only compounded his distress. When he finally received a diagnosis of ADD, he reported hat it dramatically changed his life. He started treatment with the medication Ritalin and recounted that "right after I started the treatment I saw *Awakenings* . . . I cried and cried because that was how I felt, like I had awakened" (Cowley & Ramo, 1993, pp. 48–49).

Roy has since obtained his ham-radio license and become a civil defense radio supervisor.

ADD's impact on an individual's life is cumulative. If the disorder impairs the individual's ability to concentrate and learn in school, he or she will tend to have poor academic skills. Because adults with ADD may consider the need to concentrate and pay attention too onerous and demanding, they may choose to stop their education after high school. Not wishing to expose themselves to the frustrations of postsecondary education, they may not go on to college.

Adults with ADD who had drug and alcohol problems as adolescents may continue or increase their substance abuse in their adult years. Adults with ADD may have trouble keeping a job because of their social and behavioral difficulties, even if they can do what the job requires. Marital problems can result from the ADD. Individuals who have temper tantrums may abuse their spouses or children.

RECOGNIZING ADD
IN SCHOOLS UNDER THE LAW

Until recently, most books and publications about ADD were written for health care professionals and parents; educators knew little about attention deficit disorders. In fact, ADD was not recognized as a disability in our nation's public schools, and no mention of ADD or its symptoms was made in either the special education law—the Individuals with Disabilities Education Act (IDEA), P.L. 101-476—or the earlier law, P.L. 94-142 (Parker, 1992). However, as a result of the advocacy efforts made by parents of children with ADD, together with the support of some professionals, the U.S. Department of Education finally recognized children with attention deficit disorders. In 1991, the U.S. Department of Education issued a Clarification Memorandum on ADD (U.S. Department of Education, 1991), which appears in Appendix A.

This important policy memorandum states that children with ADD may be eligible for special education and related services under the existing categories of special education. The memorandum specifically notes that children with ADD should be classified as "other health impaired" (OHI) if the ADD is a chronic or acute health impairment that results in limited alertness, which adversely affects educational performance (Aronofsky, 1992; U.S. Department of Education, 1991).

The memorandum further states that a child with ADD may also be eligible for special education services if he or she satisfies the criteria applicable to other categories of disability. Categories specifically mentioned include "specific learning disabilities" (LD) and "seriously emotionally disturbed" (SED). The memorandum implies that these may be coexisting disabilities. In addition, the memorandum explains that children with ADD who are not eligible for special education may be served under Section 504 of the Rehabilitation Act (see Chapter 3). The implications of this consequential memorandum are discussed more fully in several chapters of this book.

COEXISTING CONDITIONS

Sometimes another condition occurs concomitantly with the attention deficit disorder (Hocutt, McKinney, & Montague, 1993; McKinney, Montague, & Hocutt, 1993). In its policy memorandum on ADD, the U.S. Department of Education (1991) has recognized and addressed the issue of coexisting conditions (or associated problems or co-morbid disabilities).

LEARNING DISABILITIES

ADD is not synonymous with learning disabilities, but many children with attention deficit disorders also display symptoms of learning disabilities, further complicating identification and treatment. Estimates based on research suggest that approximately 25% of children with ADD have coexisting learning disabilities (Fowler, 1992), though such estimates range from 9% to 63% across studies (McKinney et al., 1993; Shaywitz & Shaywitz, 1988; Silver, 1990). Learning disabilities may occur more often with ADD without hyperactivity than where hyperactivity is present. Stanford and Hynd (1994) suggest that the behaviors of children with attention deficit disorders and hyperactivity are different from those of children with learning disabilities. Children with ADD with hyperactivity have distinctive behavior profiles that differ from those of children with attention deficit disorders without hyperactivity or of children with learning disabilities. Stanford and Hynd used parent and teacher rating scales to compare children with attention deficit disorders and hyperactivity with two groups: children who were identified as having learning disabilities, and children with attention deficit disorders and no hyperactivity. The children with attention deficit disorders and hyperactivity were rated as more disruptive. The children with learning disabilities or attention deficit disorders and no hyperactivity were described as more underactive and shy.

Because many students diagnosed as having ADD will also be identified and served under the classification of learning disabilities, professionals in the learning disabilities field especially need to become knowledgeable about ADD.

EMOTIONAL AND BEHAVIORAL DISORDERS

As noted, another category under IDEA, and a condition that may coexist with ADD, is serious emotional disturbance (SED). Children with ADD do not routinely show signs of serious emotional disturbance, but if not properly diagnosed and treated, they can develop significant emotional difficulties, such as behavioral disorders, depression, and even substance abuse (CH.A.D.D., 1993a).

Under the revised third edition of *Diagnostic and Statistical Manual of Mental Disorders* (DSM-III-R) (American Psychiatric Association, 1987), some children with ADD with hyperactivity may be identified as having disruptive behavior disorders (Frick & Lahey, 1991). It is estimated that 40–60% of elementary-age children with ADD have coexisting oppositional defiance disorders (ODD), while roughly 20–30% develop conduct disorders (CD) (Fowler, 1992). Children with coexisting ADD and disruptive behavior disorders often display aggression, oppositional defiance, and conduct problems (McKinney et al., 1993).

SOCIAL PROBLEMS

Social problems is not a disability category under IDEA. However, one of the most consistent findings in the literature on ADD is that children and youths with ADD have significant and persistent problems in social relationships. Children with ADD with hyperactivity are aggressive and are rejected more often than comparison subjects. Children with ADD without hyperactivity are more withdrawn and unpopular but not necessarily rejected (McKinney et al., 1993).

GIFTED STUDENTS WITH ADD

Gifted children are increasingly being referred for medical evaluations because ADD is suspected (Lind, 1993; Webb & Latimer, 1993). In fact, many of the characteristics of giftedness, such as spontaneity, inquisitiveness, imagination, boundless enthusiasm, and emotionality, are also traits of attention deficit disorders. Because of the similarity between the two categories, Lind (1993) suspects that gifted children are sometimes mislabeled as having ADD.

The nervous systems of gifted children seem to require much activity, and young gifted children are often described as hyperactive and highly distractible. Some gifted children are immovable when engaged in projects, working persistently and passionately. Gifted children may find regular classroom environments uninviting or difficult to attend to because of the slow pace. They may respond by becoming fidgety, inattentive, and even disruptive, because their learning needs are not being met.

The intensity of gifted children's concentration often permits them to spend long periods of time and much energy focusing on whatever truly interests them. Their specific interests may not coincide, however, with the desires and expectations of teachers or parents (Webb & Latimer, 1993).

Gifted children are often overexcitable, with areas of intensity in psychomotor, sensual, intellectual, imaginational, and emotional responses (Piechowski, 1991). Because these traits can mimic ADD, gifted children must be comprehensively evaluated. Some gifted children also have attention deficit disorders.

THE INFLUENCE OF PARENTS AND PARENT ADVOCACY GROUPS

All parents of children with attention deficit disorders have a strong desire to see their child succeed and be happy, and most take seriously the responsibilities and challenges of raising their child. To better meet this challenge, many parents have educated themselves about ADD and individually tried to enlighten the school and their child's teachers about their child's problem and to get their child appropriate services. These parents know that children with ADD can flourish when properly managed and taught by informed teachers. However, individually, these parents may find their success sporadic, and dependent from year to year on how much their child's teacher knows about ADD. Each school year brings a fresh battle for the help their child needs in school.

Less than 10 years ago, a small group of parents of children with ADD and a few concerned professionals, recognizing the urgent need for a support group, established an organization that is now called CH.A.D.D. (Children and Adults with Attention Deficit Disorders). CH.A.D.D. has been extremely successful in bringing the problem of ADD to the attention of other parents, professionals, and the public. Their intensive and passionate efforts also brought the disability of ADD to the attention of the U.S. Congress and the Department of Education. As a result of their endeavors, ADD is now recognized as an identifiable condition. (The legislation for ADD is discussed in greater detail in Chapter 3.) The work of CH.A.D.D. and other parent advocacy groups (such as the Attention Deficit Disorder Association) to promote understanding of ADD is a continuing effort. For example, in recent testimony before Congress, CH.A.D.D. argued for federal support of the following policies: (1) to inform our nation's educators about ADD, (2) to support ongoing neurobiological research on the causes of ADD, and (3) to disseminate nationwide current, standardized information on the recognition and education of children with ADD (CH.A.D.D., 1992).

CAUSES OF ADD

Though the causes of ADD are still not fully clear, there is widespread agreement that the disorder is neurobiologically based. Theories and research focus on neurochemical, anatomical, neuroanatomical, and genetic factors (Riccio, Hynd, Cohen, & Gonzalez, 1993). Strong evidence suggests that a likely cause of ADD is a chemical imbalance or deficiency in the area of the brain that is responsible for attention and activity. Evidence also suggests a strong hereditary disposition to ADD. The causes and the neurobiological bases of ADD are discussed further in Chapter 9.

SUMMARY

Attention deficit disorders constitute a chronic neurological condition characterized by three primary characteristics: an underdeveloped attentional capacity, causing inattention; impulsivity; and often (but not always) hyperactivity. It is conservatively estimated to affect 3–5% of the school population.

ADD affects individuals differently at various stages of life—early childhood, the elementary school years, adolescence, and adulthood. In some cases, other problems coexist with the ADD. Children with ADD can also have learning disabilities, emotional or behavioral problems, or social problems, or they may be gifted.

Parent and professional advocacy groups work to provide support for children with ADD. One effective organization is CH.A.D.D. (Children and Adults with Attention Deficit Disorder). Parent support groups have been extremely successful in bringing ADD to the attention of others, in promoting supportive legislation, and in securing governmental support in general. One achievement is the U.S. Department of Education's 1991 memorandum clarifying its policy on serving children with ADD.

There is widespread agreement that ADD is neurobiologically based.

DISCUSSION QUESTIONS

1. Name the three primary characteristics of attention deficit disorders. For each, describe a specific behavior exemplifying the characteristic.

2. Symptoms of attention deficit disorders change at various stages of life. Describe two typical traits of ADD in (a) preschoolers, (b) elementary-age children, (c) adolescents, and (d) adults.

3. Name three categories of special education under which a child with ADD may be served.

4. The term *co-morbidity* is often used in reference to children with attention deficit disorders. What does this term mean? Name another term that can be used. Name two categories of special education under which conditions co-morbid with ADD may be classified.

5. For a child with an attention deficit disorder to be eligible for special education services under the category of "other health impaired" (OHI), what criteria must be met?

CHAPTER TWO

A History of Attention Deficit Disorders

SNAPSHOT

I'm the mother of nine-year-old twin boys who have (finally) been diagnosed with ADD through our school. It has been a rough nine years. They were out of their cribs before they could even crawl. They could open any child-proof lock ever made and slept less than any human beings I have ever known. No baby-sitter has ever been willing to come more than twice. No child care center or after-school program has even been willing to keep them, so I quit my part-time teaching job and have stayed home with them since they were three. My husband has to work a second job, so most of the supervision of the boys falls on me. I almost never have any

relief. Their grandparents work full-time and live in another state. Over the last few years my health has begun to fail. Although my doctor cannot find anything wrong with me, I am constantly catching colds [and] exhausted, and have frequent headaches. I'm losing weight. I sleep very poorly. Are there other mothers of children with ADD who feel this way? Is there anything I can do about it?

Source: Richard, December 1993, p. 10.

This chapter traces the historical evolution of the recognition of attention deficit disorders. The perceptions and theories expressed in early writings became the roots of current concepts about attention deficit disorders. The terminology changed as the field of ADD evolved. Historically, the terminology at each stage reflected the ideas of the time about childhood disorders, and clinicians and researchers focused on different symptoms from each corresponding perspective. This chapter reviews the historical perspectives on this disability up to the current conceptualization of attention deficit disorders.

THE ROOTS OF ATTENTION DEFICIT DISORDERS

Only in recent years have the problems related to attention deficit disorders been acknowledged and begun to receive acceptance and recognition. Yet, this condition in children is not new. There have always been children who have displayed inattention, impulsivity, and hyperactivity. Parents and teachers knew that these children struggled to cope with the demands of their homes, school, and society. What is new is that finally the problems are being acknowledged. Today, ADD is accepted as a condition, one that professionals can distinguish from other childhood disorders.

Recognition of attention deficit disorders has been slow to develop. As views of the nature of this condition have changed and evolved over the years, a variety of terms have been used to describe it. This terminology has included *brain-damaged children, minimal brain dysfunction,* and *hyperkinetic reaction.* Currently in use are the terms *attention deficit disorders* (ADD), *attention deficit hyperactivity disorder* (ADHD), *attention deficit disorder with hyperactivity* (ADDH), and others. The current terms represent a family of disorders, with ADD being used to encompass the entire family.

A historical overview of attention deficit disorders is shown in Table 2.1 The historical events that shaped the field of attention deficit disorders are described in this chapter (Lerner & Lerner, 1993).

TABLE 2.1 Historical overview of attention deficit disorders

Date	Diagnostic terminology	Source	Characteristics
1941 1947	Brain damage syndrome	Werner & Strauss	Hyperactivity, distractibility, impulsivity, emotional instability, perseveration
1962	Minimal brain dysfunction (MBD)	Clements & Peters	Soft neurological indicators, specific learning deficits, hyperkinesis, impulsivity, short attention span
1968	Hyperactive reaction of childhood	DSM-II	Hyperactivity
1980	Attention deficit disorder with hyperactivity (ADDH)	DSM-III	1. Inattention, impulsivity, motor hyperactivity 2. Onset before age 7 3. Duration of at least 6 months
	Attention deficit disorder without hyperactivity (ADD/noH)		Inattention, disorganization, difficulty completing tasks
1987	Attention-deficit hyperactivity disorder (ADHD)	DSM-III-R	Any 8 of a set of 14 symptoms
	Undifferentiated attention deficit disorder (U-ADD)		Marked and developmentally inappropriate inattention
1991	Attention deficit disorder (ADD)	U.S. Dept. of Education policy memorandum	Eligible for services under IDEA (other health impaired, learning disabilities, emotionally disturbed) or Section 504 of the Rehabilitation Act.
1994	Attention-deficit hyperactivity disorder (ADHD)	DSM-IV	ADHD (3 subtypes) 1. IA: primarily inattentive subtype 2. HI: primarily hyperactive-impulsive subtype 3. ADHD: combined subtype

Source: From ''Attention Deficit Disorder: Issues and Questions,'' by J. Lerner and S. Lerner. In Focus on Exceptional Children, 24(3), p. 6. Copyright © 1991 by Love Publishing Co. Adapted by permission.

BRAIN DAMAGE SYNDROME

One of the first descriptions of the symptoms of ADD to appear in medical literature appeared in the early 1900s in an article by a physician (Still, 1902). Still described these children as having "morbid defects in moral control." This and other early descriptions of behaviors were remarkably similar to diagnostic criteria used today (Barkley, 1990). Moreover, investigators of that era were beginning to link this behavior to traumatic brain injury and other childhood central nervous system anomalies (Goldstein, 1936; Meyer, 1904).

Influential research in the 1930s and 1940s included the work of Werner and Strauss (1941) and that of Strauss and Lehtinen (1947). These investigators surveyed a population of mentally defective, institutionalized children, using case histories and neurological examinations. The research led the investigators to identify a behavioral syndrome that included hyperactivity in children, and they theorized that the symptomatic behaviors were linked to brain damage. They believed that these children sustained brain damage before, during, or shortly after birth. The brain-damaged children were described as hyperactive, distractible, impulsive, emotionally labile, and perseverative. Strauss and Lehtinen's influential book *Psychopathology and Education of the Brain-Injured Child* (1947) alerted many physicians and educators to an alternative diagnosis for children who previously had been otherwise labeled. Parents who had been blamed for their child's behavior welcomed this new explanation.

These beginnings provided a foundation for the recognition of what we know today as attention deficit disorders. There was, however, no vigorous follow-up at the time. After the 1940s, educators and parents seem to have turned their attention to learning disabilities, focusing on children's learning problems rather than on their behavioral symptoms. The rapid growth of the field of learning disabilities, along with special education, may have dampened professional interest in attentional problems.

MINIMAL BRAIN DYSFUNCTION (MBD)

Educators, psychologists, parents, and the medical community soon expressed dissatisfaction with the term *brain damage.* By the 1950s, the medical literature reported that verifying brain damage in children with learning and behavioral problems was difficult, because these children looked normal. To differentiate this condition from true or gross brain damage, scholars suggested other terms, including *minimal brain damage,* implying that the brain damage was slight (Cantwell & Baker, 1991; Laufer & Denhoff, 1957; Shaywitz & Shaywitz, 1991).

Clements and Peters (1962) elaborated this concept, calling the condition, *minimal brain dysfunction* (MBD). This implied that individuals with this condition did not have brain damage but rather difficulty with the way the brain functioned. In 1966, a report sponsored by the National Institutes of Health (NIH) endorsed this term (Clements, 1966). Minimal brain dysfunction was defined as afflicting

> children of near-average, average or above-average general intelligence with certain learning or behavior disabilities ranging from mild to severe, which are associated with deviations of function of the central nervous system. These deviations may manifest themselves by various combinations of impairment in perception, conceptualization, language, memory, and control of attention, impulse or motor function. (p. 9)

The concept of MBD appealed to psychiatrists, neurologists, and psychologists, because it allowed them to note subtle neurological deviations. The symptoms of MBD included specific learning deficits, hyperkinesis, impulsivity, and short attention span, and the diagnostic criteria included evidence of "equivocal" neurological signs and borderline or abnormal electroencephalogram (EEG).

HYPERKINETIC
REACTION OF CHILDHOOD: DSM-II

The concept of MBD proved in turn to be controversial, because it was not operational and it lacked sufficient guidelines for diagnosis. To better identify and classify the disorder, a more rigorous set of diagnostic criteria was needed. In 1968, the second edition of the *Diagnostic and Statistical Manual of Mental Disorders* (DSM-II) (American Psychiatric Association [APA], 1968) provided the beginnings of an answer to this need. DSM-II used the term *hyperkinetic reaction of childhood* to describe the hyperactive child. The disorder was characterized by overactivity, restlessness, distractibility, and a short attention span (Silver, 1990).

ATTENTION DEFICIT DISORDER: ADDH AND ADD/noH: DSM-III

In 1980, improved diagnostic guidelines appeared in the third edition of the *Diagnostic and Statistical Manual of Mental Disorders* (DSM-III) (APA, 1980). DSM-III is considered to have significantly advanced the validity of the diagnosis of attention deficit disorders (Cantwell & Baker, 1991; Shaywitz & Shaywitz, 1988). With the focus shifting to attentional problems rather than activity problems, the term *attention deficit disorder* was established. The role of attention in learning and within the larger cognitive system is complex. Attention affects the rest of the system in what information is allowed in at the sensory level, how information is managed in short-term working memory, how information is encoded in long-term memory, and how information is retrieved from long-term memory (Cherkes-Jukowski, Stolzenberg, & Segal, 1991; Torgesen, Kistner, & Morgan, 1987).

In DSM-III, two types of attention deficit disorders were recognized: (1) attention deficit disorder *with* hyperactivity (ADDH) and (2) attention deficit disorder *without* hyperactivity (ADD/noH). To establish the diagnosis of ADDH, the child had to show evidence of three criteria: (1) inattention, (2) impulsivity, and (3) motor hyperactivity. DSM-III specified behaviors for each of the three criteria. The diagnosis of ADD/noH was for children who exhibited symptoms of inattention and impulsivity but not hyperactivity. Other diagnostic criteria for

BOX 2.1
A CHINESE PROVERB

I hear and I forget.

I see and I remember.

I do and I understand.

both ADDH and ADD/noH included onset of the problem prior to 7 years of age and a duration of at least 6 months.

ATTENTION-DEFICIT HYPERACTIVITY DISORDER (ADHD): DSM-III-R

Further modifications in the terminology and diagnosis appeared in 1987, with the publication of the revised third edition of the *Diagnostic and Statistical Manual of Mental Disorders* (DSM-III-R) (APA, 1987). This edition recommended the term *attention-deficit hyperactivity disorder* (ADHD), to reflect recent research showing that though distractibility was primary in this disorder, hyperactivity was also an important factor (Silver, 1990). For a diagnosis of ADHD, DSM-III-R allowed any 8 symptoms to be present from a set of 14 possible symptoms. Also, DSM-III-R kept as criteria onset prior to 7 years of age and duration of the symptomatic behavior for at least 6 months. The diagnostic criteria for ADHD specified in DSM-III-R are shown in Box 2.2.

In the revised edition, ADD without hyperactivity, a type noted in DSM-III, was relegated to minor status (Barkley, DuPaul, & McMurray, 1991). Instead, DSM-III-R described a category called *undifferentiated attention deficit disorder* (U-ADD), which roughly corresponds to the ADD/noH designation. Many clinicians believe that children with U-ADD are an underidentified, underserved group who are at significant risk for long-term academic, social, and emotional difficulties. Children with ADD/noH or U-ADD are far less visible and less likely to come to the attention of parents or educators or other professionals. Even though they do not attract attention, they may be at much greater risk for school failure and social failure than children who have ADD with hyperactivity (Epstein, Shaywitz, Shaywitz, & Woolston, 1991; Shaywitz, 1987).

Some recent authorities believe that children with ADD/noH or U-ADD represent a distinct type of ADD (Barkley et al., 1991; Lahey & Carlson, 1991; Schaughency & Rothlind, 1991). In comparing children with and without hyperactivity, children with ADD without hyperactivity exhibit less-serious conduct problems, are less impulsive, and are more likely to be characterized as sluggish and drowsy. Although less rejected by their peers, they tend to be socially withdrawn, and they

BOX 2.2
SYMPTOMS OF ADHD

1. Often fidgets with hands or feet or squirms in seat (in adolescence may be limited to subjective feelings of restlessness).

2. Has difficulty remaining seated when required to do so.

3. Is easily distracted by extraneous stimuli.

4. Has difficulty awaiting turn in games or group situations.

5. Often blurts out answers to questions before they have been completed.

6. Has difficulty following through on instructions from others (not because of oppositional behavior or failure of comprehension), e.g., fails to finish chores.

7. Has difficulty sustaining attention in teaching or play activities.

8. Often shifts from one uncompleted activity to another.

9. Has difficulty playing quietly.

10. Often talks excessively.

11. Often interrupts or intrudes on others (e.g., butts into other children's games).

12. Often does not seem to listen to what is being said.

13. Often loses things necessary for tasks or activities at school or at home (e.g., toys, pencils, books, assignments).

14. Often engages in physically dangerous activities without considering possible consequences (not for the purpose of thrill-seeking), e.g., runs into street without looking.

The above items are listed in descending order of discriminating power. (DSM-III-R, p. 56)

Source: From American Psychiatric Association: *Diagnostic and Statistical Manual of Mental Disorders, Third Edition, Revised,* Washington, DC, American Psychiatric Association, 1987. Adapted by permission.

are more likely to show depressed moods and symptoms of anxiety disorders. Many authorities consider ADD without hyperactivity a clinically meaningful entity and propose including it as a distinct diagnosis.

ATTENTION DEFICIT DISORDERS: U.S. DEPARTMENT OF EDUCATION

A major step in the recognition of attention deficit disorders occurred in 1991, when the U.S. Department of Education issued a memorandum clarifying its policy with regard to children with attention deficit disorders. This significant policy memorandum was jointly signed by representatives of three offices in the Department of Education: the Office of Special Education and Rehabilitative Services, the Office for Civil Rights, and the Office of Elementary and Secondary Education. It was intended to clarify state and local responsibility under federal law for meeting the needs of children with ADD in the educational system as a whole. In the document, the term *attention deficit disorders* (ADD) was used to encompass both ADD and ADHD.

The memorandum states that a child with ADD may qualify for special education and related services under Part B of the special education law—the Individuals with Disabilities Education Act (IDEA)—within the category of "other health impaired" if the ADD constitutes "a chronic or acute health problem that results in limited alertness," thus adversely affecting educational performance. The memorandum also states that children with ADD may be eligible for services under Part B if they satisfy the criteria applicable to other disability categories, such as learning disabilities or serious emotional disturbance.

Even if a child does not qualify for special education and related services under Part B of IDEA, Section 504 of the Rehabilitation Act of 1973 (which prohibits discrimination on the basis of disability) may still apply. Under Section 504, the school must evaluate a child to determine whether or not he or she is "handicapped" as defined by the law. If the child is found to have "a physical or mental impairment which substantially limits a major life activity (e.g., learning)," then the local education agency (or school district) must make an "individualized determination of the child's educational needs for regular or special education or related aids and services." Section 504 also stipulates that the child's education must be provided in the regular classroom, "unless it is demonstrated that education in the regular environment with the use of supplementary aids and services cannot be achieved satisfactorily" (Council for Exceptional Children, 1992).

The Department of Education issued its policy memorandum in response to vigorous lobbying by concerned parent groups, in particular, CH.A.D.D. (Children and Adults with Attention Deficit Disorders), and by practitioners and researchers in education, medicine, and psychology. The process leading to the U.S. Department of Education's recognition of ADD and the legal implications in terms of eligibility for service are discussed more fully in the next chapter, on the law.

ATTENTION-DEFICIT HYPERACTIVITY DISORDER (ADHD): DSM-IV

The fourth edition of the *Diagnostic and Statistical Manual of Mental Disorders* (DSM-IV) (APA, 1994) again modifies the diagnostic criteria for ADD. In the new edition, the classification and diagnosis of ADD have changed (APA, 1994) in response to many comments from the field. (See McBurnett, Lahey, & Pfiffner, 1993, for a review of these changes.) The diagnostic criteria in DSM-IV are the result of extensive research and field trials. Revision of the criteria for attention deficit disorders was based on input gathered from parents, teachers, and children, using a structured clinical interview, a revision of the Diagnostic Interview Schedule for Children (DISC-II) (Shaffer, Fisher, Piacentini, Schwab-Stone, & Wicks, 1992). In addition, numerous studies of the factors underlying symptoms led to identification of two major factors: (1) an **inattention** factor and (2) a **hyperactive-impulsive** factor (McBurnett et al., 1993).

To provide continuity with DSM-III-R, the overall diagnostic category of ADHD has been retained in DSM-IV. Within that diagnostic category, however, criteria for three different subtypes have been established.

The Three Subtypes

1. **ADHD-IA: Primarily inattentive subtype.** In DSM-IV, the classification of
   inattentive (ADHD-IA) applies to children with at least six
   symptoms of inattention that have persisted for at least 6
   months to a degree that is maladaptive and inconsistent with
   the child's developmental level (see Box 2.3).

   Under the third edition, the diagnosis for such children
   would have been ADD without hyperactivity; under DSM-III-
   R, undifferentiated ADD.

BOX 2.3

Symptoms of Inattention

1. Often fails to give close attention to details or makes careless mistakes in schoolwork, work, or other activities

2. Often has difficulty sustaining attention in tasks or play activities

3. Often does not seem to listen to what is being said to him or her

4. Often does not follow through on instruction and fails to finish schoolwork, chores, or duties in the workplace (not due to oppositional behavior or failure to understand instruction)

5. Often has difficulties organizing tasks and activities

6. Often avoids or strongly dislikes tasks (such as schoolwork or homework) that requires sustained mental effort

7. Often loses things necessary for tasks or activities (e.g., school assignments, pencils, books, tools, or toys)

8. Is often easily distracted by extraneous stimuli

9. Often forgetful in daily activities

Source: From American Psychiatric Association: *Diagnostic and Statistical Manual of Mental Disorders, Fourth Edition, Draft Criteria,* Washington, DC, American Psychiatric Association, 1993. Adapted by permission.

2. ADHD-HI: Primarily hyperactive-impulsive subtype.   Under DSM-IV, children are identified as hyperactive-impulsive (ADHD-HI) but not clinically inattentive if they persistently display for at least 6 months at least six symptoms of hyperactivity-impulsivity to a degree that is maladaptive and inconsistent with their development level (see Box 2.4).

This category of primarily hyperactive-impulsive but not inattentive ADHD has no precedent in the earlier DSM systems.

3. ADHD: Combined subtype.   The third classification in DSM-IV includes chil dren who display both inattention and hyperactivity-impulsivity. To fit this designation, a child must have six

BOX 2.4

SYMPTOMS OF HYPERACTIVITY AND IMPULSIVITY

1. Often fidgets with hands or feet or squirms in seat

2. Leaves seat in classroom or in other situations in which remaining seated is expected

3. Often runs about or climbs excessively in situations where it is inappropriate (in adolescents or adults, may be limited to subjective feelings of restlessness)

4. Often has difficulty playing or engaging in leisure activities quietly

5. Often talks excessively

6. Often acts as if "driven by a motor" and cannot remain still

Symptoms of Impulsivity

1. Often blurts out answers to questions before the questions have been completed

2. Often has difficulty waiting in lines or awaiting his or her turn in games or group situations

3. Often interrupts or intrudes on others

Source: From American Psychiatric Association: *Diagnostic and Statistical Manual of Mental Disorders, Fourth Edition, Draft Criteria,* Washington, DC, American Psychiatric Association, 1993. Adapted by permission.

symptoms of inattention and six symptoms of hyperactivity-impulsivity.

This subtype is analogous to the diagnosis of ADHD in DSM-III-R.

OTHER DIAGNOSTIC CRITERIA

DSM-IV specifies that in addition to the criteria of symptoms of inattention, hyperactivity-impulsivity, or both, the following additional criteria must be met:

- Onset of symptoms occurs no later than 7 years of age.
- Symptoms are present in two or more situations (for example, at school, work, and home).
- The disturbance causes clinically significant distress or impairment in social, academic, or occupational functioning.
- Symptoms do not occur exclusively during the course of a pervasive developmental disorder, or schizophrenia or other psychotic disorders, and is not better accounted for by a diagnosis of a mood disorder, anxiety disorder, dissociative disorder, or personality disorder.
- Symptoms have been present for the past 6 months.

Thus, DSM-IV uses the diagnostic term *attention-deficit hyperactivity disorders* (ADHD). There are three subtypes: (1) children can display symptoms primarily of inattention, (2) children can exhibit behaviors that are primarily hyperactive-impulsive, and (3) children can display symptoms of both inattention and hyperactivity.

SUMMARY

Recognition of the condition of attention deficit disorders has evolved over the past 60 years. It was first reported in medical literature in 1902 by Still, who referred to "morbid defects in moral control." The publications of Werner and Strauss (1941) and Strauss and Lehtinen (1947) were very influential, and described a behavioral syndrome that was related to brain damage and featured symptoms of hyperactivity. Clements and Peters (1962) and Clements (1966) elaborated this concept with their description of "minimal brain dysfunction" (MBD).

The *Diagnostic and Statistical Manual of Mental Disorders* (DSM), published by the American Psychiatric Association, is the major reference source for psychiatrists and psychologists. The second edition, DSM-II, published in 1968, described "hyperkinetic reaction of childhood." The third edition, DSM-III, published in 1980, described two types of attention deficit disorders: ADD with hyperactivity (ADDH) and ADD without hyperactivity (ADD/noH). In a revision of the third edition, DSM-III-R, published in 1987, the term was changed to attention-deficit hyperactivity disorder (ADHD), and the category of undifferentiated attention deficit disorder without hyperactivity (U-ADD) was added.

In 1991, the legal status of attention deficit disorder was clarified in a policy memorandum issued by the U.S. Department of Education. It stated that children with ADD may be eligible for special education services under "other health impaired" and other existing disability categories, such as learning disabilities or serious emotional disturbance. They may also qualify for accommodations in the regular classroom under Section 504 of the Rehabilitation Act.

The most recent modification appeared in 1994, in the fourth edition of DSM. DSM-IV uses the term attention deficit hyperactivity disorder (ADHD) and notes three subtypes: primarily inattentive (ADHD-IA), primarily hyperactive-impulsive (ADHD-HI), and combined inattentive and hyperactive-impulsive (ADHD).

DISCUSSION QUESTIONS

1. An early view proposed in the 1940s by Strauss, Werner, and others was that brain damage resulted in hyperactivity, distractibility, and impulsivity. These scientists thought that such brain damage could have occurred during three periods of the children's lives. Name these three periods.

2. In the 1960s, this condition was called MBD. What do these initials stand for and how did this concept differ from that of brain damage?

3. In 1968, the term *hyperkinetic reaction of childhood* was used to identify children in DSM-II. What publication do the initials *DSM* stand for? What organization publishes it? What was the major characteristic in DSM-II identification?

4. In 1980, in DSM-III, two types of ADD were identified. What were the two types? What major characteristic was identified in the DSM-III diagnosis?

5. In 1987, in DSM-III-R, the terms *ADHD* and *U-ADD* were used. What do these initials stand for, and how did the categories relate to those of DSM-III?

6. In 1991, the U.S. Department of Education issued a policy memorandum on attention deficit disorders. Describe the existing laws under which children with attention deficit disorders may receive educational services in schools.

7. In 1994, DSM-IV was published. What changes were made in diagnosing attention deficit disorders?

CHAPTER THREE

ADD AND

THE LAW

M r. and Mrs. Brown have been worried about their daughter Sally since she was 3 years old. They recognized early that Sally's behavior was very different from that of her older sister and her younger brother. Her extreme overactivity, inability to attend, and uncontrolled impulsivity were apparent at home and at school. Their continuing apprehension and concern brought them to the medical center when Sally was 7 years old. A pediatric neurologist and a clinical psychologist conducted assessments, and the staff at the medical center diagnosed Sally's problems as an attention deficit disorder. The medical center staff urged Sally's parents

to talk to the school about referring Sally for special education services. Mrs. Brown met with the principal of the school and brought the diagnostic report from the medical center. The school told Mrs. Brown that attention deficit disorders were not recognized under special education law and that Sally was not eligible for special services. After talking with members of a local parents group, Mr. and Mrs. Brown contacted an attorney who specialized in special education law. Attorney Corrine Hopkins advised Sally's parents to request a school assessment. Their attorney attended the individualized education program

(IEP) meeting at the school, serving as an advocate for Sally. (In addition to the participants who must attend the IEP meeting, the parents or the school can bring their own experts.) Ms. Hopkins gave information on the current law in regard to attention deficit disorders, information that proved important. As a result, the IEP team determined that Sally was eligible for special education services. An individualized education program was planned for Sally, and the parents and others in attendance at the meeting signed the IEP.

This chapter discusses the laws that guide the provision of educational services to children with ADD and other disabilities and protect the child's rights to receive a free, appropriate, public education. These laws have been a long time coming, and their passage required painstaking, persistent work by many individuals and groups. Before the legislation was enacted, many children were excluded from school, or simply ignored or neglected. In 1975, a fortuitous coalition of parents, legislators, and special educators led to passage of the remarkable Public Law 94-142, the **Education of All Handicapped Children's Act.** P.L. 94-142 became the basis of much of what has happened in special education during the past 20 years. In 1990, this law was reauthorized as the Individuals with Disabilities Education Act (IDEA), P.L. 101-476, which maintains the key provisions of P.L. 94-142.

There are several federal laws, as well as state laws, that protect the rights of children with attention deficit disorders. Parents and school personnel should be familiar with the following and how they affect children with attention deficit disorders.

> *The Individuals with Disabilities Education Act (IDEA), P.L. 101-476.* This is the most significant special education legislation. It provides for the *free appropriate public education* for all children with disabilities. Part B of IDEA specifies the categories of disabilities recognized under the law.
>
> *Section 504 of the Rehabilitation Act of 1973.* This civil rights legislation enables children with ADD who are not eligible for special education to receive accommodations in regular classrooms.

The Americans with Disabilities Act (ADA). Passed by Congress in 1990, this law protects all individuals in the workplace. It can also affect services for children with ADD.

THE INDIVIDUALS WITH DISABILITIES EDUCATION ACT (IDEA)

As noted previously, the U.S. law that governs special education is the **Individuals with Disabilities Education Act,** P.L. 101-476. Passed by Congress in 1990, IDEA is a reauthorization of P.L. 94-142. This landmark legislation has tremendously influenced the education of children with disabilities. IDEA guarantees all children and youth with disabilities, ages 3 to 21, the right to a free, appropriate, public education.

Part B of IDEA defines the categories of disability recognized for special education by the Department of Education. To be eligible for special education services, a child must be identified under 1 of 13 specified categories: learning disabled, seriously emotionally disturbed, mentally retarded, hard of hearing, deaf, speech or language impaired, visually impaired, orthopedically impaired, other health impaired, autistic, deaf-blind, multihandicapped, or traumatically brain injured.

The condition of attention deficit disorders is thus not identified as a separate disability in IDEA. Concern about this omission, raised by the efforts of advocacy groups when IDEA was passed in 1990, led Congress to call for a public inquiry regarding educational services to children with ADD. More than 2000 responses were received. In reaction, on September 16, 1991, the Department of Education issued a memorandum clarifying its policy on attention deficit disorders (included here as Appendix A). Significantly, the statement was endorsed and signed by representatives of three agencies: the U.S. Department of Education, the Office for Civil Rights, and the Office of Elementary and Secondary Education.

The policy memorandum clarifies the circumstances under which children with ADD are eligible for special education services under Part B of IDEA or under Section 504 of the Rehabilitation Act of 1973. A child with ADD can be eligible for special education services under Part B of IDEA, under the other health impaired (OHI) category, or under other disability categories, including specific learning disabilities (LD), and serious emotional disturbance (SED).

ELIGIBILITY UNDER PART B, "OTHER HEALTH IMPAIRED"

Many educators are unfamiliar with the category of *other health impaired* (OHI), which currently accounts for only a small percentage of the school population (about 0.13%). The term is defined in Part B of IDEA as follows:

> "Other Health Impaired" means having limited strength, vitality, or alertness, as a result of chronic or acute health problems, such as heart conditions, tuberculosis, rheumatic fever, nephritis, asthma, sickle cell anemia, hemophilia, epilepsy, lead poisoning, leukemia, or diabetes, that adversely affects educational performance.

In its memorandum, the Department of Education affirmed that ADD may meet these criteria. Specifically, it states that "where the ADD is a chronic or acute health problem resulting in limited alertness," children with ADD "may be considered disabled under Part B solely on the basis of [the ADD] within the 'other health impaired' category in situations where special education and related services are needed because of the ADD" (U.S. Department of Education, 1991, p. 3).

ELIGIBILITY UNDER PART B, OTHER DISABILITY CATEGORIES

The policy memorandum states that children with ADD are also eligible for services under Part B if the children satisfy criteria applicable to other disability categories in Part B, such as "specific learning disabilities" or "seriously emotionally disturbed." These children would be considered to have a co-existing disability.

Specific Learning Disabilities

Children with ADD may be eligible for services under the category of "specific learning disabilities" if they meet the appropriate criteria. Part B of IDEA defines *specific learning disabilities* as:

> a disorder in one or more of basic psychological processes involved in using language, spoken or written, which may manifest itself in an imperfect ability to listen, think, speak, read, write, spell, or do mathematical calculations. The term includes such conditions as perceptual handicaps, brain injury, minimal brain dysfunction, dyslexia, and developmental aphasia. The term does not include children who have learning problems which are primarily the result of visual, hearing, or motor handicaps, of mental retardation, of emotional disturbance, or of environmental, cultural, or economic disadvantage.

Seriously Emotionally Disturbed

Children with ADD are also eligible for services under Part B of IDEA if they meet the criteria for "seriously emotionally disturbed," specified in Part B of IDEA as:

> exhibiting one or more of the following characteristics over a long period of time and to a marked extent, which adversely affects educational performance.
>
> A. An inability to learn which cannot be explained by intellectual, sensory, or health factors;
> B. An inability to build or maintain satisfactory relationships with peers and teachers;
> C. Inappropriate types of behavior or feelings under normal circumstances;
> D. A general pervasive mood of unhappiness or depression; or
> E. A tendency to develop physical symptoms or fears associated with personal or school problems.
>
> The term includes children who are schizophrenic. The term does not include children who are socially maladjusted unless it is determined that they are seriously emotionally disturbed.

Authorities' estimates of the percentage of children with ADD who have coexisting learning disabilities vary, ranging between 25% and 40%. Estimates of the percentage of children with ADD who have serious emotional disturbance in the form of oppositional defiant disorders also vary, but range from 40% to 60% of elementary-age children with ADD. Roughly half of these children—that is, 20%—will eventually develop conduct disorders (Parker, 1992). Of the two million youngsters with ADD in the United States, approximately one million will need some form of special education (McKinney, Montague, & Hocutt, 1993).

It is important to distinguish between *eligibility* for services and actual special education *service*. Service includes the actual plans and placement for services, as described in the child's individualized education program (IEP). Thus, a child could be eligible for services, but be placed in a noncategorical resource room or in the regular classroom to receive service. Eligibility and actual special education instruction will depend on the eligibility criteria used in the school, as well as on the nature and severity of the student's learning and behavior problems (Lerner & Lerner, 1991; Schiller & Hauser, 1992). Students identified as having other disabilities can be placed in special education classes, in resource rooms, or in inclusive regular education classes. (Special education methods and interventions are described in Chapter 6.)

SECTION 504 OF THE REHABILITATION ACT

The Department of Education policy memorandum clarifies that children with ADD can also be served under Section 504 of the Rehabilitation Act of 1973 (P.L. 93-112) if their condition is severe enough to be considered a handicap—specifically, if their disability "substantially limits a major life activity" such as learning (Dept. of Education, 1991, p. 6). Thus, under Section 504, children with ADD may be eligible for accommodations in the regular classroom to meet their educational needs if the condition limits a major life activity (including learning). Enforced by the Office for Civil Rights (OCR), Section 504 protects the civil and constitutional rights of handicapped persons. Section 504 is sometimes called the "curb cut" law, because it is the legal basis of the mandated curb cuts in streets that allow wheelchairs (as well as strollers, bicycles, and so on) to more easily pass from street to sidewalk. The law states:

> No otherwise qualified handicapped individual . . . shall, solely by reason of his/her handicap, be excluded from participation in, be denied the benefits of, or be subject to discrimination under any program or activity receiving federal financial assistance.

Though the Rehabilitation Act was first passed by Congress in 1973, Section 504 was expanded in 1978 to cover schools.

It requires schools to furnish children with disabilities with "regular or special education and related aids and services" (Dept. of Education, 1991, p. 6) designed to meet their educational needs as adequately as the needs of nondisabled children are met. Their education programs must be based on the least restrictive placement principle; include a full individual placement evaluation, nondiscriminatory tests, and an annual reevaluation of special education placement; and provide for procedural due process.

Section 504 has many similarities with IDEA, but it also contains some fundamental differences. Section 504 does not provide funds for state and local governments as IDEA does (Turnbull, 1993). Section 504's requirements in regard to schools and educational institutions are continually being reinterpreted under case law—that is, in accordance with court decisions in precedent cases based on this law (Rothstein, 1993; Turnbull, 1993). Section 504 covers a broader population of individuals with disabilities than IDEA. Section 504 legislation has been instrumental in increasing the number of students with learning disabilities who are successfully going on to college and postsecondary schools (Vogel & Adelman, 1993).

Students with ADD may not be receiving services from special education teachers but may still need assistance in school because of their disabilities. A child with ADD is a "qualified handicapped person" under Section 504 if (a) the child is between the ages of 3 and 21 and (b) the handicapping condition substantially limits the child's ability to learn or to otherwise benefit from his or her education program (Madson, 1990).

Many youngsters with ADD may qualify for accommodations under Section 504. For example, a student with ADD who may not qualify for services under a school district's severe eligibility specifications for learning disabilities might meet criteria to be served under Section 504. Eligible students require **reasonable accommodations** to benefit from the educational process, accommodations made by the regular teacher within the regular classroom.

School districts should be aware of their obligations under Section 504. Schools need to develop procedures for administering to the specific needs of students. They must also provide training to school staff with the techniques and procedures necessary to accommodate students under Section 504. Classroom teachers can accommodate students' needs by modifying the classroom adapting the curriculum, structuring time appropriately, and modifying assessment procedures. School administrators can provide for the needs of children with ADD without major changes in school procedures (Reeve, 1990; Teeter, 1991). (Methods for making reasonable accommodations in the regular classroom are presented in Chapter 6.)

Although Section 504 does not require the complete IEP for an individual student, Section 504 does require the school to develop a Section 504 plan for the student (see page 45).

THE AMERICANS WITH DISABILITIES ACT

The Americans with Disabilities Act (ADA), passed by Congress in 1990, explicitly prohibits discrimination in hiring and requires accessibility in public accommodations. ADA provides yet another legal means of requiring public and private educational institutions and systems to accommodate persons with disabilities. In many respects ADA mirrors the Rehabilitation Act, but it applies to employers who were not covered by Section 504. Primarily, the Americans with Disabilities Act is aimed at providing people with disabilities at the workplace, requiring employers to make "reasonable accommodations" for disabled workers, although legal remedies under ADA are also being sought for students. Much of what the ADA requires of schools is already covered by the Rehabilitation Act, but ADA provides more legal remedies (Reed, 1991; Rothstein, 1993).

Some portions of the law apply to schools, and these regulations may affect children with ADD. Title II of the Americans with Disabilities Act applies to public schools and prohibits the denial of education services, programs, or activities to all students with disabilities. It also prohibits discrimination against all such students once enrolled (Aronofsky, 1992).

Title III of ADA applies to private schools, which cannot deny access to or impose eligibility criteria that exclude persons with disabilities because of their disabilities. They must make reasonable modifications in policies, practices, or procedures, including offering auxiliary aids and services, when such modifications are needed to meet the needs of persons with disabilities. They must provide education courses and examinations in a manner likely to ensure results that reflect a disabled person's actual achievement level rather than the disability. Thus, ADA appears to impose a new set of legal obligations and rights that affect the private school education of children with ADD (Aronofsky, 1992).

ALTERNATIVE LEARNING PLAN AS PER
SECTION 504 OF THE REHABILITATION ACT OF 1973

STUDENT: _____ SCHOOL: _____ GRADE: _____

DATE OF IMPLEMENTATION: _____ TERMINATION: _____ REVIEW: _____

STATEMENT OF STUDENT'S PERFORMANCE AS IT RELATES TO THIS "PLAN": _____

INTERVENTION/ STRATEGY	IMPLEMENTOR(S)	MONITORING DATE	COMMENTS

CC: Parents
Section 504 Coordinator
Principal
Teacher
Educational Record

45

"... I can't go bowling tonight, Freddie, I'm cramming for an IQ test tomorrow..."

Source: Reprinted by permission: Tribune Media Services.

ADA stipulates that examinations or courses related to secondary or postsecondary education, professional, or trade purposes must be offered in a place and manner accessible to persons with disabilities or alternative arrangements must be made. Accessibility may mean allowing extra time, readers, or similar accommodations (Rothstein, 1993).

THE INDIVIDUALIZED EDUCATION PROGRAM

One of IDEA's major provisions is that an **individualized education program** (IEP) be written for each student identified with a disability, including children with ADD. A multidisciplinary team assesses the child, and the IEP is developed and written at a meeting that includes the parents. The IEP must indicate long-range goals and short-term objectives for the individual child. It also specifies placement for any services that may be needed. The IEP serves as a tool throughout the entire teaching and evaluating process, linking the assessment to the services and instruction that the student receives. It must, by law, be written within 30 days of the initial diagnosis. Thus, for the eligible child with ADD, the IEP is a blueprint and an entitlement to a free appropriate public education and necessary related services.

The IEP serves several purposes:

1. *The IEP is a written plan for a particular student.* Developed by the IEP team, it specifies goals, objectives, placement, and related services for an individual student.
2. *The IEP serves as a management tool* for ensuring that the education is appropriately designed for the individual student's special learning needs and that the special education services are actually delivered and monitored.
3. *The IEP is a working document* that can be modified as the child's needs change.

As illustrated in Figure 3.1, the IEP process includes three major stages:

1. The *referral stage,* consisting of prereferral activities and referral and initial planning;
2. The *assessment stage,* consisting of the multidisciplinary evaluation and the IEP meeting; and
3. The *instruction stage,* consisting of the implementing of the teaching plan and monitoring and review of the student's progress.

THE IEP MEETING

The IEP meeting occurs after a multidisciplinary team has gathered the information needed to assess the child. The parents are contacted to arrange a convenient time for the meeting.

The following persons must be included at the IEP meeting:

1. A representative of the school
2. The student's teacher
3. One or both parents
4. The student, when appropriate
5. Other individuals, at the discretion of the parents or the school, who may include professionals who participated in

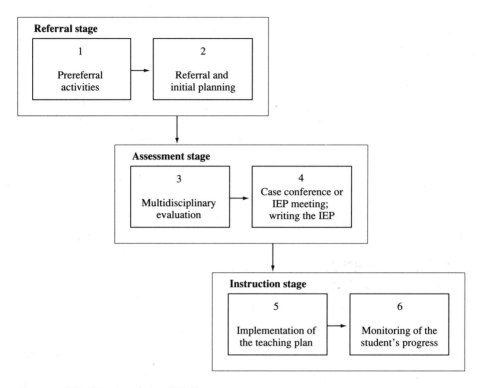

FIGURE 3.1   Stages of the IEP Process

> *Source:* From *Cases in Learning and Behavior Problems: A Guide to Individualized Education Programs*, p. 3, by J. Lerner, D. K. Dawson, and L. J. Horvath. Copyright © 1980 by Houghton Mifflin Company. Adapted with permission.

the evaluation (such as psychologists, social workers, or special educators), legal experts, private therapists, or diagnosticians

Cohen (1993) offers the following advice to parents of children with ADD:

> Never go to a meeting alone. At least one other person should accompany you, both to provide emotional support and to take notes of what transpired. Do not assume that the official records of the meeting will accurately reflect what actually transpired. In addition, wherever possible, make sure that you receive a copy of the report prepared by the school district of the meeting before you depart. (p. 7)

At the same time, the conference should be kept as small as possible so as not to overwhelm the parents. The parents must sign the IEP before it can be put into effect.

The Content of the IEP

The IEP must include the following components:

1. A statement of the student's present levels of educational performance
2. A statement of annual goals, including short-term objectives
3. A statement of the specific special education and related services to be provided to the student, and the extent to which the student will be able to participate in the regular education program
4. The projected dates for initiation of services and the anticipated duration of the services
5. Appropriate objective criteria and evaluation procedures and schedules for determining at least annually whether the short-term instructional objectives are being met

Goals and Objectives

The IEP must specify long-term goals (goals to be accomplished in one year) and short-term objectives (specific measurable steps toward those long-term goals). To determine long-term goals for students with ADD, the child's age, grade, amount of previous learning, strengths, weaknesses, and interests must be considered. Other important considerations are the severity of the child's disability and the child's academic achievement and social performance (Parker, 1992).

Long-term goals are broken down into *short-term objectives*, designed to move the student step by step to achieve the goal for the year. Each goal must encompass at least two short-term objectives. For a student with ADD and a coexisting disability, goals must be formulated for both the ADD and the coexisting disability. Goals and objectives related to the ADD can be in many areas, including: social skills, attention span, organization, listening skills, affective development, self-control, and interpersonal relationships. Objectives and goals for the coexisting disability should be relevant to the child's needs in these areas.

Related Services

Other services that will assist a student with ADD to receive an appropriate education are known as **related services.**

As designated in the law, related services include transportation and such developmental, corrective, and other supportive services as are required to assist a child with disabilities to benefit from special education (including audiology and speech pathology, psychological services, physical therapy (PT), occupational therapy (OT), recreation, early identification and assessment, counseling services, school health services, social work services in school, parent counseling and training, and medical services for diagnostic and evaluation purposes) (Turnbull, 1993).

PLACEMENT FOR SERVICES

Deciding where the student will be placed for instruction is a critical component of the assessment-teaching process. Placement refers not to a specific place but to where the special services and instruction are to be delivered. The team recommends an educational placement for services as part of the student's IEP.

Two components of the law relate to the placement of students.

THE CONTINUUM OF ALTERNATIVE PLACEMENTS

Schools must establish an array of educational placements to meet the varied needs of students with disabilities. Among the options are regular classes, resource rooms, special classes, and special schools.

THE LEAST RESTRICTIVE ENVIRONMENT (LRE)

To the maximum extent possible, children with disabilities are to be educated with typically developing children. Separate schooling should be used only when education in the regular class with the use of supplementary aids and services is not effective. The intent of this requirement is to help prepare students with disabilities for living comfortably in the larger society of individuals who do not have disabilities. In deciding placement the IEP team must consider the extent to which each student with a disability should be educated with students who do not have disabilities. Placement decisions must reflect consideration of the least restrictive environment for each student.

INCLUSION

A placement model used in many schools today is called **inclusion.** The philosophical position underlying this concept is to place and instruct *all* children in the neighborhood school, including children with all types of disabilities at all levels of severity. There is a strong movement toward inclusion in schools receiving support from certain parent groups, organizations, school boards, and legislative bodies (Fuchs & Fuchs, 1994).

To establish an inclusive setting, multidisciplinary teams of professionals must apply their collective skills and knowledge to create a unique, personal program for each student. All staff members should be involved in making decisions, teaching, and evaluating students' needs and progress.

The philosophy and goals of inclusion are controversial, with vocal supporters and opponents. The issue of where the child will receive services has become the most controversial issue in special education (Kauffman, 1993). Supporters of inclusion reason that students with disabilities are best served through placement in a regular classroom because it provides students with opportunities to experience the mainstream of society.

How does the movement toward inclusion apply to children with ADD? Some parents and educational professionals maintain that a range of placement options is needed to most appropriately meet the needs of children with ADD or children with learning disabilities (Learning Disabilities Association of America, 1993). The reasoning here is that some students with ADD need extra assistance from special educators in resource rooms or even more restrictive settings such as special classrooms. Such placements allow more intensive, ongoing interventions, with educational programs individualized to meet the child's unique needs (Parker, 1992). Gallagher (1993) notes that "Where should exceptional children be placed?" is an important political question, but two other questions are even more important: "What content should we teach?" and "What educational tools should we use?"

CH.A.D.D., an advocacy organization for children with attention deficit disorders, has adopted a position paper on the issue of inclusion, which emphasizes the need to have options in placement to meet the unique needs of the individual child. Their position paper expresses the fear that full inclusion could jeopardize the law's provision for a continuum of alternative placements and reduce the individualized instruction that many children with ADD desperately need (CH.A.D.D., 1993a). They recommend "a continued recognition of the importance of the availability of a continuum of special education services and placement settings designed to meet the individual needs of each child with a disability" (p. 11).

PROCEDURAL SAFEGUARDS

The Individuals with Disabilities Education Act includes regulations to protect the rights of students with disabilities and their families. These procedural safeguards include the following:

1. Parents must consent in writing to have their child evaluated and to the plans and placement set forth in the written individualized education program. Before a student is placed in a special education program and services begin, the parents must agree in writing to the IEP plan.

2. The assessment must be conducted in the student's native language, and the findings must be reported in the parents' native language.

3. Tests and procedures used for the evaluation and placement must be free of racial or cultural bias. (It may be virtually impossible to find a test devoid of bias. Using language is a cultural bias; in fact, taking a test is itself culture-bound.)

4. The parents have the right to see all information collected and used in the decision making.

5. Parents and students have the right to an impartial due process hearing if they disagree with the IEP decisions. If the parents or the school disagree with the findings of the impartial due process hearing, either party can ask for a higher-level impartial due process hearing. If the second hearing is unsatisfactory, the next step is a civil action lawsuit.

6. The confidentiality of all reports and records of the students is protected under the law.

The law also protects the student's right to have the individualized education plan implemented. In a recent circuit court case, the parents and student sued a high school American history teacher who refused to carry out the IEP developed by the team, which required testing modifications. As a result, the student failed the course. The Circuit Court of West Virginia found for the parents and the teacher was ordered to pay $15,000 plus legal expenses to the student ("Ignoring IEP," 1994).

DEPARTMENT OF EDUCATION INITIATIVES FOR RESEARCH ON ATTENTION DEFICIT DISORDERS

The U.S. Department of Education (1991) clarification memorandum on ADD funded research centers to further the study of attention deficit disorders and to synthesize knowledge about effective assessment and intervention practices and programs for serving students with ADD. The following centers were funded to conduct research on ADD:

University of Miami, Coral Gables, FL. Dr. James McKinney, project director.
Arkansas Children's Hospital Research Center, Little Rock, AK. Dr. Roscoe Dykman, project director.
University of California-Irvine, Irvine, CA. Dr. James Swanson, project director.
Research Triangle Institute, Research Triangle Park, NC. Dr. Tom Fiore, project director.
Federal Resource Center, University of Kentucky, Lexington, KY. Larry Carlson, project director.

CASE LAW

Laws (statutes and regulations) alone cannot provide complete guidance as to what is required in every situation. The courts are the forum for interpreting what statutes and regulations require. The judiciary has the unique functions of saying what the Constitution or a federal statute or regulation means in each case, setting forth the facts that underlie their interpretation, and commanding the parties in the case (or other courts, if the case is on appeal) to take certain actions. Jurists look to legislative history, similar laws, and the language of the statutes and regulations themselves to provide insight as to what is required in each set of circumstances. Though a court's rulings are limited to the controversy before it, the general commentaries included in judicial opinions often indicate how courts will decide other related controversies in cases with similar factual background (Rothstein, 1993). Court decisions on individual cases that set precedents for later legal disputes are collectively called *case law.*

Many special education cases have been decided by the courts, and some have gone to the U.S. Supreme Court, the highest court in the nation. For example, in a recent case decided by the U.S. Supreme Court, the parents of a child with learning disabilities and attention deficit disorders sued a school in North Carolina. The parents charged that public school officials had failed to provide their daughter with an appropriate education. They had placed their daughter in a private school and were suing for reimbursement of tuition costs. The case was appealed at several levels, and the U.S. Supreme Court ruled unanimously on November 9, 1993, that the school system can be required to reimburse parents for private school costs when public schools are unable to meet the special needs of their child ("Ignoring IEP," 1993).

When parents of children with attention deficit disorders find that schools have denied their children access to a "free appropriate public education," they often must turn to the legal system to obtain in the schools the services to which their children are entitled. Recognizing this need, attorneys and law firms are beginning to specialize in special education law.

SUMMARY

There are a number of federal laws that protect the rights of children with attention deficit disorders. The most important legislation is the Individuals with Disabilities Education Act (IDEA), which provides services for children whose ADD qualifies as a disability. Section 504 of the Rehabilitation Act of 1973 enables some children with ADD to receive accommodations in the regular classroom. The Americans with Disabilities Act (ADA) also provides some protections for children with ADD.

IDEA is the law under which all children and youth with disabilities, ages 3 to 21, are titled to a free appropriate public education. The U.S. Department of Education established that children with attention deficit disabilities are among those who can receive special education services, under the classifications of other health impaired or other disabilities, such as learning disabilities or serious emotional disturbance.

Under Section 504 of the Rehabilitation Act and also under the Americans with Disabilities Act, children with ADD may also be entitled to appropriate accommodations in the regular classroom.

The individualized education program (IEP) provides for a written plan, written by a multidisciplinary team for each child. It specifies goals and objectives, needed related services, and placement.

Participants at the IEP meeting include a representative of the school; the student's teacher; one or both parents; the student, when appropriate; and other individuals.

Specific contents of the IEP include statements of the current level of performance, special education and related services, the long-term goals and short-term objectives, the date for starting services and anticipated duration of services, and criteria for evaluation.

Placement is determined in the IEP. Two key provisions of IDEA related to placement are the continuum of alternative placements and the least restrictive environment. The term *inclusion* refers to placement in the regular class in the child's home school, an issue of controversy.

Procedural safeguards within IDEA protect the rights of the child.

Case law is the body of precedent-setting cases decided by the courts. It extends the interpretation of the law.

DISCUSSION QUESTIONS

1. The special education law was reauthorized in 1990. What are the name and acronym of the current special education law? What is Part B of the law?

2. Children with attention deficit disorders may be eligible for special education under three different federal laws. What are they?

3. What are three categories in the special education law under which children with ADD may be eligible for services? Describe the criteria for eligibility under each of the categories.

4. What kinds of individuals does Section 504 of the Rehabilitation Act of 1973 protect? What kinds of programs or organizations are affected by Section 504? What federal agency is responsible for enforcing Section 504? What kinds of services are children with ADD entitled to under Section 504?

5. Two components of the special education law are the *least restrictive environment* and the *continuum of alternative placements*. Describe the meaning of these two components of the law and their implications for children with attention deficit disorders.

PART II

ASSESSMENT, TEACHING METHODS, AND PARENTING

CHAPTER 4

ASSESSMENT

Snapshot

The Purposes of Assessment

Principles of Assessment

Clinical Assessment
The Case History and Interview
Behavior Rating Scales
Cognitive/Intellectual Assessment
Neuropsychological Assessment
Continuous Performance Tests
Academic Screening

School Assessment
Legislation
Observation
Academic Assessment
Informal and Portfolio Assessment
Public School Programs for Assessing ADD

Limitations and Concerns

Dennis W. is 8 years old and in the third grade at King Elementary School. Hyperactive and impulsive behavior and his failing grades led Dennis's mother to seek help for him at the Central Medical and Psychological Services Clinic. He was thoroughly examined by the pediatrician at the clinic and assessed psychologically by Dr. Barbara Lewis, a licensed clinical psychologist. The clinic staff reviewed the findings and diagnosed Dennis as a youngster with attention deficit disorders who needed special teaching. Dennis's mother and Dr. Lewis decided to make a referral to the special education department at King Elementary for a school evaluation

to determine his eligibility for special education services at King.

The clinical assessment. Dr. Lewis's assessment at the clinic included these procedures:

- An interview with Dennis's parents. Information was obtained on the family background.
- The taking of a case history of Dennis. Information was obtained on his development milestones, school adjustment, school problems, and home adjustment.
- The administration of behavior rating scales. Dennis's parents completed the Conners Parent Rating Scale–48, and Dennis's teacher completed the Conners Teacher Rating Scale–28.
- Obtaining cognitive/intellectual information. Dr. Lewis tested Dennis with the Wechsler Intelligence Scale for Children (3rd ed.) (WISC III).
- Academic screening. Dr. Lewis screened Dennis's reading

mathematics, and spelling achievement with the Revised Wide Range Achievement Test (3rd ed.) (WRAT-III).

■ Social, family, and emotional screening. To assess Dennis's social, family, and emotional status, Dr. Lewis interviewed his parents and administered the Parent Stress Index.

■ Continuous performance tests. These were used to assess specific aspects of Dennis's attention and impulse regulation capabilities.

■ Medical examination. The pediatrician at the clinic examined Dennis thoroughly.

After pulling together all of the assessment information, Dr. Lewis diagnosed Dennis as having attention-deficit hyperactivity disorder—primarily the hyperactive-impulsive type—using the criteria in the fourth edition of the *Diagnostic and Statistical Manual of Mental Disorders* (DSM-IV). The case history indicated that Dennis's parents have been worried about Dennis's inattention, impulsivity, and hyperactivity since his infancy. Even at age 8, he rarely sleeps through the night. His impulsivity keeps him from having friends, he requires constant supervision, and his inattention is beginning to cause problems in school. The language spoken at home is English. The test results of the WISC III show that Dennis's intellectual abilities are within the high normal range. The pediatrician at the clinic diagnosed Dennis as having ADD, but she wanted information from the school assessment before prescribing any medication.

Following the clinic's assessment, Dennis's mother and Dr. Lewis agreed to refer Dennis to the King School District Special Education Department for a school assessment and consideration for special education services.

The school assessment. Dennis was referred to the special education department of King Elementary for an evaluation. The school assessment followed the rules and regulations set forth in the Individuals with Disabilities Education Act (IDEA). The school selected a multidisciplinary evaluation team consisting of the school psychologist, Dennis's teacher, a special education coordinator, and the school counselor. The multidisciplinary team used the following procedures to obtain the assessment information:

■ Interviews with Dennis's parents and with Dennis. The school psychologist conducted the interviews.

■ Classroom observation. The school counselor and the special education coordinator separately observed Dennis in his classroom.

■ Academic achievement testing. The special education co-ordinator measured Dennis's academic achievement by administering the Woodcock-Johnson Psychoeducational Battery, by reviewing Dennis's cumulative records, and by discussing Dennis's current academic status with his teacher.

The classroom observers reported that Dennis was very talkative in class, that his activity level was very high, and that when he was expected to listen, his attention wandered. Dennis also exhibited problems relating to peers, pushing his classmates and grabbing school supplies (pencils, calculators, notebooks) from them. Dennis was "on task" only 30% of the time and "off task" 70% of the time. During the observation, his classroom behaviors included searching in his desk, talking with peers, not following directions, scooting his desk around the room, playing with a piece of paper, lying down in his desk, talking loudly, leaning back in his chair, playing with his shirt, and standing up at his desk. After the first few minutes of a lesson, he would turn away from what was happening around him, involving himself in other activities.

The special education coordinator reported that Dennis's academic skills in reading and mathematics are slightly below average for his age and grade.

Following the multidisciplinary evaluation, a team met to plan an individualized education program (IEP) for Dennis. In attendance were Dennis's parents, Dennis's teacher, the school psychologist, the principal of King Elementary, the special education coordinator, the special education teacher, and Dr. Lewis, the clinical psychologist from the Central Medical and Psychological Services Clinic. The IEP team reviewed the information obtained in the multidisciplinary evaluation and concurred that Dennis has an attention deficit disorder.

However, Dennis cannot be classified as having learning disabilities, because his discrepancy score does not meet the school's eligibility criteria for learning disabilities. He is also not eligible to be classified as seriously emotionally disturbed. Dennis *is* eligible for special education services, and the IEP team recommended that he receive such services, under the category of "other health impaired." They further recommended that he be placed in the regular classroom and also receive resource services from the special education teacher, Mr. Sanchez, who is certified to teach children with learning disabilities and those with behavior disorders. In addition, Mr. Sanchez and Dennis's regular teacher are to collaborate to design appropriate accommodations for Dennis in the third-grade class.

All participants at the meeting agreed to the plan, and all signed the IEP.

In this chapter, we review the process of assessing children suspected of having attention deficit disorders. In the assessment process, the clinician obtains pertinent information about the individual. Analysis of the information collected leads to identification of the disability and diagnosis of the problem. This chapter reviews (1) the purposes of assessment, (2) the principles of assessment, (3) clinical assessment, (4) school assessment, and (5) limitations and cautions about assessment.

THE PURPOSES OF ASSESSMENT

There are several purposes for conducting an assessment or for gathering pertinent information about a child.

1. *Assessment information provides the basis for the identification and diagnosis of ADD.* To see whether the child is eligible for special education services or for Section 504 accommodations in the regular classroom, an array of information is gathered to form a comprehensive picture of the individual's behaviors, abilities, attitudes, background, environment, family situation, school history, and so on. The process of obtaining such useful information is **assessment**; the pulling together of this information into a cohesive and meaningful whole is the **diagnosis.**

2. *The assessment information and the diagnosis provide guidelines for intervention, therapy, and teaching.* The information obtained during the assessment helps in planning intervention procedures; developing guidelines for behavior management; determining the need for further medical treatment; structuring therapy for the child and family; and determining the need for special education teaching strategies, accommodations in the regular classroom, or both. Each child needs different interventions and treatment.

3. *Assessment allows changes in the child's behavior and achievement to be monitored and reviewed.* The child's progress must be periodically checked to see whether he or she is improving; how the interventions are affecting his or her attentional, behavioral, and academic situation; and what changes should be made in the intervention plan. A review assessment

provides the means to monitor and evaluate the child's status vis-à-vis ADD and related issues. Review might show, for example, that the intervention is helping the child with certain problems but that other difficulties are now occurring. Reassessment is needed to address these new problems.

PRINCIPLES OF ASSESSMENT

Those assessing a child who may have an attention deficit disorder must comply with basic professional standards. Since the assessment information is typically gathered by several different professionals (medical specialists, clinical psychologists, school psychologists, social workers, special educators, speech and language pathologists, and so on), each professional must follow his or her own professional regulations and ethical standards. All must maintain the confidentiality of the client, keep complete records, follow standard testing criteria, and be properly licensed and certified.

Assessment requires pulling together the various pieces of information and also communicating with other specialists, with the parents and family, and with the child. Guidelines for assessing individuals with attention deficit disorders include:

1. *Assessment must be multidisciplinary.* Because so many different aspects of a child's life contribute to the problem of ADD, assessment is necessarily complex. Biological, psychological, and social dimensions of the problem, as well as medical and educational factors, must all be considered. The assessment must be multidisciplinary, involving several different professionals and specialists. In reaching the diagnosis, all of the multidisciplinary assessment information must be pulled together. Making a diagnosis is somewhat like putting together the pieces of a puzzle: information from one source should corroborate and validate information from another.

2. *A differential diagnosis must be made to rule out other psychological disorders with similar symptoms.* Not all children who are inattentive, impulsive, or hyperactive have attention deficit disorders. Other psychological disorders have similar symptoms but require different treatment approaches. A **differential diagnosis** determines whether the symptoms are due to an attention deficit disorder or another psychological problem. For example, a child's inattention may arise from frustration over schoolwork that is too difficult. Problems in the home may also

interfere with a child's concentration. Medications taken for other diseases can cause inattention, hyperactivity, or anxiety. Children with limited proficiency in English are likely to have trouble paying attention in classes conducted in English. Other serious mental conditions that may mimic attention deficit disorders, such as childhood depression, are discussed in Chapter 9.

3. *Assessment should follow a two-tiered process.* A two-tiered assessment process is recommended to (1) identify and diagnose the child with ADD and (2) plan the school instruction. The two-tiered model has been suggested by clinical psychologists; the Professional Group for Attention and Related Disorders (PGARD) (1991), an interdisciplinary group of professionals concerned about children with ADD; and Parker (1992). In this model, Tier 1 consists of the **clinical assessment**— that is, the diagnostic evaluation for ADD. Tier 2 consists of the **school assessment,** which encompasses planning for intervention by the school.

The school and clinical professionals must work out the assessment procedures for each tier. For example, psychometric evaluation and intelligence testing may be conducted at the first tier (Parker, 1992) or at the second (PGARD, 1991).

The first tier of the assessment process is focused on identification and diagnosis. At this stage, the evaluator determines whether the child shows the primary characteristics of ADD— inattention, impulsivity, and hyperactivity—and looks for other symptoms, including early onset and chronic duration, while determining that the symptoms are not due to another psychological disorder.

The evaluator also collects information about the child's home, school, and community. A case history, interviews, and rating scales are essential Tier 1 procedures. The *Diagnostic and Statistical Manual of Mental Disorders* (DSM) provides the critical criteria for making the diagnosis at this stage of evaluation. The next section, on clinical assessment, discusses Tier 1 information in greater detail.

At the next tier of assessment, the focus shifts from identification and diagnosis to using the assessment information for school-based treatment—planning the intervention, teaching strategies, classroom accommodations, and behavior management appropriate for the individual child. School-based evaluation methods include classroom observation, academic and achievement assessment, psychoeducational tests, and functional assessment. Criteria from the Individuals with Disabilities Education Act (IDEA) and Section 504 of the Rehabilitation Act of 1973 provide guidelines for school assessment.

CLINICAL ASSESSMENT

As noted, the purposes of the first tier of assessment are to identify the child's problem and make a diagnosis. Often, a child who is exhibiting behavioral problems at school, at home, or both, is referred to a psychologist—commonly, one in the private sector—who has experience and training in the diagnosis of childhood disorders. The clinical assessment can also be done in the school setting by a multidisciplinary team that includes a qualified school psychologist. Referrals can come from several different sources, including medical specialists (pediatricians, family-practice doctors, neurologists, or child psychiatrists), school personnel (teachers, therapists, counselors, or social workers), or parents. The referral may be made for a variety of reasons: the child's behavior at home or at school may have become unmanageable; he or she may be having serious academic difficulties or may be failing to complete tasks or turn in homework; or his or her grades may have declined markedly. Obvious social difficulties, a marked change in the child's mood, or serious concern about the child's emotional functioning or low self-esteem may also lead to a referral.

During the clinical assessment, a variety of information is obtained through various means. The family and child are interviewed to learn about the child's family background, past and present symptoms, developmental and medical history, school history, social adjustment, and general day-to-day adaptive functioning. The child is also given a standardized intelligence test and screened for academic achievement (Barkley, 1990; Barkley & Murphy, 1993). In some cases, he or she may be given psychological projective tests to assess his or her personality. The child's parents and teachers complete rating scales.

Also useful to know are the parents' perceptions of the child's problems, the child's perceptions of his or her problematic behavior, the types of school programs in the local area, and the child's adjustment and behavior at home.

THE CASE HISTORY AND INTERVIEW

Much needed information comes from a comprehensive interview with the parents. In conducting the interview, the psychologist explains the nature and purpose of the testing and obtains the parents' consent to proceed. The interview provides the psychologist with an opportunity to talk with and establish a collaborative relationship with the parents. With young children, only the parents attend the initial interview, but with older children, often both the child and the parents participate.

Family Background

During the initial interview, it is important to recognize how the parents perceive the child's presenting problems. Specifically, what are the child's difficulties? What is the frequency, intensity, and duration of the problematic behaviors? For example, if the presenting problems involve aggressive behavior toward siblings, the interviewer would try to determine under what circumstances the aggression occurs, when it began, and how severe it has become.

The psychologist also learns about the family background during the parent interview, gathering information about the parents' health history and genetic history, the family membership, and the family's stability. The family's cultural and language background are important considerations.

The Child's History

During the interview, the child's developmental history is elicited. Information about the child's birth, early development, and temperament as an infant is important, since symptoms of ADD can be evident very early in a child's life. The child's medical history is critical. Some medications produce side effects that diminish a child's attentional capabilities. The medical history may also reveal information about such events as seizures, a head injury, or an ear infection that may have caused a temporary hearing loss. All of this information helps the psychologist determine whether other conditions may be the cause of the child's problems.

It is also important to know about the child's school background and school experiences. What experiences has the child had in various school settings—in day care, preschool, primary, or secondary school? What specific behavioral problems have interfered with his or her adjustment at school? What kinds of school interventions have been tried, and how effective have they been?

The child's adjustment in the home environment is another important part of the picture. What specific behavioral difficulties are evident at home or in other nonschool environments (such as in social groups, church groups, scout groups, or during recreational activities)?

BEHAVIOR RATING SCALES

Behavior rating scales offer valid and reliable means of measuring a child's behavior and adjustment and comparing them to those of other children of the same sex and age. In using such scales, a person familiar with the child (such as a parent or teacher) answers a series of questions about the child's behavior (McKinney, Montague, & Hocutt, 1993). For example, in the ADHD Rating Scale (DuPaul, 1991) the parent and the teacher separately answer 14 questions on the child's behavior, taken from DSM III-R.

Examples of parent and teacher rating scales are shown on pages 68–72. The clinician interprets the rating scales using guides that are included with the scales.

Some rating scales are specifically designed to be answered by a child's parents. The Child Behavior Checklist for Parents (Achenbach, 1991) is one example (see page 68). Such scales measure the child's behavior at home and also the parents' perceptions of the child.

Other rating scales are specifically designed to be answered by the child's teacher; examples include the Conners Teacher Rating Scale–28 (Conners, 1989; see Table 4.1, p. 72) and the Teacher Report Form (Achenbach, 1991; see page 70). These scales concern the student's behavior at school. Elementary school teachers are likely to know their students better than high school teachers. Special education teachers who work with the student in small groups may rate a child differently than a classroom teacher who observes the child in a larger social setting.

Evaluators find comparing the rating scales from different sources useful. For example, how do the parents' ratings of the child compare to the teacher's? How do the special education teacher's ratings compare to those of the regular teacher?

The Achenbach Child Behavior Checklist for Parents

Below is a list of items that describe children and youth. For each item that describes your child **now or within the past 6 months**, please circle the **2** if the item is **very true** or **often true** of your child. Circle the **1** if the item is **somewhat** or **sometimes true** of your child. If the item is **not true** of your child, circle the **0**. Please answer all items as well as you can, even if some do not seem to apply to your child.

0 = Not True (as far as you know)   **1 = Somewhat or Sometimes True**   **2 = Very True or Often True**

0 1 2	1.	Acts too young for his/her age
0 1 2	2.	Allergy (describe): _____
0 1 2	3.	Argues a lot
0 1 2	4.	Asthma
0 1 2	5.	Behaves like opposite sex
0 1 2	6.	Bowel movements outside toilet
0 1 2	7.	Bragging, boasting
0 1 2	8.	Can't concentrate, can't pay attention for long
0 1 2	9.	Can't get his/her mind off certain thoughts; obsessions (describe): _____
0 1 2	10.	Can't sit still, restless, or hyperactive
0 1 2	11.	Clings to adults or too dependent
0 1 2	12.	Complains of loneliness
0 1 2	13.	Confused or seems to be in a fog
0 1 2	14.	Cries a lot
0 1 2	15.	Cruel to animals

0 1 2	32.	Feels he/she has to be perfect
0 1 2	33.	Feels or complains that no one loves him/her
0 1 2	34.	Feels others are out to get him/her
0 1 2	35.	Feels worthless or inferior
0 1 2	36.	Gets hurt a lot, accident-prone
0 1 2	37.	Gets in many fights
0 1 2	38.	Gets teased a lot
0 1 2	39.	Hangs around with others who get in trouble
0 1 2	40.	Hears sounds or voices that aren't there (describe): _____
0 1 2	41.	Impulsive or acts without thinking
0 1 2	42.	Would rather be alone than with others
0 1 2	43.	Lying or cheating
0 1 2	44.	Bites fingernails
0 1 2	45.	Nervous, highstrung, or tense
0 1 2	46.	Nervous movements or twitching (describe): _____

0	1	2	16.	Cruelty, bullying, or meanness to others	
0	1	2	17.	Daydreams or gets lost in his/her thoughts	
0	1	2	18.	Deliberately harms self or attempts suicide	
0	1	2	19.	Demands a lot of attention	
0	1	2	20.	Destroys his/her own things	
0	1	2	21.	Destroys things belonging to his/her family or others	
0	1	2	22.	Disobedient at home	
0	1	2	23.	Disobedient at school	
0	1	2	24.	Doesn't eat well	
0	1	2	25.	Doesn't get along with other kids	
0	1	2	26.	Doesn't seem to feel guilty after misbehaving	
0	1	2	27.	Easily jealous	
0	1	2	28.	Eats or drinks things that are not food—*don't* include sweets (describe): _____	
0	1	2	29.	Fears certain animals, situations, or places, other than school (describe): _____	
0	1	2	30.	Fears going to school	
0	1	2	31.	Fears he/she might think or do something bad	

0	1	2	47.	Nightmares	
0	1	2	48.	Not liked by other kids	
0	1	2	49.	Constipated, doesn't move bowels	
0	1	2	50.	Too fearful or anxious	
0	1	2	51.	Feels dizzy	
0	1	2	52.	Feels too guilty	
0	1	2	53.	Overeating	
0	1	2	54.	Overtired	
0	1	2	55.	Overweight	
			56.	Physical problems without known medical cause:	
0	1	2	a.	Aches or pains (*not* headaches)	
0	1	2	b.	Headaches	
0	1	2	c.	Nausea, feels sick	
0	1	2	d.	Problems with eyes (describe): _____	
0	1	2	e.	Rashes or other skin problems	
0	1	2	f.	Stomachaches or cramps	
0	1	2	g.	Vomiting, throwing up	
0	1	2	h.	Other (describe): _____	

The Achenbach Child Behavior Checklist for Teachers

Below is a list of items that describe pupils. For each item that describes the pupil **now or within the past 2 months**, please circle the **2** if the item is **very true** or **often true** of the pupil. Circle the **1** if the item is **somewhat** or **sometimes true** of the pupil. If the item is **not true** of the pupil, circle the **0**. Please answer all items as well as you can, even if some do not seem to apply to this pupil.

0 = Not True (as far as you know) 1 = Somewhat or Sometimes True 2 = Very True or Often True

0 1 2	1. Acts too young for his/her age	
0 1 2	2. Hums or makes other odd noises in class	
0 1 2	3. Argues a lot	
0 1 2	4. Fails to finish things he/she starts	
0 1 2	5. Behaves like opposite sex	
0 1 2	6. Defiant, talks back to staff	
0 1 2	7. Bragging, boasting	
0 1 2	8. Can't concentrate, can't pay attention for long	
0 1 2	9. Can't get his/her mind off certain thoughts; obsessions (describe):	
0 1 2	10. Can't sit still, restless, or hyperactive	
0 1 2	11. Clings to adults or too dependent	
0 1 2	12. Complains of loneliness	
0 1 2	13. Confused or seems to be in a fog	
0 1 2	14. Cries a lot	
0 1 2	15. Fidgets	

0 1 2	33. Feels or complains that no one loves him/her
0 1 2	34. Feels others are out to get him/her
0 1 2	35. Feels worthless or inferior
0 1 2	36. Gets hurt a lot, accident-prone
0 1 2	37. Gets in many fights
0 1 2	38. Gets teased a lot
0 1 2	39. Hangs around with others who get in trouble
0 1 2	40. Hears sounds or voices that aren't there (describe):
0 1 2	41. Impulsive or acts without thinking
0 1 2	42. Would rather be alone than with others
0 1 2	43. Lying or cheating
0 1 2	44. Bites fingernails
0 1 2	45. Nervous, highstrung, or tense
0 1 2	46. Nervous movements or twitching (describe):

0 1 2	16.	Cruelty, bullying, or meanness to others
0 1 2	17.	Daydreams or gets lost in his/her thoughts
0 1 2	18.	Deliberately harms self or attempts suicide
0 1 2	19.	Demands a lot of attention
0 1 2	20.	Destroys his/her own things
0 1 2	21.	Destroys things belonging to others
0 1 2	22.	Difficulty following directions
0 1 2	23.	Disobedient at school
0 1 2	24.	Disturbs other pupils
0 1 2	25.	Doesn't get along with other pupils
0 1 2	26.	Doesn't seem to feel guilty after misbehaving
0 1 2	27.	Easily jealous
0 1 2	28.	Eats or drinks things that are not food—*don't* include sweets (describe): _____
0 1 2	29.	Fears certain animals, situations, or places other than school (describe): _____
0 1 2	30.	Fears going to school
0 1 2	31.	Fears he/she might think or do something bad
0 1 2	32.	Feels he/she has to be perfect

0 1 2	47.	Overconforms to rules
0 1 2	48.	Not liked by other pupils
0 1 2	49.	Has difficulty learning
0 1 2	50.	Too fearful or anxious
0 1 2	51.	Feels dizzy
0 1 2	52.	Feels too guilty
0 1 2	53.	Talks out of turn
0 1 2	54.	Overtired
0 1 2	55.	Overweight
	56.	Physical problems without known medical cause:
0 1 2		a. Aches or pains (*not* headaches)
0 1 2		b. Headaches
0 1 2		c. Nausea, feels sick
0 1 2		d. Problems with eyes (describe): _____
0 1 2		e. Rashes or other skin problems
0 1 2		f. Stomachaches or cramps
0 1 2		g. Vomiting, throwing up
0 1 2		h. Other (describe): _____

TABLE 4.1 Sample items from the Conners Teacher Rating Scale–28

Not at all	Just a little	Pretty much	Very much	Item
0	1	2	3	1. Restless in the "squirmy" sense
0	1	2	3	2. Makes inappropriate noises when s/he shouldn't
0	1	2	3	3. Demands must be met immediately
0	1	2	3	4. Acts "smart" (impudent or sassy)
0	1	2	3	5. Temper outbursts and unpredictable behavior
0	1	2	3	6. Overly sensitive to criticism

Instructions: Read each item . . . carefully, and decide how much you think the child has been bothered by this problem during the past month.

Source: © Copyright 1989, Multi-Health Systems, Inc. In the U.S.A.: 908 Niagara Falls Boulevard, North Tonawanda, NY 14120, (800) 456-3003. U.S.A. or Canada: (416) 424-1700. In Canada: 65 Overlea Boulevard, Suite 210, Toronto, Ontario M4H 1P1, (800) 268-8011. Reprinted by permission.

Advantages of Rating Scales

Rating scales offer several distinct benefits in assessment (McKinney, Montague, & Hocutt, 1993; Parker, 1992). Many of the commonly used rating scales:

- offer a quick and easy method of gathering information.
- standardize the set of behaviors to be evaluated, ensuring that specific behaviors will be assessed.
- are economical in terms of both cost and time.
- reduce rater bias and subjectivity by using a standardized presentation of questions.
- provide a means of evaluating the frequency and severity of specific behaviors and provide age- and gender-graded norms for comparison with the child's peers.
- can be given to both parents and teachers, thereby allowing a comparison of home and school behaviors.
- have a normed sample that includes children from all socioeconomic and racial and ethnic populations.
- are multifactorial, reflecting a broad assessment of the child's emotional (internal) and behavioral (external) problems, as well as measuring relevant features of ADD or ADHD.

Disadvantages of Rating Scales

Rating scales have some shortcomings and, as noted earlier, should not be the only source of information for assessment. The value of a rating scale score depends on the respondent's familiarity with the student. For example, high school teachers will generally not be as familiar with their students as elementary teachers, and their ratings should accordingly carry less weight. In addition, unrelated characteristics of the child can bias the rater's responses, so a likable child may receive higher ratings than a less pleasant child). The rater's characteristics can also affect his or her responses: Depressed mothers rate their children as having more behavior problems than mothers who are not depressed (Parker, 1992).

Selecting Rating Scales

A good rating scale should be easy to give and score. It should be reliable and valid and should provide information on the standardization population. It should also include standardized scores for a number of factors, such as attention span, self-control, learning ability, hyperactivity, aggression, social behavior, and anxiety. A rating scale with more questions will be more useful than one with fewer questions.

Commonly Used Rating Scales

Conners rating scales.   The original Conners Rating Scale (Conners, 1969) has a parent and teacher form. The Conners Teacher Rating Scale measures six factors: hyperactivity, conduct problems, emotionality-overindulgence, anxiety-passivity, asociality, and daydreaming/attention problems (see Table 4.2). Five other Conners scales have been used extensively to assess ADD: the revised Conners Parent Rating Scale (Goyette, Conners, & Ulrich, 1978); the Abbreviated Symptom Questionnaire, parent and teacher versions (Conners, 1973; Goyette et al., 1978); and the IOWA-Conners Scale (Loney & Milich, 1982). The Conners scales are often used in clinical practice and research.

Child behavior checklists.   These scales include the Child Behavior Checklist (Achenbach & Edelbrook, 1983) and the Teacher Report Form (Edelbrook & Achenbach, 1984). These instruments remain well-normed across socioeconomic and racial and ethnic populations. They are commonly used in clinical practice and research.

Behavior Problem Checklists.   The revised version of the Behavior Problem Checklists (Quay & Peterson, 1987) measures six factors: conduct problems, socialized aggression, attention problems–immaturity, anxiety-withdrawal, psychotic behavior, and motor

TABLE 4.2 Commonly used rating scales for ADD and ADHD

Rating scale	Parent or teacher	Number of items	Factors	Comments	Age span	Publisher
Conners Teacher Rating Scale–39 (CTRS-3)	Teacher	39	*5 factors:* Daydreaming-Inattentive, Hyperactivity, Conduct problems, Anxious-Fearful, Social Cooperative		3–17	Multi-Health Systems; ADD Warehouse
Conners Teacher Rating Scale–28 (CTRS-28)	Teacher	28	*4 factors:* Conduct Problems, Hyper-activity, Inattentive-Passive, Hyperactivity Index	Shortened version of above	3–17	Same
Abbreviated Symptom Questionnaire	Teacher	10	Hyperactivity	10 items from the Hyper-activity Index of CTRS-39 & CTRS-28	3–18	Same
Conners Parent Rating Scale–93	Parent	93	*8 factors:* Conduct Disorder, Anxious-Shy, Restless-Disorganized, Learning Problems, Psychosomatic, Obsessive-Compulsive, Antisocial, Hyperactive-Immature		3–17	Same
Conners Parent Rating Scale–48	Parent	48	*6 subscales:* Conduct Problems, Learning Problems, Psychosomatic, Impulsive-Hyperactive, Anxiety, and Hyperactivity Index		3–18	Same

Instrument	Rater	Items	Scales	Comments	Age/Grade	Source
Teacher Report Form (Achenbach)	Teacher	118	*8 problem scales:* Anxious, Social Withdrawal, Depressed, Unpopular, Self-Destructive, Inattentive, Nervous-Overactive, and Aggressive		6-11 and 12-16	University of Vermont Dept. of Psychiatry
Child Behavior Checklist—Parent (Achenbach)	Parent	113	*8 problem scales:* Anxious, Social Withdrawal, Depressed, Unpopular, Self-Destructive, Inattentive, Nervous-Overactive, and Aggressive	Useful for assessing anxiety and depression	2-3 and 4-16	Same
Attention Deficit Disorders Evaluation Scale—Home Version	Parent	46	*3 scales:* Inattentive Impulsive Hyperactive	Separate norms for boys & girls Inexpensive computer scoring	4-20	Hawthorne Educational Services
Attention Deficit Disorders Evaluation Scale—School Version	Teacher	60	*3 scales:* Inattentive Impulsive Hyperactive	Separate norms for boys & girls Inexpensive computer scoring	4-20	Same
ADHD Rating Scale	Teacher and Parent	14	DSM III-R list of 14 ADHD symptoms	Normative data for teachers & parents	6-12	DuPaul, G., 1991
ADD-H Comprehensive Teacher's Rating Scale	Teacher	24	*4 scales:* Attention Hyperactivity Social Skills Oppositional		Grades 5-8	MetriTech

Sources: DuPaul (1991); DuPaul, Rapport, & Perriello (1991); Koutnik (1992); Parker (1992); and Sharp (1993).

tension excess. It provides normative data on students with serious emotional disturbances, students with learning disabilities, and students without learning disabilities. It is one of the most extensively used instruments in special education for assessing emotional and behavioral problems.

Other rating scales.   Many other rating scales are commonly used in clinical diagnosis. Some of their characteristics and special features are listed in Table 4.2.

COGNITIVE/INTELLECTUAL ASSESSMENT

Standardized measures of intelligence, tests of informational processing skills, and observations made during the diagnostic process provide information about the child's cognitive and intellectual functioning. These data offer insight into the student's learning style, strengths and weaknesses in learning abilities, and evidence of a coexisting disability (such as learning disabilities). The most commonly used tests for school-age children are the Wechsler scales: the third edition of the Wechsler Intelligence Scale for Children (WISC III) (Wechsler, 1991) and the earlier revised edition of this test (WISC-R) (Wechsler, 1981). A commonly used intelligence test for preschool children (ages 4 to 6) is the revised Wechsler Preschool and Primary Scale of Intelligence (WPPSI-R) (Wechsler, 1989). All of the Wechsler scales of intelligence yield scores on verbal and nonverbal (or performance) intelligence, and a full-scale intelligence score.

NEUROPSYCHOLOGICAL ASSESSMENT

Neuropsychology is a discipline that combines psychology and neurology by focusing on the relationship between brain function and human behavior. Though most neuropsychological research has studied the behavior of adults with brain injury, some recent work in this specialized field has focused on childhood disorders, including attention deficit disorders. Child neuropsychologists are concerned with perceptual, cognitive, and motor deficits that occur during childhood and the relationship of these deficits to brain structure and function (Gaddes, 1985).

Many neuropsychologists believe that ADD involves impairment of the prefrontal cortex, the connections between the prefrontal and limbic systems, or both (Barkley, 1990). Neuropsychological measures of frontal lobe functions may be useful in assessing children with ADD. Tasks of vigilance (such as continuous performance tests, which are discussed in the next section) can be sensitive to frontal lobe injuries, as well as to symptoms of ADD. Other neuropsychological tests that may be used in assessing ADD include the Wisconsin Card Sort Test (Grant & Berg, 1948); the Matching Familiar Figures Test (Kagan, 1966); the Stroop Word Color Test (Stroop, 1935); the Stroop Neurological Screening Test, a recent version of the Stroop Word Color Test (Trennery, Crosson, DeBoe, & Leber, 1989); and the Hand Movements Test, a subtest of the Kaufman Assessment Battery for Children (Kaufman & Kaufman, 1983). Some researchers are cautious about the value of several of these tests in discriminating ADD from other disorders (Barkley, 1990; Barkley & Murphy, 1993).

CONTINUOUS PERFORMANCE TESTS

Continuous performance tests use computers or computerized devices to test attention. One such device is the Gordon Diagnostic System (Gordon Systems, Inc.). This is a portable computerized instrument that can be programmed to administer any of three tasks for a child to perform: the Delay Task, a measure of impulse control; the Vigilance Task, a measure of sustained attention; and the Distractibility Task, a measure of sustained attention in the presence of distracting stimuli.

Another continuous performance test is the Test of Variables of Attention, or TOVA (Universal Attention Deficits, Inc.), a visual test that can be used as part of a multimodal assessment for ADD. It also can be used to determine a child's response to medication given to treat ADD. This test is easily administered, with versions available for IBM-compatible, Apple II, and Macintosh computers.

A recently published continuous performance test is *The Conners Continuous Performance Test Computer Program* (Multi Health Systems). This measure permits examiners to use their

CLOSE TO HOME   JOHN McPHERSON

"In the last couple of months, we've noticed
a big improvement in her motor skills."

Source: Reprinted by permission, Universal Press Syndicate.

own computers to produce results instantly. It is a 14-minute computerized test that can be used with any IBM PC or compatible desktop or notebook computer. The measure compares an individual case with an ADHD reference group by age and sex.

ACADEMIC SCREENING

Because many children with attention deficit disorders have school-related and academic difficulties, assessment of academic achievement is an essential part of the diagnosis. Clinical psychologists often use a quick academic screening test, such as the revised Wide Range Achievement Test (WRAT-III) (Jastak & Wilkinson, 1993), which measures achievement in reading (letter recognition, letter naming, and pronunciation of words in isolation), spelling, and arithmetic. More in-depth academic testing is provided during the school assessment.

SCHOOL ASSESSMENT

The **school assessment** constitutes the second tier within the two-tiered assessment model. The purpose of this phase of the assessment is to determine the effects of the attention deficit disorder on the child's academic achievement and to develop a teaching and intervention plan, based on the assessment information, that is the most appropriate for this particular student with ADD. For some children, this will be the only assessment they receive.

According to a recent statement issued by the Department of Education, schools do not have to consult physicians when outlining special education services for children with ADD ("Doctors Not Needed to Diagnose Attention Deficit Disorder, ED Says," 1992). A school must, however, convene a multidisciplinary team to collect information from which an individualized education program (IEP) can be developed. The team must include someone with specific knowledge of how to identify and treat ADD—a psychologist, special educator, or other professional. However, some states may require schools to include licensed physicians in assessing students before preparing IEPs.

LEGISLATION

School assessments of students with ADD are guided by specific legislation that includes safeguards for the child.

The Individuals with Disabilities Education Act: IDEA

The primary law guiding the assessment of students with disabilities is the Individuals with Disabilities Education Act (IDEA). A Department of Education policy memorandum (1991) clarifies that under Part B of IDEA, children with attention deficit disorders may be eligible for special education services under the category other health impaired (OHI), "where the ADD is a chronic or acute health problem that results in limited alertness that adversely affects educational performance." Children may also be eligible for special education services if they meet the criteria for other disabilities, such as specific learning disabilities (LD) or serious emotional disturbance (SED). Since many students with disabilities are placed in inclusive educational settings (regular classrooms) for much of the time, appropriate accommodations also need to be made in the regular classroom through collaboration between regular and special educators.

Section 504 of the Rehabilitation Act

The second law under which students with ADD may receive services is Section 504 of the Rehabilitation Act. Section 504 is civil rights legislation protecting persons with handicaps. Students with ADD who are not eligible for services under Part B of IDEA may be eligible for accommodations under Section 504, if their condition "substantially limits a major life activity," such as learning. Section 504 law requires that reasonable accommodations be made in the classroom to meet the needs of many students with attention deficit disorders.

The legal and educational implications of both IDEA and Section 504 for assessing students with ADD are discussed in greater detail in Chapters 3, 5, and 6.

OBSERVATION

IDEA requires that students who are being assessed for special education must also be observed. As Yogi Berra once said, "Sometimes you observe a lot just by watching." Information gathered through observation in the classroom can contribute much to the assessment. Many of a child's characteristics and behaviors are not adequately identified through testing or case study interviews but can be detected by a skillful observer in the classroom setting. Often, observation will corroborate the findings of the assessment measures.

ACADEMIC ASSESSMENT

The school assessment includes a comprehensive assessment of the child's academic achievement and performance in several areas of the curriculum. A child's individualized education program (IEP) must include a statement of the child's current level of performance, and the long-term goals and short-term objectives that the child can be expected to accomplish.

One widely used standardized comprehensive battery is the revised version of the Woodcock-Johnson Achievement Tests (Woodcock & Johnson, 1989). This instrument has nine tests that measure reading, mathematics, written language, and knowledge. The assessment usually includes other standardized tests of reading, mathematics, spelling, and language, as well.

INFORMAL AND PORTFOLIO ASSESSMENT

In addition to using formal standardized tests for assessment, the use of informal measures of performance is becoming quite popular. Called *portfolio assessment, authentic assessment,* or *functional assessment,* informal evaluation methods are useful and practical, for they assess students on the ordinary materials and procedures that they encounter in school. These methods are valuable ways of appraising a child's academic growth and progress. Their major benefit is that the assessment and curriculum activities are closely linked.

Portfolio assessment (or authentic or functional assessment) is done by collecting multiple samples of a student's actual classwork over an extended period of time. This portfolio is used to evaluate the student's current achievement level and provides an overview of progress over time. A portfolio might contain the following kinds of materials: selected samples of daily work accomplished in the classroom, classroom tests (for example, in spelling, reading, or arithmetic), samples of writing projects, checklists of behavior, science projects, art samples, a teacher's observational notes, or the results of group projects. These portfolios are particularly useful during parent-teacher conferences, as the parent can actually see what the child has accomplished and his or her progress over a semester (Wolf, 1989).

PUBLIC SCHOOL PROGRAMS FOR ASSESSING ADD

Schools are just beginning to develop procedures for assessing ADD. Until the Department of Education's clarification memo was issued in 1991, most schools did not recognize their obligation to consider ADD as an eligible disability under special education law or Section 504. The programs of two school systems are described in the following paragraphs.

Jefferson County Public Schools, Louisville, Kentucky

One school system that has developed a formal procedure for assessing ADD is that of the Jefferson County Public Schools in Louisville, Kentucky. The Jefferson County schools have generously shared their procedures and materials with the public at large. The following description is based on their procedures and materials in their ADHD Assessment Packet.

The Jefferson County Public Schools enroll more than 90,000 students, and officials estimate they serve 2,500 to 4,500 children with ADD (using a prevalence rate of 3–5%). There are several elementary, middle, and high schools in the Jefferson County Public School District, with one psychologists' office, located in the administrative offices. A clerk in this office serves the psychologists for the entire school district.

A flowchart of the procedural steps followed in the Jefferson County Public Schools for school assessment of ADD is shown in Figure 4.1.

Eight steps are followed when an assessment for ADD does not include a referral to special education. The school district has informally adopted a 45-day time line for completion of the assessment.

1. *Referral or written parental permission received.* A referral for a school assessment can come from any of several sources: the school (teacher), the parent, the physician, or others. The referral is sent to the school counselor.

2. *Request sent to the clerk in the school psychologists' office.* After the school counselor obtains the parents' permission to assess the child, the counselor forwards this request to the clerk in the school psychologists' office.

3. *Information packet assembled.* The clerk puts together an information packet and sends it to the school. This packet may include rating scales for teachers and parents, parent information forms (asking about the child's social and developmental history, for example), and classroom observation forms.

4. *School counselor gathers information.* Upon receipt of the packet from the school psychologists' office, the school counselor coordinates the gathering of the needed information from teachers and parents. Qualified school personnel observe the child in the classroom at least once.

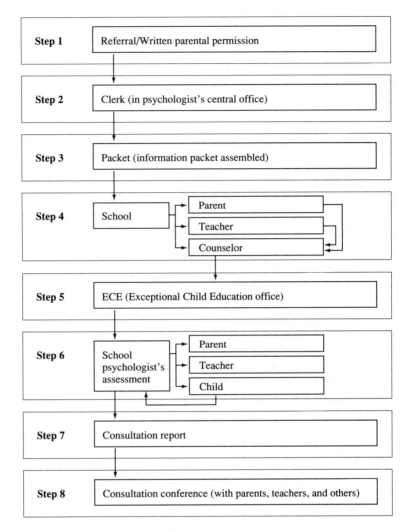

FIGURE 4.1   Flowchart of Jefferson County Public Schools' ADHD process

Source: From *Serving Children with Attention Deficit Disorders (ADD).* Adapted by permission of Federal Resource Center for Special Education, Louisville, KY.

5. *Exceptional Child Education (ECE) Office.* Upon completion of the packet, the counselor returns the information to the psychologists' office, formally known as the Exceptional Child Education (ECE) Office. A school psychologist arranges the assessment.

6. *Psychologist's assessment.* The school psychologist observes the child in the classroom at least once, interviews teachers and parents and has them complete rating scales, analyzes the child's school records (report cards, attendance records), and may directly assess the child. A direct assessment may include cognitive and academic screening, interviews, visual-motor testing, drawing, and self-concept questions.

7. *Consultation report.* The school psychologist then collects all information and writes a report.

8. *Consultation conference.* The school counselor arranges for a follow-up conference with the parents, teachers, school psychologist, and appropriate others.

The written report is shared at this meeting, and suggestions and recommendations are discussed. A written record of this meeting is made, copies of which are kept in a district file and in the child's folder at school. The need for follow-up with parents, physicians, teachers, counselors, and other mental health professionals is determined on an individual basis.

Kenosha Public Schools, Kenosha, Wisconsin

The procedures used by the schools in Kenosha, Wisconsin, to provide services to students with attention deficit disorders are described by Hubbard (1993).

The schools first conducted a survey and found that 3% of their students had been diagnosed with ADD. Of these students, 15% were in the learning disabilities program, 11% were in the program for emotional disturbances, and 72% were in regular education. School psychologists and social workers were then specially trained to evaluate students with ADD and to score and analyze behavior rating scales, as well as being instructed on the policies and procedures established for students with ADD under IDEA and Section 504. The school system also added an ADD program consultant to the staff. The consultant is responsible for: (1) coordinating and monitoring the services offered through the schools' ADD program, (2) developing and conducting the ADD teacher training and the parent education program, (3) observing students in the classroom, (4) modeling strategies for teachers, (5) collaborating with teachers and parents, (6) providing staff with current research on ADD, and (7) teaching strategies and behavior management. In addition, each school has a regular education teacher who volunteers to act as the ADD teacher liaison, serving as the contact person for the ADD program consultant.

Teachers or parents may consult the school psychologist regarding the need for an ADD screening for a child. The ADD screening is a formal evaluation conducted by the school psychologist and school social worker. This screening involves completing behavior rating scales, taking a social and medical history, testing intellectual functioning, interviewing the parents and the child, and observing the child in several settings. Upon completion of the ADD screening, a conference is held with the parents to discuss the findings and make recommendations. If ADD is suggested by the screening, the parents are advised to see a specialist (a pediatrician, clinical psychologist, or psychiatrist) for formal diagnosis of the neurobiological condition. Upon receipt of the ADD diagnosis from the specialist, the regular education teacher writes an attention deficit education plan for the student. This plan identifies desired goals and suggests teaching strategies, behavioral interventions, and classroom accommodations. (If the parent does not take the child to a specialist for the diagnosis, the school can choose to write an educational plan based solely on the findings of the school's screening).

LIMITATIONS AND CONCERNS

There are several concerns inherent in the assessment of children with ADD.

One concern relates to the differences between the two sources of the criteria and procedures used in assessment. The editions of the *Diagnostic and Statistical Manual of Mental Disorders* (DSM) are a psychiatric and medical tool for diagnosing ADD. IDEA, the special education law, addresses the assessment of ADD for educational purposes. The two are designed for different practitioners and for different purposes, and their assumptions and procedures may not always mesh. For example, Reid, Maag, and Vasa (1994) question the wisdom of using a medical-psychiatric model for educational classification.

In addition, some statistical experts have concerns about the statistical properties of behavior rating scales (Reid, Maag, & Vasa, 1994) and question the scales' objectivity, reliability, and validity.

Finally, cultural and linguistic factors greatly affect a child's behavior. Therefore, social and cultural factors, as well as genetic and biological factors, should be considered in the assessment process (Ortiz, 1991; Reid, Maag, & Vasa, 1994).

SUMMARY

The purposes for conducting an assessment include (1) gathering information for the diagnosis, (2) providing guidelines for teaching, and (3) monitoring and reviewing progress. The assessment should, as a matter of principle, conform to professional standards; be multidisciplinary, considering biological, psychological, and sociological factors; and rule out other psychological disorders with similar symptoms.

A two-tiered process is recommended, with a clinical assessment done to identify and diagnose the child's condition and a school assessment done to guide educational planning.

Measures and methods used in the clinical assessment phase include the case history and interview, behavior rating scales, cognitive assessment, continuous performance tests, and academic screening.

The school assessment phase is guided by the requirements of IDEA and Section 504 of the Rehabilitation Act. It includes observation, academic assessment, and informal and portfolio assessment. Two public school programs are described as models.

DISCUSSION QUESTIONS

1. Discuss the three main purposes of assessment. How are assessment, diagnosis, and intervention related?

2. Describe the principles underlying assessment of a student with ADD. What is meant by the term *differential diagnosis*? Why is it important?

3. What are the two tiers of assessing students with ADD? Give three examples of types of assessment methods that may be used at each level.

4. Describe *behavior rating scales* and explain how they are used in assessing ADD. Give two examples of commonly used rating scales.

5. What specific legislation guides the process of school assessment for students with ADD? Describe how children with ADD may be eligible for services under this legislation.

CHAPTER 5

TEACHING STUDENTS WITH ADD IN THE REGULAR CLASSROOM

Juan is 9 years old and in the fourth grade at Kennedy Elementary. He has been diagnosed as having attention deficit disorders. The multidisciplinary and IEP teams concluded that Juan is not eligible for special education services under Part B of the Individuals with Disabilities Education Act (IDEA). However, he is eligible for services under Section 504 of the Rehabilitation Act, because his "physical or mental disability substantially limits a major life activity"—learning. Under the protection of Section 504, he is entitled to reasonable accommodations in the regular classroom, and related aids and services, to meet his educational needs.

An accommodation plan for Section 504 services was written by a team at Kennedy Elementary with the consent of and consultation with Juan's parents. This plan was implemented by his fourth-grade classroom teacher, Mr. Diamond. It included modifications in the class's organization and structure, adaptations in the curriculum, time management plans, strategies to improve Juan's listening, and steps to facilitate coordination between the home and school.

To increase Juan's organizational abilities, Mr. Diamond developed a structured routine and schedule for Juan to follow. Juan was given his own copy of the class schedule, a list of required materials for each task, and notebooks for each subject.

In adapting the curriculum, Mr. Diamond selected high-interest reading materials at Juan's instructional reading level.

This change helped motivate Juan to improve his reading skills, which were below his age level. Worksheets were color coded and modified so that there was less material on each page but the overall content was not changed. This modification improved Juan's attention, and he was able to successfully complete the task. Because of his difficulty with handwriting, he was encouraged to use a computer word-processing program to complete assignments. The plans included teaching Juan the needed keyboarding skills. Juan was also encouraged to tape-record assignments.

To assist Juan in time management, his assignments were shortened and he was allotted more time to complete them. Because Juan often had difficulty following instructions, Mr. Diamond used short and simple sentences and tried to present one instruction at a time (instead of numerous instructions at one time) for Juan to follow.

To facilitate cooperation between the school and Juan's family, Mr. Diamond made sure that he communicated frequently with Juan's parents. He also worked with the parents to plan a behavior management program in which Juan was rewarded for positive behaviors both at home and at school. Thus, Juan was rewarded at home for cooperating at school by being allowed to choose his favorite dessert after dinner.

With these accommodations in his regular school activities, Juan's attention improved, and he became better organized, more cooperative, and better able to follow directions.

> There is absolutely no substitute for a teacher who loves his or her job and wants to make a difference in the lives of our children. Trust and believe in your ability to change the future of a child. Dare to make a difference. Celebrate the magnificent gift of uniqueness in every child. A plaque I once saw summed it up this way: "Teachers affect eternity/One can never tell where their influence ends." (Rief, 1993, p. 153)

These heartening words from a mother of a child with ADD underscore the value of the teacher. This chapter and the next spotlight the power of teachers to make a difference in the lives of children and adolescents with attention deficit disorders. In this chapter, we examine what regular classroom teachers can do, particularly to accommodate students in their classrooms. In the next, we describe methodologies, strategies, and interventions used in special education.

LAWS SUPPORTING REGULAR CLASS PLACEMENT

In Chapter 3, we refer to the U.S. Department of Education policy memorandum (1991) that clarified the eligibility of children with ADD for special services in the schools. Depending on the nature and severity of the problem, a child with ADD may qualify to receive either special education services under the Individuals with Disabilities Education Act or accommodations in the regular classroom under Section 504 of the Rehabilitation Act of 1973.

As noted in Chapter 3, under IDEA, children with ADD may be eligible for special education services under the category of other health impaired or another of the categories of Part B, such as specific learning disabilities (LD) or serious emotional disturbance (SED). Children with ADD who do not meet the criteria for special education may be eligible for services under Section 504 of the Rehabilitation Act, if they have a disability that "substantially limits a major life activity," such as learning. Under Section 504, students with ADD may be accommodated in the regular classroom and may receive related aid and services. Figure 5.1 illustrates how the provisions of IDEA and Section 504 are related.

A key phrase in Section 504 is: "Otherwise qualified individuals with handicaps may not be discriminated against by any institution receiving federal financial assistance." Section 504 also states that eligibility applies to persons whose physical or mental impairment substantially limits one or more major life activities, and the act of *learning* is recognized as a necessary life activity (Fowler, 1992; Rothstein, 1993).

The policy memorandum highlights the critical role of regular classroom teachers in meeting the needs of children with ADD. To be knowledgeable about the adaptations and accommodations that can be made in regular classrooms for students with ADD, classroom teachers need special training and preparation. Schools are obligated to take the necessary steps to develop awareness of ADD among all school personnel, especially regular classroom teachers (Parker, 1992).

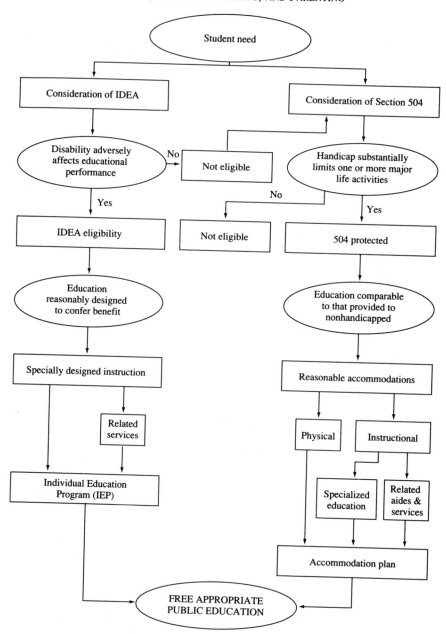

FIGURE 5.1 Flowchart showing the relationship between the provisions of IDEA and those of Section 504

Source: From *Student Access: A Resource Guide for Educators,* by the Council of Administrators of Special Education, 1992, Albuquerque, NM: Author. Reprinted with permission.

Rights of Children
with ADD under Section 504

The Office of Civil Rights (1994) issued a clarification on Section 504 coverage for students with ADD. Box 5.1 shows the questions and answers given in this clarification ("Office of Civil Rights Issues Clarification," 1994):

BOX 5.1
Questions and Answers: Office of Civil Rights' Section 504 Clarification

Q: What is ADD?

A: Attention Deficit Disorder (ADD) is a neurobiological disability. It is characterized by attention skills that are developmentally inappropriate; impulsivity; and in some cases hyperactivity.

Q: Are all children with ADD automatically protected under Section 504?

A: *No.* Some children with ADD may have a disability within the meaning of Section 504; others may not. Children must meet the Section 504 definition of disability to be protected under the regulation. Under Section 504, a "person with disabilities" is defined as any person who has a physical or mental impairment which substantially limits a major life activity (e.g., learning). Thus, depending upon the severity of their condition, children with ADD may or may not fit within that definition.

Q: Must children thought to have ADD be evaluated by school districts?

A: *Yes.* If parents believe that their child has a disability, whether by ADD or any other impairment, and the school district has reason to believe that the child may need special education or related services, the school district must evaluate the child. If the school district does not believe the child needs special education or related services and thus does not evaluate the child, the school district must notify the parents of their due process rights.

(continued)

BOX 5.1

QUESTIONS AND ANSWERS
(continued)

Q: Must school districts have a different evaluation process for Section 504 and IDEA?

A: *No.* School districts may use the same process for evaluating the needs of students under Section 504 that they use for implementing IDEA.

Q: Can school districts have a different evaluation process for Section 504?

A: *Yes.* School districts may have a separate process for evaluating the needs of students under Section 504. However, they must follow the requirements for evaluation specified in Section 504 regulation.

Q: Is a child with ADD, who has a disability within the meaning of Section 504 but not under the IDEA, entitled to receive special education services?

A: *Yes.* If a child with ADD is found to have a disability within the meaning of Section 504, he or she is entitled to receive any special education services the placement team decides are necessary.

Q: Can a school district refuse to provide special education services to a child with ADD because he or she does not meet the eligibility criteria under IDEA?

A: *No.*

Q: Can a child with ADD, who is protected under Section 504, receive related aids and services in the regular education setting?

A: *Yes.* Should it be determined that a child with ADD has a disability within the meaning of Section 504 and needs only adjustments in the regular classroom, rather than special education, those adjustments are required by Section 504.

Q: Can parents request a due process hearing if a school district refuses to evaluate their child for ADD?

(continued)

BOX 5.1

QUESTIONS AND ANSWERS

(continued)

A: *Yes.* In fact, parents may request a due process hearing to challenge any actions regarding the identification, evaluation, or educational placement of their child with a disability, whom they believe needs special education or related services.

Q: Must a school district have a separate hearing procedure for Section 504 and IDEA?

A: *No.* School districts may use the same procedures for resolving disputes under both Section 504 and IDEA. In fact, many local school districts and some state education agencies are conserving time and resources by using the same due process procedures. However, education agencies should ensure that hearing officers are knowledgeable about the requirements of Section 504 regulations.

Q: Can school districts use separate due process procedures for Section 504?

A: *Yes.* School districts may have a separate system of procedural safeguards in place to resolve Section 504 disputes. However, these procedures must follow the requirements of the Section 504 regulation.

Q: What should parents do if the state hearing process does not include Section 504?

A: Under Section 504, school districts are required to provide procedural safeguards and inform parents of these procedures. Thus, school districts are responsible for providing a Section 504 hearing even if the state process does not include it.

Source: Office of Civil Rights. (1994). *OCR Facts: Section 504 Coverage of Children with ADD.* Washington, DC: Office of Civil Rights, Department of Education.

SCHOOL PLACEMENTS
FOR STUDENTS WITH ADD

Many students with ADD will be served in the regular class under the rules and regulations of either Section 504 or IDEA. IDEA's provision for a continuum of alternative placements means that some children eligible for special education under IDEA will receive instruction in the regular classroom, with the support and collaboration of special education teachers. Children with ADD who need other placement options, such as resource rooms or special classrooms, will, of course, have those options. Those children with ADD who are eligible for services under Section 504 will be served in the regular classroom through appropriate modifications and accommodations.

If teachers are trained to recognize the special needs of students with ADD and to provide appropriate classroom modifications, it is estimated that about 50% of students with ADD can be appropriately served within the regular education program (Fowler, 1992). The other 50% of the students will need some degree of special education and related services. Many in this group can also be served in the regular class by having regular and special educators work together as a collaborative team. Some students will benefit from instruction in a resource room for part of the day while remaining in the regular classroom for most of the day. Some of these students may have coexisting disabilities (Fowler, 1992).

Those pupils with the most severe ADD (about 15%) may need placement in special classes (Fowler, 1992). These youngsters are likely to have coexisting disabilities, such as serious emotional disturbances and learning disabilities, that require specialized instruction from teachers who are knowledgeable about and experienced with special intervention strategies.

Figure 5.2 shows the percentage of children with ADD estimated to be served in the three alternative instructional environments.

EFFECTIVE TEACHERS
OF STUDENTS WITH ADD

What characterizes teachers who work successfully with children with ADD? In many respects, they are simply good teachers.

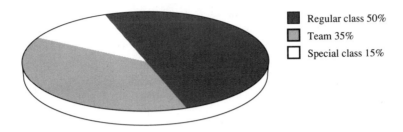

Regular class 50%
Team 35%
Special class 15%

FIGURE 5.2   The placement of children with ADD

Extensive research has been conducted to determine the qualities of a good teacher. The effective teaching studies show that the following teacher characteristics are good indicators of successful education outcomes for children (Berliner, 1984; Bickel & Bickel, 1986; Brophy & Good, 1986; Kauffman & Trent, 1991; Rosenshine & Stevens, 1986). Effective teachers:

1. Strongly engage students within academically focused, teacher-directed classrooms, using sequenced, structured materials.
2. Focus on academic matters using activities with goals that are clear to students.
3. Allocate sufficient time for instruction.
4. Frequently monitor student performance and check student work.
5. Plan lessons and questions to obtain many correct responses from students.
6. Offer immediate feedback to students on academic tasks.

Teachers who work successfully with students with ADD also possess the following characteristics:

■ *Positive attitudes toward mainstreaming and inclusion.* Teachers must believe that children can benefit from being in an integrated learning environment. An inclusive classroom helps prepare children to live in an integrated society as adults. Such teachers welcome diversity among the children in their classes and help their students learn to appreciate the contributions that each child has to offer. They are willing to be flexible and modify their instruction to meet the unique needs of students with ADD so that they can succeed in the regular class. A student's success or failure may depend on small changes in a teacher's approach.

■ *The ability to collaborate on an interdisciplinary team.* Children with attention deficit disorders need the support and collaborative efforts of regular and special educators. Effective classroom teachers are also effective team members. They know how to work with others.

■ *Knowledge of behavior management techniques.* Many children with ADD need behavior management to learn how to control their inattention, impulsivity, and hyperactivity. Classroom teachers should understand the concepts underlying the basic principles of reinforcement and behavior theory, and be able to apply behavior management strategies.

■ *Personal characteristics.* Teachers who work well with children with ADD are fair, firm, warm, and responsive, have patience and a sense of humor, and are able to establish a rapport with pupils. Rapport refers to a harmonious relationship between the teacher and the child, a feature of paramount importance. When a strong rapport exists between teacher and pupil, learning often occurs despite inappropriate techniques or materials, or other shortcomings. Effective teachers provide structure and expectations for students that students realize are fair and just. Effective teachers know that learning may take a long time and requires many repetitions, but they have the patience to wait as the child learns. Finally, teaching children with ADD is hard work. Teachers need a good sense of humor to maintain their diligence and forbearance.

ACCOMMODATIONS FOR THE PRIMARY TRAITS OF ADD

To accommodate children with attention deficit disorders, regular classroom teachers must provide ways of managing the three primary traits of ADD: inattention, impulsivity, and hyperactivity. To manage the behaviors that typify these traits, teachers must directly modify the classroom and their instruction. Ways of helping children overcome and cope with these behaviors are discussed in this section.

INATTENTION

Inattention is a major symptom of individuals with ADD. The student with ADD may be attending, but attending to the wrong stimuli, such as what is going on outside, noises in the room, or even their own thoughts. There are several distinct but interrelated phases of attention.

1. **Coming to attention,** the first phase, requires students to be alert, ready, and motivated for the lesson.
2. **Focusing attention** requires vigilance and the energy to examine problems carefully and to develop an interest in the problem to be solved. Children with ADD must learn to focus their attention, to slow down, to become more deliberate and reflective, and to monitor their responses before answering.
3. In **sustaining attention,** students must concentrate for an extended period of time. The ability to focus and attend to a task for a prolonged period is essential for the student to receive necessary information and complete certain academic activities. To learn many academic skills (such as reading), the pupil must work hard and keep attending over many days, weeks, or even months.

Individuals with ADD may encounter problems in any, or several, of these phases of attention. Ways to strengthen attention include (1) improving organizational skills, (2) improving sustained attention, and (3) improving the student's ability to listen.

Improving Organizational Skills

Many children with ADD appear to be totally unable to organize their lives. They cannot differentiate major from minor tasks, viewing details of assignments and major activities as equally important. They may accordingly feel so overwhelmed by all they must do that they do nothing. Lack of organization results in uncompleted assignments. These students need structure in their lives to eliminate some unnecessary distractions, enabling them to better attend to school tasks. They need to learn how to plan ahead, how to gather appropriate materials together for a task, how to prioritize the steps to complete an assignment, and how to keep track of their work.

Because they lack internal structure, these students need external structure to assist them in prioritizing tasks and improving their organizational skills. Teachers can supply structure by adhering to a well-planned schedule, by establishing a consistent method of collecting assignments, by directly teaching organizational skills, and by modeling efficient procedures (Mather & Jaffe, 1992).

     Consistent routines and clear classroom rules are essential. Not only do classroom rules add structure to the classroom, but they provide the student a framework and they communicate clear teacher expectations.

     Strategies for cultivating a student's organizational skills include (Friedman & Doyal, 1992; McCarney, 1989):

1. Reward the student for being prepared by allowing him or her to participate in favorite activities, conferring classroom privileges, giving tangible rewards, and so on.
2. Train the parents to reinforce the student as she or he prepares for school activities.
3. Establish routines for placing objects—especially routinely used objects such as books, assignments, and outdoor clothes—in designated places so that they can be found readily. Encourage parents to establish similar routines at home.
4. Point out the overall structure and salient features of assignments (for example, topic sentences, headings, table of contents).
5. Provide the student with a list of materials needed for each task. Limit the list to only those materials necessary to complete the task.
6. Improve the clarity of your instructions. Repeat as often as necessary in a calm tone of voice. (Inattention may have prevented the student from hearing the assignment.)
7. Provide a schedule so that the student knows exactly what to do for each class period.

8. Teach the student to use the learning strategy of self-questioning—for example, to ask themselves before starting work, "Do I have everything I need?"
9. When allotting time for assignments, allow the student to pace his or her own completion of the work.
10. Make sure the student has all homework assignments before leaving school. Write each assignment on the board and have the student copy it. Or write the assignment for a student in a pocket notebook.
11. Tape "prompt" cards (or reminders) to books or assignment folders.
12. Use specific procedures to delineate transition times between activities. (For example, to indicate a transition time, use an agreed-upon signal, or allow a short break between one activity and the next.)
13. Provide students with pocket folders to organize their materials. For example, place new work on one side and completed, graded work and class notes in chronological order on the other. Assignment notebooks and colored folders for each subject are useful. Many students find that a structured assignment notebook helps them remember and organize their homework. A sample page for such an assignment notebook is on page 102.

Increasing Sustained Attention

Students with ADD are likely to have a short attention span. They may initially attend to a task, but their attention soon begins to wander. Teachers can take steps to keep such students' attention, and prolong their concentration on the tasks at hand.

■ *Shorten the task.* Teachers can accommodate students with attentional problems by shortening tasks.

1. Break one task into smaller parts to be completed at different times. Allow quiet talking during work.
2. Give two tasks, with the task the student prefers to be completed after the less preferred task.
3. Assign fewer problems; for example, fewer spelling words or mathematics problems.
4. Try to use fewer words when explaining tasks. Give concise verbal directions.
5. Use distributed practice rather than massed practice for rote tasks; that is, set up more short, spaced practice sessions

HOMEWORK ASSIGNMENT

NAME _____   DATE _____

SUBJECT	ASSIGNMENT	DATE DUE
Language Arts	_____	
Math	_____	
Reading	_____	
Social Science	_____	
Spelling	_____	
Other	_____	
Other	_____	

Remember to take home

1. _____

2. _____

3. _____

4. _____

Remember to bring to school

1. _____

2. _____

3. _____

4. _____

instead of fewer but longer and more concentrated sessions. Plan several short periods for work rather than one long period.

6. Give fewer and shorter homework assignments.

■ *Make tasks more interesting.* When students are intensely interested in something, their attention span can be amazingly long. For example, a child will spend hours at a video game or a favorite hobby. Remember that obtaining "on-task" behavior is not in itself a useful goal. Attention should be a natural result, not a goal to be observed, so change the nature of the task or the learning environment as needed. The following strategies make tasks more engaging.

1. Encourage children to work with partners, in small groups, or at interest centers.
2. Alternate highly interesting and less interesting tasks.
3. Use visual aids (such as an overhead projector) when teaching.

■ *Increase the novelty of the task.* Tasks that are new, unique, or unusual are inherently more appealing and more likely to capture a child's attention. For longer tasks or tasks that are done later in the day or tasks that are necessarily repetitive, increasing the novelty value is especially important. To add novelty, try using a game format for the task. Games add fun and novelty to learning, especially when material must be overlearned to develop automaticity (such as with word recognition or math facts).

Improving the Student's Ability to Listen

Students with ADD frequently miss important instructions and information because of their inattention; often, they are even unaware that instructions have been given. When teachers ask students to listen, they want them not just to hear or recognize the words that are spoken. They expect the students to comprehend the messages.

The following classroom strategies can help students acquire better listening skills (Fowler, 1992; McCarney, 1992; Parker, 1992):

1. Use short, simple sentences when speaking to the child. Make certain the vocabulary you use is developmentally appropriate.

2. Give one instruction at a time. Slow your rate of presentation. Repeat as often as necessary. Paraphrase using similar language to assist comprehension.

3. Prompt the student to repeat instructions after listening to them.

4. Alert the student by using key phrases: "This is important," "Listen carefully," and the like. Use prearranged signals, such as hand signals or turning the lights on, before giving directions.

5. Write a short outline or summary of the directions on the chalkboard for easy reference.

6. Use visual aids (such as charts, pictures, graphs) to illustrate and support verbal information.

7. Make certain the student is sitting near the teacher when oral instructions are given.

8. Place the student in the least distracting location in the classroom. This may be in front of the class, away from high-traffic areas. Eliminate extraneous noise and visual stimuli whenever possible.

9. Reduce the emphasis on competition in the class. Competition may overstimulate the student, distract him or her from listening to information, or both.

10. Have students repeat to themselves information they have just heard to build listening and memory skills.

IMPULSIVITY

Impulsive behavior is recognized as a major characteristic of attention deficit disorders. Experts hypothesize that an underdeveloped inhibitory mechanism within the nervous system causes overarousal, making suppressing behavior difficult for the child. Impulsive children act out physically and verbally. Often, they will shout out answers, without waiting for recognition or raising their hands. Particularly challenging for impulsive children are transition times, when class activities shift from unstructured to structured. After a stimulating activity, such as recess or a physical education period, impulsive children have difficulty settling down (Parker, 1992). General ways of dealing with impulsivity in the regular classroom include: (a) adapting the curriculum, (b) helping students learn to wait, (c) helping students manage time, and (d) encouraging compliant behavior.

Adapting the Curriculum

Many parts of the curriculum can readily be changed, modified, or adapted, without sacrificing the integrity of the basic curriculum. In many cases, even small changes will greatly benefit students with ADD, who in general, need a stimulating, active curriculum that will captivate their attention and motivate them to complete the activity at hand. General guidelines for adapting a curriculum are (Lerner & Lowenthal, 1993; Mather & Jaffe, 1992; McCarney, 1992):

1. Use high-interest curriculum materials.
2. Check the difficulty level of the reading material and textbooks to make sure it is appropriate for the child's reading level. A level that is too easy leads to boredom; a level that is too difficult leads to frustration.
3. Select manipulable, hands-on material whenever possible.
4. Establish a solid, concrete experiential base before teaching abstract concepts. Demonstrate how new information relates to material already learned.
5. Introduce new vocabulary before beginning a lesson.
6. Use visual aids to supplement oral and written information. Also, use learning aids such as computers, calculators, and tape recorders to structure learning and increase motivation.
7. Create curriculum activities that require active participation, such as talking through problems and acting out steps.
8. Use multiple modalities when presenting information; for example, combining a visual-tactile approach with verbal information.
9. Modify curriculum worksheets so there is less material on each page. Use color-coded worksheets to attract attention and increase the novelty of the task.
10. Break assignments into small chunks. Give feedback on each one immediately.
11. Avoid pressures of speed and accuracy.
12. Modify tests, allowing the student to take tests orally instead of writing the answers. Avoid a large amount of written work for students who have difficulty with visual-motor integration. Help the student with test directions by using color, circles, or underlining.
13. Teach the child how to cross out incorrect answers on multiple-choice tests.

Helping Students Learn to Wait

One symptom of impulsivity is an inability to wait. Preschoolers who cannot wait for their turn to use a toy or to paint on the easel may throw temper tantrums in class. Elementary school students in physical education classes who cannot wait for their turn to use a ball may grab it from another child. Adolescent drivers may not wait for slower or more cautious drivers ahead of them and simply pass them, even if it endangers others.

The concept of "wait" can be learned very young. Three-year-olds who use a computer soon learn that they must "wait" until the software is loaded or they will not be able to play the computer game. The following strategies are designed to help children learn to wait:

1. Give the child substitute verbal or motor responses to use while waiting.
2. Instruct the child on how to continue on easier parts of tasks (or do a substitute task) while awaiting the teacher's help.
3. Have the child underline or rewrite directions before beginning, or provide colored markers or colored pencils for the child to mark directions or relevant information.
4. Encourage the child to doodle or play with clay, paper clips, or pipe cleaners while waiting or listening to instructions.
5. Encourage note taking (even just of cue words).
6. Allow the child, rather than the teacher, to pace activities.

The inability to wait is often manifested as impatience and bossiness. Teachers should understand the underlying causes of this disruptive behavior and should not assume that impulsive statements or behavior are aggressive in intent. The following strategies can help check more disruptive behavior:

1. Suggest and reinforce alternative ways to get attention (such as being a line leader or paper passer).
2. Teach children who interrupt to recognize pauses in conversations and how to hang onto ideas.
3. Let the child know about upcoming difficult times or tasks for which he or she will need extra control.
4. Teach and reinforce social routines (such as saying *hello, goodbye,* and *please*).

Helping Students Manage Time

Many children with ADD have habitual trouble managing time. Their impulsiveness pulls them away form the task at hand and they become involved with new challenges. These youngsters are unable to adapt their behavior to a task or particular setting. They become procrastinators, a trait they retain into their adult lives (Fowler, 1992; Frick & Lahey, 1991). Regular classroom teachers can assist children with time management (CH.A.D.D., 1988; Lerner & Lowenthal, 1993).

1. Increase the time allotted to complete assignments.
2. Shorten assignments and tests and reduce the amount of work involved.
3. Adjust the level of difficulty of assignments to fit the student's learning ability and preferred response style.
4. Use behavioral contracts with students that specify the amount of time allotted for specific activities.
5. Make lists that will help students organize their tasks. Let them check off tasks as they complete them.
6. Alternate short work periods with breaks or change of tasks.
7. During the school day, alternate activities that are done while sitting with those that involve standing and moving about.
8. Set up a specific routine and adhere to it. If unavoidable disruptions occur, explain the situation to the students and the appropriate behavior expected from them.

A time management log is shown on page 108. Such a log can help students develop a sense of time and what must be accomplished in a given time span.

HYPERACTIVITY

For some students with ADD, hyperactivity is a prominent characteristic. These children may be classified as having ADHD (attention-deficit hyperactivity disorder). Students who are hyperactive in the classroom are the most challenging for the classroom teacher. These students cannot sit in their seats for prolonged periods; they may get up to sharpen their pencils 12 times each class; they need to move and be active. They may simply pace back and forth, because they cannot sit quietly.

TIME MANAGEMENT LOG

NAME _____

ACTIVITY	TIME SPENT				
	Monday	Tuesday	Wednesday	Thursday	Friday	Total
Class						
Study						
Individual time						
Social time						
Exercises						
Work (if any)						
Sleep						

Source: From "Time Management Instruction for Students with Learning Disabilities," by R. Manganello. In *Teaching Exceptional Children, 26*(2), p. 61. Copyright © 1994 by Council for Exceptional Children. Reprinted by permission.

Accommodating Excessive Activity

The need for physical movement and activity must be taken into account in planning classroom accommodations. In general, such accommodations involve trying to channel excessive activity into acceptable endeavors, using activity as a reward, and encouraging the students to respond to instruction actively. The following principles can guide teachers in managing and accommodating for students with excessive activity (Zentall, 1991a, 1991b).

Simply telling the child to stop his or her disruptive hyperactive behavior may not work. Helping students find other ways to use their high activity levels—that is, channeling their excessive activity into acceptable behaviors—may be more fruitful.

1. Encourage nondisruptive, directed movement in the class-room.
2. Allow standing during seat work, especially near the end of a task.
3. Use activity as a reward. Permit specific activities (such as running an errand, cleaning the board, organizing the teacher's desk) as an individual reward for improvement.
4. Encourage participation in small- and large-group discussions.
5. Use teaching activities that encourage active responding (such as talking, moving, working at the board).
6. Encourage diary writing, painting, and so forth.
7. Teach the child to ask questions that relate to the topic.
8. Encourage note taking (even just of cue words).

Fostering Compliant Behavior

One of the most trying responses of some students with ADD is their noncompliant behavior. At school, they act so impulsively and inappropriately that their behavior disrupts the class, getting them into trouble. They ignore teacher warnings and refuse to follow class rules. Noncompliant students cause their parents much worry, too. Many parents relate that every time the phone rings, they are afraid someone is calling to report that their child has again broken the rules or landed in some kind of predicament.

The following guidelines are designed to reduce non-compliant behavior (Zentall, 1991a):

1. Limit the choice of tasks, topics, and activities.
2. Try to determine the student's preferred activities and then use them as incentives.
3. Bring the student's interests into assignments.
4. Praise the student for improved work.

Recognizing and appreciating students' accomplishments and efforts can also foster compliance.

1. Call attention to the student's strengths and abilities. Set aside a regular time each day or week during which the student can display his or her talents. For example, if Joseph does particularly well with art, make sure he has the opportunity to practice his craft.
2. Recognize that excessive activity can also mean increased productivity.
3. Recognize that bossiness can also be leadership potential.
4. Recognize that attraction to novelty can also lead to creativity.
5. Recognize that impulsiveness can also mean increased energy.
6. Increase feelings of success by helping students develop their skills.
7. Recognize the child's playfulness and use it to develop his or her skills.
8. Mark the child's correct performance, not his or her mistakes.

Creating a Stimulating Learning Environment

As previously noted, individuals with ADD respond well to novelty. A number of investigators report that students with ADD benefit from increased stimulation and novelty on easy and repetitive tasks but not on new or difficult ones (Zentall, 1985; Zentall, Falkenberg, & Smith, 1985). Research shows that simple modifications can increase the novelty and stimulation of tasks presented to students with ADD (Zentall, 1991a). For example, adding shape, color, or texture to an activity increases its novelty value. With a stimulating learning environment, students attend better to the learning activity (Zentall, 1989; Zentall & Dwyer, 1989). Other relatively simple modifications that make activities more stimulating include:

1. Eliminate unnecessary repetition of tasks.
2. Add action to the task (for example, have the student work with others, talk, move materials).

Calvin and Hobbes

by Bill Watterson

Source: Reprinted by permission, Universal Press Syndicate.

3. Shorten assignments.
4. Develop routines aimed at completing the task (for example, establish a specific place to put finished materials).

Building Self-Esteem

Much of the discussion in this chapter is focused on modifying the school environment to change student behavior. Sensitivity to the feelings and emotions of students is also important. Too often, students with ADD suffer academic and social failures day after day, week after week, and year after year. The student is bewildered by behaviors that are difficult to control. It is not surprising that all of these frustrations begin to take their toll on the student's self-esteem. It is important to build the student's self-concept and self-assurance, and to provide experiences of success. The student's strengths and the efforts they put forth should be recognized and appreciated.

IMPLICATIONS OF CURRENT EDUCATIONAL APPROACHES FOR CHILDREN WITH ADD

In this section, we review four educational approaches currently being used in the schools and consider their effects on students with attention deficit disorders: content mastery classes, cooperative learning, peer tutoring, and home-school coordination.

CONTENT MASTERY CLASSES

The content mastery program was designed some 10 years ago to help children with learning disabilities succeed in the regular classroom (Meisgeier, personal communication, December 9, 1993). The program won awards in Texas as an exemplary inclusion model and has been expanded to include a broader group of special-needs students. Although widely used in Texas, the program is not well known outside the state.

In the content mastery program, students are taught by an appropriately trained and certified special education teacher in a separate classroom. The content mastery class (CMC) teacher works closely with the regular classroom teacher to enable students who come to the content mastery class for assistance to meet the demands of the regular class. The CMC teacher is proactive, actively obtaining tests and materials such as lesson plans and handouts from the regular teacher ahead of time to plan a system of support that specifically meets the desires of the regular classroom teacher and the needs of each student. In this way, the CMC model unites the efforts of the regular classroom teacher and the special education teacher.

Goals

The content mastery program has six goals (Meisgeier, no date):

1. To assist the regular class teacher in establishing a system of support for special education students in regular class settings.
2. To adapt the methods of presenting information in the regular classroom to accommodate the specific needs of each student.
3. To adapt the methods of assessing a student's knowledge of a subject in the regular classroom to accommodate the specific needs of each special education student.
4. To adapt the regular classroom environment to accommodate the special education student.
5. To help the student determine and demonstrate appropriate behavior in the regular classroom.
6. To assign the special education student a student mentor who will provide academic tutoring and social cues.

Modifications

The content mastery teacher modifies the instruction in the following ways:

1. *Altering the way information is presented:*
   - Textbooks recorded on audiotape
   - Highlighted readings
   - Advance organizers for lectures, readings, audiovisual presentations

2. *Altering the way information is assessed:*
   - Alternative test formats (matching instead of essay, for example)
   - Shorter tests
   - Oral presentations and responses
   - Redesigned tests

3. *Managing academics and behavior:*
   - Specifically prescribed classroom alterations for certain students (seating, individual instruction, and so on)
   - Behavior management techniques (positive reinforcement, student conferences, behavior contracts, and so on)
   - Student partners/mentors

COOPERATIVE LEARNING

Cooperative learning is a method of promoting learning through student cooperation rather than competition. Essentially, students work together to seek solutions to problems instead of competing against one another. Through cooperative learning, students develop more positive attitudes toward a subject area than they do through competitive learning (Johnson & Johnson, 1983). According to Johnson and Johnson (1986), students perceive learning in which they are rewarded as a group as being fairer than being rewarded on a competitive or individual basis.

In a typical cooperative learning system, students are divided into groups and work together to master an assigned lesson. Usually, students are tested individually on their mastery of the subject matter, but rewards are based on group accomplishments. Cooperative methods are most often compared with competitive procedures in which students compete for awards or work individually to better their previous performance (Lloyd, Crowley, Kohler, & Strain, 1988).

Some studies on cooperative learning experiences in the regular classroom show that cooperative learning methods foster more achievement and stronger positive relationships between typically developing children and those with special learning needs than competitive methods (Johnson & Johnson, 1984, 1985, 1986; Johnson, Johnson, & Maruyama, 1983; Slavin, 1983). More research is needed to know the effects of cooperative learning for students with ADD. However, Johnson and Johnson (1986) suggest that cooperative learning could help children with ADD succeed academically, because this method increases motivation and persistence in completing academic tasks (Johnson & Johnson, 1986).

Steps for structuring cooperative learning in the regular classroom are (Johnson & Johnson, 1986): (1) clearly specify the objectives for the lesson, (2) selectively group the students, (3) clearly explain the learning activity to the students, (4) monitor the effectiveness of the learning groups, (5) intervene to assist groups with the task as needed, (6) evaluate the students' achievements, and (7) encourage the students to discuss how well they collaborated. These steps can structure the regular class environment so that students must cooperate to attain a common goal (Lloyd et al., 1988). Cooperative learning may prove a useful modification in the regular classroom to help children with ADD achieve more positive peer interaction and academic success.

PEER TUTORING

When one student teaches another student, this is called peer tutoring. Peer tutoring is a method of offering individual (one-on-one) instruction in the regular classroom by using peers (or classmates) to teach target students. The student who teaches is the *tutor,* and the student being taught is the *tutee.* The tutor helps the tutee learn, practice, or review an academic skill. For example, the tutor may say the spelling words as the tutee writes them, or the tutor may read sentences to the tutee or listen while the tutee reads the sentences, or the tutor may demonstrate how to solve a mathematics problem. The peer tutor may be the same age as the tutee or older.

Research shows that both the tutor and the tutee benefit from peer tutoring. The tutee is often able to learn more effectively from a fellow student than from the teacher. The tutor benefits because (as teachers well know) one of the best ways to learn something is to teach it to others (Slavin, 1991). Among the other advantages of peer tutoring are that the tutor models appropriate academic and nonacademic behaviors for the tutee, and the relationship between the two students offers both opportunities to build social relationships within the classroom.

Peer tutoring is simple to implement, it requires little time and effort from teachers, it is a practical way to meet the special academic needs of a few children in a class, and students like it (Fowler, Dougherty, Kirby, & Kohler, 1986; Lloyd et al., 1988; Slavin, 1991).

Peer tutoring may benefit students with ADD who are in regular classes, and may offer several advantages (Abramowitz & O'Leary, 1991). By giving the students more opportunities to observe and practice the positive behaviors of their peer tutors in the classroom, learning may then generalize to other settings (the lunchroom, library, playground, and so forth).

Peer tutors provide instruction, feedback, and reinforcement based on the target child's mastery of an academic assignment. Research with children with and without disabilities indicates that adequate training and supervision are essential to the success of peer tutoring programs. When peers provide some of the instruction, teachers cannot assume that they will have more free time initially. Sometimes, at the beginning of the program, more time must be spent on the training than on the tutoring itself. However, with proper training, peer tutoring has shown positive results (Eiserman & Osguthorpe, 1985; Osguthorpe & Scruggs, 1986; Scruggs & Osguthorpe, 1986).

In summary, peer tutoring is a promising approach to accommodating students with ADD in regular classes. More research is needed to ascertain its effects on youngsters with ADD and the extent to which students with ADD could be effective peer tutors for other children.

HOME-SCHOOL COORDINATION

Programs of home-school coordination are intended to improve the behavior of students with ADD in regular classes by combining school and home efforts (Abramowitz & O'Leary, 1991). Behavioral goals are established for the child, and each day the teacher checks off a list of the behavioral goals the student has met. The checklists are sent home, signed by the parents to acknowledge the teacher's comments, then returned to the school. In addition, the student is reinforced at home for the positive behaviors he or she has displayed at school. A sample checklist used to promote cooperation between home and school is shown on page 117.

Some advantages of home-school coordination programs are: (1) they foster regular communication between the home and school, (2) they do not require teachers to substantially alter their teaching styles, (3) the system is easy to implement for both the teacher and the family, (4) the use of these techniques with reinforcers can improve parent-child relationships, and (5) parents often have access to a wider variety of reinforcers than the teacher does. Parental reinforcers can include favorite foods, television programs, and trips to restaurants, museums, movies, and the like (Kelley & Carper, 1988).

COLLABORATION: REGULAR AND SPECIAL EDUCATION TEAMWORK

As noted earlier, most students with attention deficit disorders are placed in the regular classroom. This means that regular classroom teachers and special education teachers must collaborate to make sure that children with ADD receive the instruction and support that they need. A growing responsibility of special education teachers is that of collaboration, consultation, and supportive services. When students with ADD are placed in regular classes, cooperative working relationships among regular and special education teachers and other school personnel is key to the students' success (West & Cannon, 1988).

There is a subtle but important distinction between **consultation** and **collaboration.** In consultation, the consultee (usually the regular teacher) seeks guidance from an expert professional (such as the special education teacher). In collaboration, the two teachers bring together their equal levels of expertise and work together to solve classroom problems (West & Idol, 1990).

HOME/SCHOOL DAILY RECORD

NAME OF STUDENT _____

DATE _____

BEHAVIORS	NO CHANGE	BEGINNING TO IMPROVE	GOOD IMPROVEMENT
RAISES HAND			
FOLLOWS DIRECTIONS			
WAITS FOR TURN			
FINISHES WORK			

(Signed) _____
                          Teacher

(Signed) _____
                          Parent

Dear Parent:

This rating scale shows how your child behaved in school today. The check (✓) shows progress toward behavioral goals.

Please sign this form and return.

Thank you.

_____
        Teacher

Friend and Cook (1992) conceptualize collaboration as a style of interaction. What distinguishes collaboration for them is how individuals or groups work together. Six characteristics define successful collaborations: (1) mutual goals, (2) voluntary participation, (3) parity among participants, (4) shared responsibility for participating and decision making, (5) shared accountability for outcomes, and (6) shared resources (Friend & Cook, 1992; Sugai & Tindal, 1993; Vandercook, York, & Sullivan, 1993). Table 5.1 presents a summary of the characteristics of successful collaboration, along with what works and what does not, for each characteristic.

1. *Mutual goals.* Successful partners must share mutual goals and a common philosophy about students with attention deficit disorders. They must establish a relationship by initially engaging in short-term efforts.

2. *Voluntary participation.* Collaboration cannot be forced. It cannot be controlled by directives from superiors. Successful collaboration requires individuals to take mutual responsibility for a problem and freely seek solutions to it.

3. *Parity among participants.* Each person's contribution to an endeavor is equally valued and each person has equal power in decision making. Rather than one leader, a team of individuals shares equal responsibility for facilitating movement toward a common goal. To achieve a sense of equality, it is suggested that first names (Sam, Sarah) be used instead of titles (Dr. Smith, Superintendent Brown). Also, the primary support roles (facilitator, timekeeper, and recorder) for these meetings should be rotated among all team members.

4. *Shared responsibility for participation and decision making.* Individuals involved in a collaborative effort are expected to share the responsibility for both participation and decision making. Shared responsibility means each is committed to participating in the activity and making any decisions necessary. It does not imply that the tasks must be divided equally or that everyone must participate fully in every activity required to reach the goal (Friend & Cook, 1992).

5. *Shared accountability for outcomes.* Everyone involved in the activity shares in the outcomes, whether successful or not. When successful, all share in the celebration; when unsuccessful, all share responsibility for any shortcomings or failures. No one person is responsible for either successes or failures. As a result, all participants are more willing to acknowledge and learn from failures, rather than covering them up.

TABLE 5.1 Characteristics for collaboration

Defining characteristics	What works?	What doesn't?
Mutual goals	• Developing a relationship • Engaging in small-scale efforts initially • Sharing the same philosophy	• Engaging in a long-term commitment without having established a relationship
Voluntary participation	• Involving key stakeholders • Inviting participation	• Working with only one or two individuals on something that will impact many
Parity among participants	• Using names, not titles, when interacting • Rotating and sharing team roles (e.g., facilitator, timekeeper, recorder) • Structuring ways to facilitate participation	• Calling John Jacob, Professor Jacob, instead of John. • Reserving the role of facilitator for a select few
Shared responsibility for participation and decision making	• Sharing perspectives about decisions • Brainstorming before decision making • Balance between coordination of tasks and division of labor • Clear delineation of agreed-upon actions as follow-up	• Assuming that tasks must be divided equally and that each party must participate fully in each activity • Placing decision-making responsibility with one individual or party
Shared accountability for outcomes	• Acknowledging risks and potential failure • Celebrating successes together • Embracing failures together, adopting a "learning from failures" mindset	• Trying to determine *who* to blame • Giving awards to individuals for team efforts
Shared resources	• Identifying respective resources • Having mutual goals • Highlighting the benefits of sharing • Joint decision making about resource allocation	• Protecting, not revealing, resources • Having no mutual goals and disparate benefits • Using own resources after depleting others' resources

Source: From "True or False? Truly Collaborative Relationships Can Exist Between University and Public School Personnel," by T. Vandercook, J. York, and B. Sullivan. In *OSERS News in Print, 5*(8), p. 3. Copyright 1993 by U.S. Department of Education. Reprinted by permission.

119

6. *Shared resources.* Individuals engaged in collaborative activities each have resources that can be contributed to reaching the shared goals. Indeed, the fact that resources never seem to be adequate motivates individuals to collaborate, and pool their resources.

Research indicates that collaborative consultation will be most effective if the participants follow a set of problem-solving strategies (Idol, 1989; West & Cannon, 1988). The steps include:

1. *Establishing goals.* Objectives and responsibilities are negotiated.
2. *Defining the student's problem.* Both the specialist and the regular teacher develop common perceptions about the student's difficulty.
3. *Generating intervention methods.* Written objectives are developed with specific interventions for each part of the problem. Criteria for evaluation are developed, and needed resources are identified.
4. *Assigning responsibilities for both teachers.* The student's instruction will be implemented by both the regular teacher and the special education teacher, with specific responsibilities assigned to each.
5. *Evaluating the program from several points of view.* The success of the intervention is evaluated from the perspective of the child, the family, and the teachers.
6. *Modifying the procedures as necessary.* The intervention is continued or changed in accordance with the evaluation.

Teachers who are good collaborators have certain personal characteristics, which include: empathy, patience, a respect for diversity, an open and positive attitude, and a willingness to learn from others. To help students with ADD succeed in inclusive placements requires collaboration and a good working relationship between regular and special educators.

SUMMARY

Most children identified as having attention deficit disorders will be served through placement in a regular classroom. The school placement depends on the type and severity of the student's disorder. The continuum of alternative placements includes placement in a regular class; placement in a resource room, with a team approach taken to instruction; and placement in a special class. Students with ADD can be accommodated in the regular classroom in many ways.

Teachers who work effectively with students with ADD are, in essence, simply good teachers. Studies of effective teaching have identified the characteristics of good teachers. Also described are other characteristics of effective teachers of children with ADD.

There are specific ways for teachers to make accommodations relative to the primary characteristics of ADD—inattention, impulsivity, and hyperactivity. Specific suggestions for meeting children's needs with regard to each of these characteristics are described.

Several current educational approaches can be effective with students with ADD. These include content mastery classes, cooperative learning, peer tutoring, and home-school coordination. Collaboration and teamwork between regular and special educators are essential for meeting the needs of students with ADD in the regular classroom.

DISCUSSION QUESTIONS

1. Name and describe each of two federal laws under which students with attention deficit disorders can be eligible to receive services in the regular classroom. What conditions must students with ADD meet to receive services in the regular classroom under each?

2. Identify three characteristics of regular education teachers who are effective with students with attention deficit disorders.

3. Describe three strategies that regular classroom teachers can use to increase the attention of students with attention deficit disorders.

4. Discuss three strategies that regular classroom teachers can use to decrease impulsivity and hyperactivity.

5. What is *collaboration* and who is involved in the collaborative process with respect to teaching students with ADD? Name two characteristics of teachers who are effective collaborators.

SPECIAL EDUCATION INTERVENTIONS

Mike S., who is 8 years old, was referred for a special education assessment. The multidisciplinary team identified Mike as having an attention deficit disorder with coexisting learning disabilities and judged that Mike is eligible for special education services. The IEP team, which included the school's special education director, the learning disabilities teacher, Mike's parents, and the regular classroom teacher, then met to write Mike's individualized education rogram. The IEP team agreed that Mike would receive most of his education in the regular third-grade classroom and that for reading and mathematics, he would also receive services

in a resource room with the learning disabilities teacher. The learning disabilities teacher would also collaborate with Mike's third-grade teacher. The IEP plan included a periodic review of Mike's progress and reevaluation of the program to ensure that progress was being made toward the annual goals and short-term objectives. All participants at the meeting signed the IEP.

Special teaching plans were made to deal with Mike's learning disabilities in reading and mathematics. The plan also specified interventions to manage Mike's ADD behaviors, specifically to reduce Mike's inattention, distractibility, and aggressive behaviors. In addition, Mike would be trained in social skills to improve his relationships with peers and adults. The resource room teacher and the regular classroom teacher would collaborate in implementing these plans, with the goal of transferring and generalizing academic and social skills developed in the resource room to the regular classroom. The plan called for establishing a close collaboration to coordinate school efforts with home management procedures. Mike's parents would extend the school's interventions by rewarding improvements in his behavior at home. Mike's parents will be continually informed about measures being taken in school and Mike's progress toward meeting objectives.

The plan included establishing a token economy system as part of the behavior management program. Mike would be given at least ten "good work" stickers each day and contingent teacher attention for positive behaviors (such as displaying a good attitude, paying attention, working cooperatively, and so on). Class observations would be instituted to ensure that at least twice as many positive statements as reprimands were addressed to Mike. Mike could exchange the "good work" stickers for preferred activities. His favorite activities are computer games and extended art periods.

This chapter continues the discussion of ways of teaching students with attention deficit disorders. In the previous chapter, we concentrated on accommodations in the regular classroom. In this chapter, we focus on special education interventions. This chapter examines the framework of special education, the psychological foundations of special education, techniques of behavior management, and ways to teach academic skills in special education.

THE FRAMEWORK
OF SPECIAL EDUCATION

Historically, the field of special education developed because the needs of children with disabilities were not being met in the schools. Public schools either ignored or, in too many cases, even excluded youngsters with disabilities. The distressed parents of children with disabilities, along with concerned professionals in the field of special education, worked arduously over many years to obtain public educational services for these children. Only through their constant, strenuous efforts were supportive special education laws finally passed by Congress in 1975. These special education laws have played a primary role in enabling children with disabilities to receive educational services in public schools. Now called the Individuals with Disabilities Education Act (IDEA), the legislation specifies twelve different categories of disability under which individuals are eligible to receive special education services. Three of these disabilities are mentioned in the policy memorandum issued by the U.S. Department of Education (1991) as a way of serving students with ADD. They are: other health impaired (OHI), specific learning disabilities (LD), and serious emotional disturbance (SED).

THE DEFINITION OF SPECIAL EDUCATION

The term *special education* refers to instruction that is specially designed to meet the unusual needs of exceptional learners. Special materials, teaching techniques, equipment, or facilities may be required. Special education also includes related services the child may need, such as audiology and speech pathology, social services, physical and occupational therapy, adapted physical education, or counseling. The special education and related services must be specified in the child's individualized education program.

CHILDREN WITH ADD WHO REQUIRE SPECIAL EDUCATION SERVICES

As emphasized in the previous chapter, many children with attention deficit disorders do not require special education services. For these children, placement in the regular class with suitable accommodations and modifications is appropriate and sufficient. Other youngsters with ADD, however, need more intensive help and may be eligible for special education services. These children are likely to have more severe disabilities related to their inattention, impulsivity, or hyperactivity, and may have a coexisting disability that requires special education methods and teaching strategies. Competency with

methods used to teach children with learning disabilities, emotional disturbances, or both, is useful for teaching children with
ADD.

Special Education Law
and Children with ADD

In Chapter 3, we discuss many of the parameters of the
special education laws that affect students with attention deficit
disorders. Throughout the book, we frequently refer to the important policy memorandum, issued by the U.S. Department
of Education in 1991, clarifying the law with regard to children
with ADD. The memorandum clarified that students with ADD
may be eligible for special education and related services, if they
meet the eligibility criteria under Part B of IDEA. The memorandum specifically mentions three categories of Part B under
which youngsters with ADD may be eligible for special education services. The first is other health impaired (OHI). Children
with ADD are eligible for services under OHI if their attention
deficit disorder constitutes a chronic or acute health problem
resulting in limited alertness. Two other Part B disability categories under which children with ADD may be eligible for
special education services are *specific learning disabilities* (LD)
and *serious emotional disturbance* (SED). If the child has such a
coexisting disability along with the ADD and meets the criteria
for these categories, he or she is entitled to educational services that meet the specific needs arising from both disabilities.

IDEA defines these three disability categories as follows.
Other health impaired (OHI) means:

> having *limited* strength, vitality, or *alertness, as a result of chronic
> or acute health problems,* such as heart conditions, tuberculosis,
> rheumatic fever, nephritis, asthma, sickle cell anemia, hemo-
> philia, epilepsy, lead poisoning, leukemia, or diabetes, *that
> adversely affects educational performance.* [italics added]

Specific learning disabilities (LD) include:

> having a disorder in one or more of the basic psychological pro-
> cesses involved in understanding or in using language, spoken
> or written, that may manifest itself in an imperfect ability to
> listen, think, speak, read, write, spell, or do mathematical calcu-
> lations. The term includes conditions such as perceptual handi-

caps, brain injury, minimal brain dysfunction, dyslexia, and developmental aphasia. The term does not include children who have learning problems that are primarily the result of visual, hearing, or motor handicaps, of mental retardation, or of environmental, cultural, or economic disadvantage.

Seriously emotionally disturbed (SED) means:

exhibiting one or more of the following characteristics over a long period of time and to a marked degree that adversely affects educational performance:

- an inability to learn that cannot be explained by intellectual, sensory, or other health factors;
- an inability to build or maintain satisfactory interpersonal relationships with peers and teachers;
- inappropriate types of behavior or feelings under normal circumstances;
- a general pervasive mood of unhappiness or depression; or
- a tendency to develop physical symptoms or fears associated with personal or school problems.

The term *seriously emotionally disturbed* includes children who are schizophrenic. The term does not include children who are socially maladjusted, unless it is determined that they are seriously emotionally disturbed.'

There is currently a proposal to change the category of seriously emotionally disturbed to emotional and behavioral disorders [EBD].

As noted earlier, estimates of the percentage of children with ADD who have coexisting disabilities vary, ranging from 25% to 40% for those who have coexisting learning disabilities, and from 40% to 60% for those who have serious emotional disturbances (Parker, 1992). Of the estimated two million youngsters with ADD in the United States, approximately one million will need some form of special education (McKinney, Montague, & Hocutt, 1993).

CLINICAL TEACHING

Special education teachers use a variety of different teaching methods, which are collectively referred to as: remediation, special education teaching methods, intervention, educational therapy, learning strategies, instructional strategies, or, simply, good teaching. Some methods are adaptations of those used in regular classes; others are very distinctive. To differentiate special education teaching from regular teaching, it is helpful to think of it as "clinical teaching."

THE CLINICAL TEACHING PERSPECTIVE

Clinical teaching implies an attitude, perspective, or philosophy about teaching. Clinical teaching does not require any particular instructional system, educational setting, or style of teaching. It can be applied in any placement—a regular classroom, a resource room, a special class, or one to one. It can be used by special education teachers, regular classroom teachers, or in collaboration, and it can encompass many different teaching methods, materials, and strategies.

The goal of clinical teaching is to tailor learning experiences to meet the unique needs of a particular student. Using all of the information gained through assessment of the student and through analysis of the student's specific attentional, learning, and behavior problems, the clinical teacher designs a special teaching program for that student. Assessment and clinical teaching are continuous and interlinked, with the clinical teacher modifying the instruction as new needs become apparent.

Clinical teaching is unique in several ways:

■ It requires flexibility and continual decision making.
■ It is planned for an individual student.
■ It can be accomplished in a variety of placements.

THE CLINICAL TEACHING CYCLE

It is useful to view clinical teaching as a cycle, as diagrammed in Figure 6.1. The phases of the clinical teaching cycle are (1) assessment, (2) planning, (3) implementation of the teaching plan, and (4) evaluation, leading to (5) a modification of the assessment and then to new planning, new forms of implementation, and a continuing cycle of clinical teaching. If the student performs well, the clinical teacher knows the plan has succeeded and plans for the next step. If the student

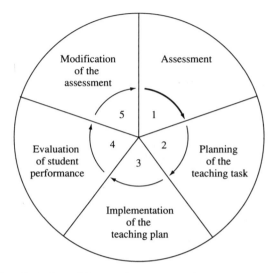

FIGURE 6.1   The clinical teaching cycle
Source: From *Learning Disabilities,* by Janet Lerner. Copyright ©
1993 by Houghton Mifflin. Reprinted by permission.

has difficulty, the clinical teacher reevaluates and modifies the teaching
plan.

PSYCHOLOGICAL BASES FOR SPECIAL EDUCATION INSTRUCTION

Special education instruction is based on several distinct
psychological theories of learning. The theories underlying developmental psychology, behavioral psychology, and cognitive
psychology lead to different beliefs about learning and different
methods of teaching. Each of these fields of psychology has implications for teaching students with attention deficit disorders.

DEVELOPMENTAL PSYCHOLOGY

Developmental psychology focuses on the nature of
human growth and development. The foundations of developmental psychology lie in the inspirational ideas of Jean Piaget,
who, more than 50 years ago, observed that the ways children

think differ qualitatively from the ways adults think. Further, Piaget observed that cognitive abilities develop sequentially; as children mature, their ways of thinking continually change (Piaget, 1970).

The concepts of developmental psychology have profound implications for understanding and teaching children with ADD. For instance, developmental psychology champions the notion of **readiness,** which refers to the state of maturational development that is needed before a desired skill can be successfully learned. The readiness needed for walking, for example, includes a certain level of neurological development, adequate muscle strength, and the development of certain prerequisite motor functions. Until an infant has acquired these prerequisite abilities, attempts to teach him or her to walk are futile. Similarly, though in a very different area, a student must have acquired certain mathematics skills and knowledge to profit from a course in calculus.

An important goal in teaching students with ADD stems from developmental psychology: that of strengthening the child's thinking and cognitive abilities. Developmental psychologists suggest that in some cases a school actually hinders rather than assists the child's learning by making intellectual demands for which the child is not yet ready. These school-related demands may require cognitive abilities that the child has not yet developed. Such demands not only set up the child to fail but also may cause stress-related emotional problems. Behaviors such as school phobias or acting out may be rooted in academic demands (such as reading) for which the child is not ready.

The lesson from developmental psychology is that the clinical teacher must design learning experiences to enhance the child's natural development. Children with ADD may need special instruction to develop readiness for their next step in learning.

Behavioral Psychology

Behavioral psychology has had a pivotal influence on special education, affecting research, assessment, instruction, and behavior management of students with ADD. Since the initial work of B. F. Skinner more than 50 years ago, the concepts of behavioral psychology have flourished, helping special educators understand how modifications in the environment can shape learning and behavior. For children with ADD, behavioral theory can be applied to both teaching academic skills and managing behavior.

For improving academic performance, behavioral theory provides a method of teaching academic skills called **direct instruction.** Direct instruction is a carefully structured and sequenced, teacher-planned and teacher-controlled method that has proved a useful and efficient means of teaching academic skills to students with disabilities (Winograd & Hare, 1988). Direct instruction provides structure and organization that enable students with ADD to acquire needed academic skills.

Direct instruction:

■ is academically focused, teaching academic skills directly;
■ is teacher-directed and teacher-controlled;
■ is carefully sequenced, using structured materials;
■ gives students mastery of basic skills;
■ sets goals that are clear to students;
■ allocates sufficient time for instruction;
■ uses continuous monitoring or curriculum-based assessment of students' performance;
■ provides immediate feedback to students;
■ teaches a skill until it is mastered.

Behavioral theory also provides a workable system of strategies for managing the behavior of students with ADD. Applied behavioral analysis and behavior modification techniques utilize a systematic arrangement of environmental events to produce specific changes in observable behavior. Systematically used behavior management techniques can strengthen or maintain desirable behaviors in students with ADD, and diminish undesirable behaviors. The behavior management procedures of reinforcement, punishment, extinction, shaping, and contingency management have proved particularly useful for students with ADD (Barkley, 1990; O'Leary & O'Leary, 1977). Behavior management techniques are described later in this chapter.

COGNITIVE PSYCHOLOGY

The field of cognitive psychology deals with the human processes of thinking, knowing, and learning. Cognitive abilities are clusters of mental abilities essential to human functions, enabling one to know, be aware, think, conceptualize, use abstractions, reason, criticize, and create.

Cognitive learning theories emphasize approaches to teaching that promote active student learning and encourage students to direct their own learning. The focus of instruction is to stimulate and nourish students' own mental constructs for acquiring knowledge and to help them grow in their capacity to monitor and guide their own learning and thinking (Palinscar & Klenk, 1991; Resnick & Klopfer, 1989; Scruggs & Mastropieri, 1991; Wong, 1992).

Some of the key principles of cognitive learning theories serve as guidelines for instruction:

1. *Learning is a constructive process.* Knowledge cannot be given to a student. Instead, each person must construct or build his or her knowledge.
2. *Learning is linking new information to previous knowledge.* What a student learns depends on the experiences and knowledge he or she brings to the learning situation.
3. *Learning is strategic.* Learning is more than simply remembering. People need strategies to learn something.
4. *Learning requires motivation.* Much of schooling requires hard work over a long period of time. It requires students to be actively involved, committed, and interested over a period of time. Motivation energizes and directs behavior.

Students with ADD need instruction to help them focus, take responsibility for their own learning, and learn strategies they can use to manage their own learning. They must become independent, rather than dependent, learners.

In summary, each of these psychological theories has implications for teaching individuals with ADD. First, from developmental psychology we learn that the child's maturational level and readiness for learning must be considered. Second, behavior management techniques borrowed from behavioral psychology have proved very effective for individuals with ADD, both in learning academic skills and in managing behavior. Finally, cognitive psychology suggests that individuals with ADD must learn to control, regulate, and direct their own behavior and learning.

Source: Reprinted by permission, Universal Press Syndicate.

METHODS OF BEHAVIOR MANAGEMENT

Behavioral methods offer indispensable tools for modifying the behavior of students in special education. Applied behavior management strategies are often used with students with disabilities. Behavioral techniques are especially useful for modifying the behavior of students with attention deficit disorders (Barkley, 1990). The terms *behavior management, behavior therapy, behavior modification,* and *contingency management* all refer to strategies designed to establish appropriate behaviors or reduce inappropriate ones. The methods are centered on increasing on-task behavior, completing work, improving compliance and impulse control, and building acceptable social skills. Behavioral methods are also used to decrease hyperactivity, reduce off-task behavior and disruptive behavior, and curtail acts of aggression (Fiore, Becker, & Nero, 1993).

Discussed in this section are the following aspects of behavior management, as they apply to students with ADD:

FIGURE 6.2   The components of a behavioral unit

(1) key concepts of behavior theory, (2) applied behavior analysis strategies, (3) cognitive behavior modification, and (4) social skills training.

KEY CONCEPTS OF BEHAVIOR THEORY

At the core of the behavioral unit in behavior theory are three key components: the **stimulus** (*S*), the **response** (*R*), and the **consequence** (*C*), as illustrated in Figure 6.2. The target behavior is *R*—the response. It is helpful to think of the target behavior as an event sandwiched between two sets of environmental influences—those that precede the behavior (stimulus or antecedent events) and those that follow the behavior (consequent events or reinforcements). Changing a student's behavior requires analysis of these three components. Figure 6.2 illustrates how these three components are related.

Here is a simple example of the three behavioral events: The teacher asks Jenine to read silently. This action is the stimulus (or antecedent event). The response (or target behavior) occurs when Jenine reads for two minutes. The consequence (or reinforcement) follows the target behavior: In this case, the teacher may reinforce Jenine's reading behavior by giving her praise or a sticker.

Some of the key concepts of behavior theory are described in the following paragraphs.

Reinforcement

Reinforcement is a means of strengthening or increasing the likelihood of a behavior desired from a subject. **Positive reinforcement** involves responding to the desired behavior with a reward. Positive reinforcement serves to increase the probability that the target behavior will occur again. To illustrate, praise can be a reinforcer for children who wait their turns to play a game. If they are rewarded with compliments, the next time the game is played, the children will tend to await their turns again to receive the praise. In another example, Susan's teachers use positive reinforcement to strengthen the behavior of remembering to bring her assignment. Susan, who usually forgets her assignment, is rewarded for remembering it, thereby strengthening the desired behavior (Parker, 1992).

Various social and tangible reinforcers may be used, including classroom privileges, free time, praise, attention, favorite activities, food, toys, and games. A good reinforcer is simply one that works for the individual student.

Negative reinforcement also increases the likelihood of a behavior occurring. When an unpleasant or aversive event is withdrawn, the desired behavior will increase. An example of negative reinforcement is a teacher's clanging a bell to get children to take their seats. To stop the unpleasant event of the ringing of the bell, the children sit in their seats. The persistent beeping your car makes when you leave the lights on can also be viewed as a negative reinforcer. The sound continues until you turn your lights off, the desired behavior.

Schedules of reinforcement (which specify the conditions under which reinforcement will occur) can be continuous or intermittent. A continuous schedule reinforces the target behavior each time it happens. An intermittent schedule can deliver the reinforcement either at intervals (reinforcers given at certain times) or on a ratio basis (reinforcers given after a certain number of responses).

Sometimes teachers inadvertently reinforce inappropriate behavior. For example, if Billy clowns around and the teacher pays attention to him, the teacher's negative attention to his actions can reinforce the undesirable behavior.

Punishment

The purpose of **punishment** is to stop or diminish undesired behavior, reducing the probability that an unwanted behavior will occur. Studies on the use of punishment with subjects with ADD have employed mildly aversive punishments, such as reprimands or ignoring (Fiore et al., 1993). In fact, the reprimand is probably the most frequently occurring teacher response in the classroom (Barkley, 1990). Research on children with ADD shows that effective reprimands are immediate, unemotional, brief, and consistently backed up with time-out or a loss of privilege for repeated noncompliance. In contrast, ineffective reprimands are delayed, long, emotional, and occur without concrete backup consequences (Rosen et al., 1984). In using punishment, the following principles should be applied (Parker, 1992; Rosen et al., 1984):

■ Punishment should be used in conjunction with a plan for reinforcement.
■ Punishment alone will not establish a desired behavior.
■ Punishment should be administered calmly and consistently.
■ Punishment needs to be administered sparingly. Over-punishment can demoralize and anger students, resulting in more negative than positive effects.
■ The number of reinforcing events should greatly exceed the number of punishing events.

Extinction

Extinction is the process of gradually decreasing or diminishing the intensity or frequency of an undesired behavior. Extinction occurs when the sources of reinforcement that followed a specific behavior have been removed; for example, when Lenny's teacher ignores his clowning around instead of rewarding him with attention—albeit negative attention. Ignoring works best in the initial stages of inappropriate behavior, before too much attention has been called to it.

Shaping

Shaping is a technique of gradually building a desired behavior by reinforcing each small step toward the target behavior. To use the shaping technique, the teacher must first break the target behavior down into a sequence of small steps. The child receives a reinforcer for a behavior he or she can already do, then reinforcers are provided for each step closer to the target behavior. This procedure is sometimes called *successive approximations*. For example, if the target behavior is for Charlene to sit in her seat and work for 15 minutes, at first Charlene is reinforced for being near her seat. Later, she is reinforced for kneeling at her desk, then for sitting in her seat for 1 minute. The time she must spend in her seat before receiving a reinforcer is gradually lengthened until she sits in her seat doing her work for 15 minutes.

Applied Behavior Analysis Strategies

Several applications of behavioral theory that are important in managing the behavior of children with attention deficit disorders are described in this section.

Contingency Management

Contingency management is a behavioral system that is often used with children with attention deficit disorders in school or at home. With this technique, the rewards or negative consequences that the child receives are contingent on (or an immediate response to) the child's behavior. Research shows that contingency management methods work with children with ADD, increasing appropriate behaviors and decreasing inappropriate ones (Abramowitz & O'Leary, 1991; Barkley, 1990; Fiore et al., 1993). Positive consequences for appropriate behavior may include praise or recognition. Negative consequences for inappropriate behavior may include ignoring or reprimands. The combination of praising appropriate behavior while ignoring inappropriate behavior has been shown to reduce disruptions in the classroom (Pfiffner & O'Leary, 1987). Other studies show that a combination of praise for desired behaviors and reprimands for undesirable behaviors work in managing the behaviors of ADHD children (Rosen et al., 1984).

Some principles guiding the effective use of contingency management are (Abramowitz & O'Leary, 1991; Barkley, 1990):

- The immediate consequences of a specific behavior can either strengthen or weaken that behavior.
- Praise should be delivered as soon as possible following the appropriate behavior.
- Reprimands should be straightforward and delivered immediately after off-task behavior.
- Teachers should use calm, firm, and consistent reprimands (instead of overly emotional or delayed reprimands).
- Eye contact and close proximity seem to increase the effectiveness of reprimands.

Token Economies

Another commonly used behavioral strategy is that of establishing a **token economy** in the classroom. This involves systematically awarding or withdrawing from children tokens or points, contingent on their display of appropriate or inappropriate behaviors. The children accumulate these tokens (or points) and can exchange them at a later time for rewards such as desired activities, privileges, toys, food, and games. Research shows that token economies help motivate children, keeping them on task and increasing their attention spans (Shores, Gunter, Denny, & Jack, 1993). Token economy programs can target a wide variety of behaviors or a single specific inappropriate behavior such as aggression or noncompletion of assignments (Abramowitz & O'Leary, 1991).

Response Cost

Response cost involves the loss of positive reinforcers when the child exhibits inappropriate behavior. Lost reinforcers can include a wide range of privileges and activities (Fiore et al., 1993). In one study, points were subtracted for aggressive behavior and earned by actions that were incompatible with aggression. In this study of a response cost procedure, children significantly decreased their aggressive behaviors (DuPaul, Guevremont, & Barkley, 1992).

A commercially available electronic device simplifies the response cost procedure for the teacher. The Attention Training System (Gordon, Thomason, Cooper, & Ivers, 1991) is a small electronic box that is placed on a child's desk. It automatically credits children with points, and teachers can use a remote control device to deduct points. A few studies suggest that using such an electronic device leads to improvement in the child's behavior (DuPaul, Guevremont, & Barkley, 1992; Gordon et al., 1991).

Whether children will generalize behavior learned through token economies and response cost procedures needs further study. When a child is transferred from a special education setting that employs a token system to a regular class that does not, increases in appropriate behavior achieved through the token system often disappear. More studies are needed on methods that will enable children with ADD to maintain and generalize the gains from token economies as they move into more regular settings.

Time-Out

Another application of behavior theory is the **time-out** procedure, in which a disruptive student is removed from instructional activities. Time-out can be a powerful technique for managing disruptive behaviors with children who do not respond to other behavior management methods, but it should be used cautiously. If implemented properly, time-out offers an effective means of managing the behavior of youngsters with ADD (Abramowitz & O'Leary, 1991).

Exclusionary time-out involves placing the child in a designated, isolated area for a short period of time. Marion (1991) describes several conditions that will increase the likelihood of success with this method. Teachers are cautioned to warn the child only once, to state clearly the broken rule, and to actively assist the student's return from time-out by directly engaging the child in ongoing activities. Time-out should be brief, from 1 to 10 minutes, with younger children requiring the least amount of time. A common rule of thumb is no more than 1 minute for every year of the child's age. During a time-out, the teacher and the other children should ignore the student. The goal is to eliminate all potential reinforcers (CH.A.D.D., 1992; Parker, 1992). To implement time-out fairly and ethically, certain guidelines should be followed (Abramowitz & O'Leary, 1991):

1. Both the target behaviors and the methods of implementing time-outs should be clearly stated on the pupil's IEP.
2. A written record of the number of time-outs and their effectiveness should be kept.
3. The staff (teachers, aides, related service personnel, and so on) need to be fully trained and able to carry out time-outs consistently.
4. The staff should determine in advance how noncompliance with a time-out should be handled. For instance, will the time-out start right away or after the child is quiet?

Meeting the requirements of time-outs can be difficult in regular classes. Therefore, special educators may be needed to follow through on recommended procedures.

Contingency Contracting

Contingency contracting is based on what is known as "Grandma's Rule" because grandmothers are alleged to bargain:

"If you finish what's on your plate, you can have your dessert." Contingency contracting is a bit more formal and involves negotiating a written agreement in which the student agrees to perform a task and the teacher, in return, agrees to provide something the child wants. The contract must specify the exact target behavior or task, a time limit for completion, the student's reward for completion, and the people responsible for the agreement (in this case, the teacher and the student). An example of a contingency agreement is: If Steve stays in his seat for 10 minutes during reading time, he can have 10 minutes of extra time for art (an activity he enjoys). An example of a contingency contract is shown on page 141.

Cognitive Behavior Modification

Cognitive behavior modification is a strategy that combines behavioral techniques with cognitive strategies. Based on the work of Meichenbaum and Goodman (1971), cognitive behavior modification is designed to teach students strategies for modifying their own behavior. The method addresses some of the core problems of ADD—namely, impulse control, higher-order problem solving, and self-regulation (Fiore et al., 1993). Cognitive-behavioral strategies can help students with ADD develop their own coping strategies to improve their behavior.

The goal is for students to spontaneously ask themselves such questions as (Haake, 1991):

1. What is the problem, or What am I supposed to do?
2. What is my plan?
3. Am I using my plan?
4. How did I do?

The teacher models the thinking process through overt verbalization—talking out loud. For example, after writing an assignment on the board, the teacher might say out loud (Haake, 1991, p. 267):

> Let's see. What am I supposed to do? Wow, that's confusing! OK, first I'll find the page—there—now, what else? Alternative rows—I know that means every other one—beginning with which–Oh, yeah—number 2. I better mark those rows before I start. How, what's my plan? Last time I really messed up; I didn't pay attention to my +s and −s. This time I think I'll circle each one before I do it—that way, I'll *have* to look at it.

Contract

SEAL OF
AGREEMENT

_____ and _____
Student   Teacher

agree on the following;

If _____ completes the arithmetic problem sheet,
_____ will allow_____ to
use the computer for 30 minutes.

Signatures:

_____   _____
Student   Teacher

_____   _____
Date   Date

Through **self-monitoring** and **self-reinforcement** strategies, children learn to observe their own behavior. Self-reinforcement involves children rewarding themselves based on their self-monitoring. Several studies indicate that self-monitoring and self-reinforcement are more effective methods of improving social and academic behaviors of youngsters with ADD than external reinforcements and monitoring by teachers (Barkley, Copeland, & Sivage, 1980; Whalen & Henker, 1986).

Self-instructional problem solving enables students to control their own learning. Through training and rehearsal, the student is taught to follow a series of steps (Camp, 1980; Kendall & Braswell, 1984). The following are guidelines for using cognitive behavior modification:

1. Repeat the instructions.
2. Describe the task.
3. Verbalize an approach to the task.
4. Think about the consequences of the approach.
5. Decide how to proceed.
6. Perform the task.
7. Evaluate the success of the approach.
8. Replace verbalizations with self-instruction.

The results of research on the effectiveness of cognitive behavior modification are mixed (Abikoff, 1987). Some studies show that the method leads to positive changes in sustained attention, impulse control, hyperactivity, and self-concept, and that some children with ADD benefit from these strategies (Barkley et al., 1980; Fiore et al., 1993; Kendall & Braswell, 1984). Other clinical studies of self-instruction and self-instructional problem solving show greater improvements when these techniques are used in clinical settings than when they are used in actual classrooms (Abikoff, 1987; Barkley et al., 1980).

The following statements are generalizations about cognitive behavior modification:

1. Self-instruction and self-monitoring can reduce such symptoms of ADD as inattention, distractibility, impulsivity, difficulty in following rules, and poor social skills.
2. When students learn to regulate their own behavior, they may no longer require external reinforcement and external behavior control by teachers (Barkley et al., 1980).

Calvin and Hobbes   by Bill Watterson

Source: Reprinted by permission, Universal Press Syndicate.

3. When children develop their own strategies to improve their behavior in one setting, they must learn to generalize the strategies to other settings.

SOCIAL SKILLS TRAINING

One of the most consistent findings in the literature on ADD is that many students identified as having ADD exhibit significant and persistent problems in social relationships. Studies show that children with ADD and hyperactivity are aggressive and rejected more often than other children. Children with ADD without hyperactivity are more withdrawn than other children. Children with ADD without hyperactivity are more withdrawn and unpopular but are not necessarily rejected (McKinney, Montague, & Hocutt, 1993).

Many children with ADD have trouble acquiring age-appropriate social skills because of their persistent problems with impulse control, inattention, distractibility, and sometimes hyperactivity. A child who is overactive may stand out negatively in the classroom and be perceived as annoying and demanding by classmates. Often, children with ADD are rejected by others, especially if they display aggression (Schaughency & Rothlind, 1991). These students are described as being bossy, intrusive, and intimidating, all characteristics that lower their social status (Whalen & Henker, 1986). In contrast to the more positive interactions experienced by popular children, children with ADD receive more negative feedback from their peers. Prolonged peer rejection leads to poor self-esteem (Whalen & Henker, 1986). Characteristics that are common to children with ADD and that may interfere with positive peer interactions include:

- Frequent intrusive behaviors
- Deficient communication skills
- Biased or deficient social cognitive skills
- Poor emotional regulation

Because of their social difficulties, students with ADD need instruction in social skills. Methods of instruction can include direct instruction, prompting, modeling, rehearsal, and reinforcement (Landaw & Moore, 1991; Strain, Kerr, & Ragland, 1981). Several activities useful in teaching social skills are:

- *Judging behavior through stories.* Read or tell an incomplete story that involves social judgments. Have the student anticipate the ending and complete the story. Discuss the consequences to the people in the story.
- *Grasping social situations through pictures.* Let the child arrange a series of pictures depicting a social situation. Have the student describe how the people might feel in this situation. The teacher can assist the child with feedback on his or her perceptions.
- *Distinguishing reality from make-believe.* Help children differentiate between reality and make-believe by asking them questions such as, "Do flowers and trees talk for real or just for pretend?"
- *Learning to generalize to other situations.* After the students have practiced specific social skills in one setting, they need direct practice in other situations as well. Feedback on their performance is essential. This will require collaboration between regular teachers, special educators, other school personnel, and family members, who can assist the children with these skills at home.
- *Learning how to communicate effectively.* Students with ADD may need assistance in improving their conversational skills; for example, in learning to extend greetings, to stay on a topic, to take turns with their conversational partners, and to develop effective listening abilities.
- *Developing friendships.* Some children will need help making and keeping friendships. Acquiring skills in initiating play, giving compliments, and cooperating will be valuable for them.

Some popular social skills training programs that regular and special education teachers can use for students with ADD are listed in Box 6.1.

TEACHING ACADEMIC SKILLS

In addition to dealing with ways of managing behavior, special education methods are used to improve academic achievement. Many children with ADD have academic problems in the areas of listening, oral language, reading, writing, and mathematics. They tend to receive lower grades in academic subjects and lower scores on standard measures of reading (more than 80% of 11-year-olds with ADD are at least 2 years behind in reading), spelling, mathematics, and written language (Zentall, 1993). If the child has coexisting learning disabilities, academic problems are even more likely. Many of the special education strategies are useful in teaching academic subjects to children with ADD (Lerner, 1993).

PREACADEMIC LEARNING

Children with attention deficit disorders may encounter academic difficulties because they lack readiness skills needed for academic learning, such as motor skills, language skills, and

BOX 6.1
SOCIAL SKILLS TRAINING PROGRAMS

DUSO (Developing Understanding of Self and Others) (American
   Guidance Service)

Getting Along with Others (Research Press)

Skillstreaming in Early Childhood (Research Press)

Skillstreaming the Elementary Child (Research Press)

Skillstreaming the Adolescent (Research Press)

The Social Skills Curriculum (American Guidance Service)

TAD (Toward Affective Development) (Research Press)

Walker Social Skills Curriculum: The ACCEPTS Program (PRO-ED)

auditory and visual processing skills. While many children readily acquire these essential developmental skills before they enter school, some children need to be taught them (Kirk & Chalfont, 1984; Lerner, 1993).

Motor Skill Development

Some children with ADD need direct instruction to improve motor function. Poor motor development can adversely affect academic learning. Learning to write, for example, requires proficiency in eye-hand coordination, vivid sequential memory images, visual perception skills, fine motor abilities, and so on. To learn to write, children may need instruction in those skills.

Language Development

Language learning is an essential area of developmental learning. Any child who does not understand language or cannot use language effectively will be jeopardized. Underlying language disorders can also affect learning to read and write. Therefore, children who exhibit developmental problems in language need specific instruction in language learning.

Auditory Processing Deficiencies

Auditory perception is an important pathway for learning. Many poor readers have auditory, linguistic, and phonological difficulties. These children do not have a hearing or auditory acuity problem but one in auditory perception, the ability to recognize or interpret what they hear. Many children do not realize that words and language are patterns of sounds; they lack what is referred to as phonological awareness. These children do not understand that language is comprised of words, syllables, and phonemes (letter sounds). Completely unaware of how language is put together and unable to recognize or isolate the sounds of a word, they consequently have great difficulty learning to read. With instruction, children who lack phonological awareness can develop the skills needed to process the sounds that shape language and reading. Methods of increasing phonological awareness include playing word games, learning rhyming words, and learning to break words into syllables and sounds.

Visual Processing Deficiencies

Visual perception plays a significant role in academic learning, particularly in reading and mathematics. Students with deficiencies in visual perception have difficulty performing tasks that require visual discrimination of letters, words, numbers, geometric designs, or pictures. These children may need instruction in visual perception, visual discrimination, and spatial relationships. Instruction should be as closely related as possible to the academic task the student is required to do.

ACADEMIC LEARNING

Listening

The act of listening requires the ability to select out and attend to a message while ignoring competing information. The inclusion of much detail and description increases the difficulty of the task of listening. Students who have difficulty with auditory processing will have problems understanding lectures. To help children concentrate on the elements of a lesson, teachers should make sure that oral presentations are simple, well organized, and incorporate visual materials (Zentall, 1993).

Speaking

Many children with ADD lack proficiency in language production—that is, in speaking. Though they may be more talkative than their classmates when they initiate a conversation, they tend to be less talkative when asked to respond. They may need props or visual cues, such as pictures, to sustain their attention during activities requiring speech.

Reading

Many children with ADD have difficulty with reading. About 80% of children with learning disabilities encounter problems in learning to read. Zentall (1993) conjectures that about 9% of students with ADD have a reading disability, when it is defined as a discrepancy between reading achievement and reading potential.

Reading is an extremely complex task, and learning to read requires sustained attention over a long period. Learning to read well takes several years, and teachers must plan to engage the interest of beginning and poor readers during this long span. It is important that students not lose hope that they will eventually be able to read well. Unfortunately, poor readers often lose motivation, becoming inattentive, giving up easily, and not completing their work. Teachers should try to make reading enjoyable and convey to students the belief that they will learn to read.

Special methods not typically used in regular classrooms are effective with students with severe reading problems. Among them are multisensory techniques (combining auditory, visual, and tactile stimuli), computer applications, direct instructional approaches, and modifications of standard methods of phonics and language experience. These methods often are successful with poor readers who have been unable to learn to read using other methodologies.

Writing

Students with ADD tend to have slower motor responses and slower perceptual responses (Zentall, 1993). As a result, they have more difficulty than other children with the physical act of handwriting. Like other academic tasks, learning to write requires sustained attention and concentration. Many children with ADD do better with word processing than with writing. Typing is inherently easier and neater than handwriting, especially for children with fine motor problems. For efficient computer word processing, students need to learn typing or keyboarding skills. Students with ADD will need special instruction to learn keyboarding skills. Teachers have found that third or fourth graders are able to learn keyboarding, if it is a planned part of the curriculum.

Written expression and spelling are two other components of the writing curriculum. Competent writing requires many related abilities, including facility in spoken language, ability to read, spelling skills, legible handwriting, knowledge of the rules of written usage, and cognitive strategies for organizing and planning the writing. Producing a piece of written work also requires sustained attention and effort over a long period of time. The writing process consists of several stages, which include: (1) prewriting, when the writer gathers ideas; (2) drafting, when the writer expresses his or her ideas in rough form; (3) revising, when the writer organizes and polishes his or her ideas and their actual expression; and (4) sharing with an audience, which gives value to the entire writing process. The teacher plays a key role in keeping the student motivated and interested throughout the writing process.

Mathematics

Both word problems and computations require selective attention, and students with ADD often have difficulty in mathematics. Zentall (1993) reports that students with ADD often do poorly on mathematics tests, and that they are slower than their peers in doing calculations. Off-task behavior prevents them from concentrating on learning computation facts. To teach mathematics to students with ADD, teachers can use a variety of special education methods, including using concrete, hands-on materials; direct instruction; math learning strategies instruction; arithmetic computer programs; and problem-solving techniques. Students must have acquired basic prerequisite math concepts, be given ample opportunity for practice and review, learn the vocabulary of mathematics, and be able to generalize to new situations.

SPECIAL REMEDIAL METHODS

Several special methods are not typically used in the regular classroom. These require intensive instruction in small groups or one-to-one instruction and are not practical for the regular classroom. Special education teachers may use these special methods for teaching children with ADD. The methods include VAKT, the Fernald method, the Orton-Gillingham method, Reading Recovery, and the neurological impress method. Special education teachers need to know these methods, which are explained in various books on learning or reading disabilities (see Lerner, 1993).

LEARNING STRATEGIES INSTRUCTION

Learning strategies instruction is a method of teaching students with attention deficit disorders that comes from cognitive psychology. This approach focuses on *how* students learn rather than on *what* they learn and is built on the belief that good learners have a repertoire of cognitive learning strategies that help them learn and remember. In contrast, students with attention deficit disorders may lack such strategies. They do not know how to control and direct their thinking to learn, how to gain knowledge, or how to remember what they learn.

Fortunately, learning strategies can be taught, and research shows that students who receive instruction in learning strategies do improve. Learning strategies facilitate learning and remembering in every area of the curriculum—in reading, writing, mathematics, social studies, and science. When teachers help students acquire learning strategies, the students learn how to learn (Ellis et al., 1991).

One widely used model of instruction in learning strategies is the Strategies Instruction Model (SIM). It was developed by Deshler, Schumaker, and their colleagues through many years of programmatic research with adolescents with learning disabilities at the University of Kansas Institute of Research on Learning Disabilities. Central to this model is a series of eight stages of instruction (Ellis et al., 1991):

1. The teacher gives students a pretest and obtains a commitment from the student to learn the strategy.
2. The teacher describes the learning strategy.
3. The teacher models the learning strategy for the students.
4. The students verbally practice the strategy.
5. The students engage in controlled practice and get feedback on their performance.
6. The students engage in advanced practice and get feedback on their performance.
7. The teacher gives students a posttest and obtains a commitment from the student to generalize.
8. The students generalize the learning strategy in a classroom situation.

SUMMARY

Many children with attention deficit disorders, such as those with a codiagnosis of other health impaired, learning disabilities, or serious emotional disturbance, will need special education. More intensive, ongoing educational techniques include behavior modification, cognitive-behavioral interventions, parent training, social skills training, and special education methods for academic instruction.

The term *special education* refers to instruction that is specially designed to meet the unusual needs of exceptional learners. Special education methods and strategies can be useful with children and adolescents with attention deficit disorders. Special materials, teaching techniques, equipment, or facilities may be required.

Special education teachers are clinical teachers in that they tailor instruction to a unique student. The psychological theories on which special education instruction is based come from developmental psychology, behavioral psychology, and cognitive psychology.

Special education methods are used to manage behaviors, to develop self-instruction and self-monitoring skills, and to teach social skills. They can also be used to teach preacademic skills and the academic skills of listening, speaking, reading, writing, and mathematics. Special remedial methods and learning strategies instruction are also an important part of special education.

DISCUSSION QUESTIONS

1. The U.S. Department of Education policy memorandum of 1991 described the conditions under which students with attention deficit disorders may be eligible for special education services under the Individuals with Disabilities Education Act (IDEA). Name the three categories of disability mentioned in the policy memorandum. What conditions must students with ADD meet to be eligible under each of these categories?

2. What is meant by *clinical teaching*? Describe the five phases of the clinical teaching cycle.

3. Name three different fields of psychology that provide a theoretical base from which to approach the teaching of students with attention deficit disorders. What does each field have to offer with regard to teaching such students?

4. Describe three applications of behavioral theory for managing the behaviors of children with attention deficit disorders.

5. Describe a special education method used to teach students with ADD in each of the following academic areas: speaking, reading, mathematics, and writing.

CHAPTER 7

THE FAMILY SYSTEM: PARENT TRAINING, COUNSELING, AND HOME MANAGEMENT

Tabetha M. is a 14-year-old ninth grader. Her teachers describe her behavior in school as oppositional and defiant; her mother says her behavior at home is uncontrollable and unpredictable. An interview with her mother and a review of school records indicate that this behavior pattern began in early childhood. According to her mother, Tabetha was extremely active, impulsive, and aggressive, even as a child. During her elementary school years, she was described as a hyperactive pupil with social-emotional disorders, and she received special education services. At present, she is failing in many subjects but doing well in music and mathematics, two

subjects that she likes. Tabetha's oppositional behavior has increased in high school; she was suspended twice this year because of aggression toward her classmates and teachers.

According to Tabetha's mother, there is serious family discord in the home, because the mother and stepfather blame each other for their inability to control Tabetha's behavior. Her 11-year-old sister complains bitterly about Tabetha's verbal and physical aggression toward her and her friends. Because of Tabetha's behavior, the atmosphere in the family is tense, charged with endless arguments.

The IEP assessment team at the high school met with Tabetha and her mother. Tabetha was identified as having an attention deficit disorder and a coexisting disability classified as a serious emotional disturbance (SED). The team determined that she was eligible for special education services and also recommended related services, including weekly psychological counseling, assistance from a social worker for Tabetha and her family, and continued special education instruction in a resource room.

The school told Tabetha's parents about a parent training program at the high school that emphasized behavior management techniques, and her parents agreed to attend. Her parents also decided to seek assistance from a family therapist, and her sister would be included in many of the sessions. The family counseling sessions were designed to help each family member better understand Tabetha's disabilities and their effects on her behavior.

The combination of counseling, the behavior management program, and the efforts of the family and school team seem to be helping Tabetha control her aggressive behavior both at home and at school. The individual counseling sessions are designed to help Tabetha understand her problems and accept her limitations and build on her strengths. The goal is to help her learn ways of managing her impulsive and aggressive behaviors. The support services and the efforts of family members will help the family relationship become more positive and functional. As family members emphasize mutual solutions to their problems instead of blaming each other, the home atmosphere will improve.

The focus of this chapter is the family system—the pattern of interactions between the parents and other family members and the child or adolescent with an attention deficit disorder. The major topics discussed in this chapter are: parent training, family counseling, and home management strategies.

THE CHALLENGES OF
RAISING A CHILD WITH ADD

Children with ADD present special challenges to parents. The usual modes of parenting are ineffective with such a child. If he or she is a first or only child, the parents may begin to believe that they are bad parents. If the child has siblings who do not have problems, the parents may conclude that the child is defective, and the child may eventually come to believe this as well. Thus, a layer of negative, emotional, and inappropriate judgments surrounds an already demanding situation. Family therapy and behavior management for children with ADD require cognizance of the special nature of families, knowledge of family systems theory, and compassionate understanding of the impact of ADD on a child and the family (Reeve, 1991).

Parents of children with attention deficit disorders face many of the same problems as teachers, but for parents the problems are greatly magnified. Teachers have a child for a few hours a day in a limited, controlled situation, whereas parents are challenged 24 hours a day, 7 days a week, in all kinds of situations and by all types of demands. And there are no vacations. Moreover, it is not uncommon for ADD to occur over several generations, and a parent may also have a history of attention deficit disorders. When parents begin to understand the problem of attention deficit disorders, they begin to grasp what may have been incomprehensible behavior in themselves.

Parents can play a crucial role in helping a child with ADD. They must be informed consumers, always working to learn more about the baffling condition of attention deficit disorders. They must become assertive advocates, continually seeking the right programs for their child at home, in school, and out of school. Even after a suitable program is found, parents must often fight to make sure that their child's legal rights are being recognized. Parents must be firm in managing their child's behavior while remaining empathetic to their child's feelings, failures, fears, and tribulations. In between, they must also give time and attention to other members of the family and try to make a life for themselves. There are no easy answers and no simple solutions for parents of children with attention deficit disorders.

Raley (1993) gives the following advice for parents of children with ADD:

> 1. You will be sorely tempted to: yell, scream, nag, nag some more, lecture, moralize, debate. Don't. It doesn't work.
>
> 2. You will be vulnerable to thinking that each and every "problem" area is important to tackle—for his/her sake. For both of your sakes, don't. Choose your battles carefully and gauge your response according to how important this issue will be in 20 years.
>
> 3. At times you will think that you are highly anxious, depressed, and close to insanity—you're right. Parents (especially mothers) and teachers of children with ADD have a harder job than usual. Take care of yourself and your relationships.

4. You will need to be a continual student. Do your homework and learn as much as you can about ADD. Know in the core of your being that this is a legitimate disorder.

5. You will need to become a specialist in behavior modification techniques: Keep the overall behavior plan as simple as possible, focus on one behavior at a time, be creative in setting up a positive reinforcement system with celebrations for his/her hard work, set up a negative consequence system for major battles and minor battles (time out; natural and logical consequences; loss of privileges; and response cost programs). Let the small skirmishes go, and carry out the above plan with a great deal of consistency and without a lot of emotion.

6. Know full well that when you're about to act in anger . . . you're about to mess things up in a big way. Use time out for yourself and find healthy outlets for your anger and your sadness.

7. Try (as hard as you possibly can) not to battle over homework. This child has already put in a very long, very hard day in a job at school, attending to routine, repetitive tasks, as well as organizational and self-control skills. Homework represents being sentenced to a second job, a second shift of the same. Parents and teachers need to work hard to help modify school work as needed.

8. Your own sense of worth and happiness must never be dependent upon how well any treatment program is working at any point in time. It's not fair to make children feel responsible for our sense of happiness or for our self-esteem—it's not their job and it's too heavy a burden for them.

9. Find *5 minutes* out of every *24 hours* to let this child know in some way that you're really glad he's/she's part of your universe. We have to let kids know what's right and good about them, because the rest of the world will often tell them what's wrong.

10. Remind yourself frequently that the most powerful way to show respect to a child is to listen—really listen not only to the words, but also to the emotions hiding slightly below the surface of those words.

11. Look for ways of encouraging a sense of mastery and self-confidence in your child. Keep looking, keep searching for some hobby or activity or anything your child does well, and then nurture it.

12. Never give up. Expect periods of relapse. Know that the course of this disorder includes times when symptoms are more difficult to bring under control. But also know that studies and experience show that a combination of school intervention, these behavioral guidelines, and medication can positively alter the overall course of attention deficit disorders for your child.

PARENT TRAINING

Parent training and behavior management programs are often recommended to teach parents how to help their child. Parents can learn to become effective agents of change for their children. Through training sessions, parents discover how to be integral members of the interdisciplinary team working to alleviate the difficulties and shape the behavior of the child with ADD. Many of the systematic parent training programs were initially developed as interventions for children with behavior problems, such as aggression or tantrums. But these programs also effectively train parents to modify the behavior of children with ADD. Research shows that acting-out behaviors such as aggression, impulsivity, and noncompliance decrease through parent training (Barkley, 1990; Barkley, Fischer, Edelbrock, & Smallish, 1990).

GUIDELINES FOR PARENT TRAINING

Parent training programs teach parents ways of interacting and working with their child. The following guidelines are suggested (Newby, Fischer, & Roman, 1991; Silver, 1993b; Whitman & Smith, 1991).

1. *Provide consistency in home management.* The procedures used in the home should be consistent. If there are two parents in the family, both are encouraged to attend counseling sessions. By learning together, both parents will be consistent in their management styles.

2. *Emphasize methods to decrease noncompliant behavior.* The child's noncompliant behavior is the most common reason that parents come to parent training programs (Barkley, 1990). Noncompliance is the most frequent parent complaint, and it leads to many negative parent-child interactions and much tension in the family. Decreasing noncompliant behavior is an appropriate goal for children with ADD. Noncompliance is often a precursor to social maladjustment.

3. *Foster feelings of self-esteem in your child.* A priority in any intervention is to bolster the child's self-esteem and sense of competence. Brooks (1992) suggests that parents consider the following when working to build their child's self-esteem.

- All children have strengths and competencies and these strengths must be identified and reinforced.
- Parents who convey hope provide a major force in helping children overcome adversity and become resilient.
- Parents can help children develop a feeling of responsibility and sense of making a contribution to the family and the world.
- Parents can provide opportunities for their child to make choices and decisions and promote self-discipline.
- Parents can help children deal effectively with mistakes and failures.

4. *Learn about parent training programs in your community.* Parent training programs teach parents and families home management skills. They teach the key concepts of behavior management and what parents can do in various situations. Since groups of parents of children with ADD usually attend these training sessions, the sessions also serve as a parent support group.

Several parent training programs are briefly described in Box 7.1.

THE EFFECTIVENESS
OF PARENT TRAINING PROGRAMS

Research suggests that parent training programs can be helpful (Newby et al., 1991). One study used a combination of the Barkley and the Forehand and McMahon parent training programs (Pisterman et al., 1989). Both child compliance and parent-child interactions improved. In this study, families of children with ADD were randomly assigned to either a treatment condition or a waiting condition. Treatment involved ten weekly group sessions and two individual family sessions. The child's compliance and parents' management techniques significantly improved for those in the treatment group. Treatment gains were maintained at a three-month follow-up evaluation.

A study of the Patterson Parent-Training Program showed that the children of 78% of the families who had completed the program had significantly fewer problem behaviors at the conclusion of the study. A follow-up study one year later showed similar success (Patterson & Fleischman, 1979).

BOX 7.1
Parent Training Programs

The Barkley Parent-Training Program. A major goal of this program is to improve parent management skills and competence in dealing with child behavior problems, particularly noncompliance. Another goal is to further parents' knowledge of the causes of the child's misbehavior. The final goal is to improve child compliance to parents' appropriate rules and commands.

This program emphasizes that incentive programs should be established by parents before punishment is introduced and that misbehavior should be anticipated and planned for. The program also stresses the importance of positive interactions between the parent and the child. (Barkley, 1987).

The Patterson Parent-Training Program. The main goal of this program is to reduce negative interactions between parents and children. The program targets a wide assortment of child misbehavior, including those associated with ADD, such as inattention, impulsivity, hyperactivity, and aggression. The program consists of several phases: In Phase 1, the parent monitors the child's behaviors to determine if they are compliant or noncompliant. In Phase 2, a reward program is set up for the child based on his or her positive behaviors. In Phase 3, the parent is taught appropriate methods of punishment. The underlying objective of the program is to teach the parents more effective techniques of child management (Patterson, 1982).

The Forehand and McMahon Parent-Training Program. The major goals of this program are to improve children's compliance with family rules and to make family interactions more pleasurable. The initial evaluation includes extensive family interviews, a brief child interview, and a number of questionnaires completed by parents about their parenting styles and their child's behaviors. Then

(continued)

BOX 7.1
PARENT TRAINING PROGRAMS
(continued)

parent-child interactions are observed in the clinic setting and at home in 45-minute sessions.

The program consists of training the parents and children in the clinic using role-playing, direct instruction, and coaching by the therapist. These behaviors are then practiced at home. Parents learn to attend to the child's positive behaviors and to ignore negative behaviors. Parents are taught to give clear, specific commands one at a time to the youngster and then to give the child sufficient time to respond. A time-out procedure is used to reinforce compliance.

Although this program was not specifically designed for children with ADD, it can be useful for parents whose children have difficulty with compliance. The program is highly structured and focuses on improving daily parent-child interaction (Forehand & McMahon, 1981).

The Educators In-Service Program on Attention Deficit Disorders. This multimedia training program for educators provides in-service preparation for teaching children with attention deficit disorders. It is also effective as a parent-training program. The program is based on the *CH.A.D.D. Educators Manual* (Fowler, 1992). The package contains a script, color transparencies, and a copy of the *CH.A.D.D. Educators Manual*. It covers educational implications of the disorders, identification and assessment protocols, intervention practices, and problem-solving techniques (CH.A.D.D., 1993).

1-2-3 Magic: Training Your Preschooler and Preteen to Do What You Want Them to Do. This is an excellent video and training book for parents to learn a behavioral technique for home management (Phelan, 1990).

COUNSELING

A child with ADD affects the entire family system. Counseling is often recommended to help family members learn to cope with the situation and to ease their emotional reactions (Robbins & Wolfe, 1987).

STAGES OF PARENTAL GRIEF

When parents are faced with the quandary of a child who has serious problems, they are likely to pass through a series of predictable stages. Counselors should recognize signs of these stages and know that parents live through each as they cope with the problem.

The predictable stages that parents go through when confronted with a child with special needs are apparently universal, applying to anyone who experiences a loss. The basis for this paradigm comes from the seminal work of Kübler-Ross (1969) in her analysis of patients who were in the final stages of terminal illnesses. Klauss and Kennel (1981) elaborated her ideas, applying them to parents of children born with obvious and severe medical problems. The loss these parents faced, and parents of children with ADD face, is the loss of their hoped-for and dreamed-of normal child. This dream is shattered when attention deficit disorders complicate the lives of the child and the parents (Whitman & Smith, 1991).

1. The first stage is characterized by shock, disbelief, and *denial*. During this time, the parents cannot grasp that their child has a disability. They feel that it's all unreal, and they block the problem from their minds. Denial buys the parents time—time they need to come to terms with this difficult problem.

2. The second stage is one of *anger* and resentment. Parents who have moved past denial often become enraged. "Why did this have to happen to me, and to my child?" They may displace this anger onto teachers, the doctor, the psychologist, or the therapist.

3. The next stage involves *bargaining*. Parents may try to make some kind of pact with themselves or others, sometimes through their religion. "If I only do this or that, then surely my child will be all right."

4. The next stage brings *depression* and discouragement. This stage is very difficult for the parents, and they may despair of finding a solution to their problems. They often feel sad and helpless during this time.

5. On a positive note, depression heralds the final stage: *acceptance*. Acceptance does not mean that the parents are satisfied with their child's disability. Acceptance means that despite the disability, the parents can fully love their child as he or she is, and that they can see hope for the future.

These stages of grief are universal; experienced by anyone who has suffered loss. The emotions parents express over their child's disability, and the behaviors they exhibit, are normal, not pathological. Teachers, counselors, and others who deal with the parents must understand that one cannot accelerate the grieving process. Individuals move through the stages at their own pace, and not necessarily in the sequence presented (Silver, 1992).

When under stress, parents will often return to the denial stage. Situations that may provoke this response include the child's birthday, the birth of another sibling, the discovery of another medical or educational problem for the child, and transitions of the child from one educational placement to another.

Reactions of Family Members

The entire family system is affected by a child with attention deficit disorders (Ingersoll, 1990). Day-to-day living with children who have ADD is extremely stressful. From the start, infants with ADD are often irritable, demanding, and difficult to soothe. Parents who have trouble coping with their baby's demands may feel incompetent, confused, and helpless. As these children grow up and develop, their often-unpredictable, negative behavior may arouse in the parents guilt, shame, and embarrassment. The parents may become frustrated and blame each other for their youngster's inappropriate behavior. One parent may accuse the other of being too strict or too lenient in raising their child, putting extra strain on the marital relationship.

Siblings and other family members are also affected when a family member has an attention deficit disorder. Siblings may be embarrassed by their brother's or sister's behavior. They may feel angry or jealous because their parents seem to pay more attention to the child with ADD than to them. The siblings may even worry that the ADD condition is contagious and they could "catch" it and begin to act like their sister or brother.

COUNSELING FOR THE FAMILY SYSTEM

Counseling may be needed by the entire family system: family counseling for the family as a whole, couple counseling for the parents, child or adolescent counseling for the individual with ADD. The type of counseling that is used will depend on the needs within the family.

Family counseling therapy.   This is directed toward the family as a unit. The initial stages of family counseling therapy focus on helping the child to gain control of his or her behavior and the parents to gain confidence in their ability to manage the child (Ostrander & Silver, 1993). Parents can learn to use behavior management skills that are similar to the behavior management techniques special education teachers use in school (see Chapter 6). Contingency management, time-outs, and contingency contracting are particularly useful in home situations. Parents learn how to set appropriate limits for their child.

Once the family becomes more functional, the educative process begins. Family members learn more about the condition of ADD so that they can understand and be more supportive of the child. The parents learn how to identify and build on their child's strengths, how to avoid failures, and how to select activities at which their child can succeed. Parents can guide their child toward finding successful activities at home. For example, children who have difficulty in competitive team sports may enjoy individual sports, such as swimming, biking, or jogging. If the child is expected to set the table at home but cannot remember where the dishes are to be placed, the parents can provide a picture of a table setting to assist in recall. If the child has difficulty playing with his or her peers, the parents can encourage him or her to play with younger children for a while, creating situations that are less competitive and more enjoyable (Silver, 1989).

During all stages of the counseling, the youngster with ADD must feel a part of the process. He or she needs to understand the helping process and feel that his or her opinions are important. The child is asked what situations and settings are difficult for him or her. Family members are then guided as to how to modify or adjust their demands and teach their child ways of adapting to stressful events. The child needs enjoyable activities, because such pleasant experiences help build self-esteem and motivation. Through such efforts, family relationships become more positive and functional (Ostrander & Silver, 1993).

Couple counseling therapy.   This is therapy for the two parents and does not include the full family. It is typically used when there is marital discord. Coping with a youngster with ADD places additional stress on the marital relationship, as parents often blame each other for the child's misbehavior. The purpose of the counseling is to help the couple reduce their stress and improve their ability to cope with the situation. If one spouse is clinically depressed or has other psychiatric problems, more intensive individual psychotherapy may be needed.

The couple must realize that ADD may be a familial pattern. One of the parents may have an attention deficit disorder that has been unrecognized until now. This could explain, for example, why the father is disorganized and impulsive or why the mother cannot finish tasks. Once the two better understand themselves, they become more empathetic and supportive of their child with ADD (Silver, 1992).

Child counseling therapy.   This is therapy for the child with ADD. Two models of child therapy are commonly used: the dynamic model and the behavioral model.

The dynamic model of child therapy emphasizes guiding children to understand themselves, to learn better methods of coping with stress, and to express their inner feelings. For one child, the attention deficit disorder may be the primary problem, and emotional problems, secondary. For another youngster, emotional problems may be more urgent than the ADD. Both children need to recognize their conflicts, comprehend their use of defense mechanisms, and recognize their nonproductive coping strategies.

In the initial phase of counseling, the goal is to establish a trusting relationship between the child and the counselor or therapist (Ostrander & Silver, 1993). The parent should view the counselor as a supportive advocate for the youngster as the counselor works to help the child accept and understand the disability and its impact on his or her behavior. During the middle stages of counseling, the child comes to know the causes of his or her stress and to recognize ineffective coping strategies and defense mechanisms. The goal now is to help the child develop more effective behavior strategies. Some children will need more intensive psychotherapy to resolve deeper conflicts and to build self-esteem. In the final stage of counseling, children learn that they can master the difficulties related to ADD and cope with them productively (Ostrander & Silver, 1993).

The behavioral model of child therapy employs environmental modifications to establish appropriate behaviors. The first step is to identify the problem behaviors that the child needs to change, such as aggression, noncompliance, or noncompletion of tasks. Second, the antecedents and consequences of the problem behaviors are determined. Antecedents are the events that precede the target behavior, and consequences are the events that follow it. To increase a desired behavior, behavioral methods can be used to change the antecedents, with powerful reinforcements used as consequences. What reinforcers or rewards will be effective must be determined individually for each child. In the case of children with ADD, rewards need to be changed frequently, as they lose their reinforcement value quickly for such children (Zentall, 1992). Rewards can improve behavior in youngsters with ADD in areas such as completing tasks, following directions, and the like. Other behavioral interventions are used to decrease negative behaviors such as aggression and rule breaking (Goldstein & Goldstein, 1990). Misbehavior must be decreased, but at the same time, appropriate behavior must be modeled for youngsters with ADD. They need to know *what* to do as well as what *not* to do. (Chapter 6 suggests specific techniques for managing behavior.)

Adolescent counseling therapy.   Both the dynamic and behavioral models of therapy can benefit the adolescent with ADD, but there are additional considerations for adolescents. Adolescents need counseling to understand the nature of their ADD condition. Many teenagers with ADD have difficulty accepting their disabilities. Counseling can help them accept and adjust to their limitations while encouraging them to build on their abilities and strengths (Barkley, 1990; Robin & Foster, 1989).

The counselor needs to be sensitive to the adolescent's striving for independence and self-identity. Robin and Foster (1989) advocate focusing on individual differences. Every person has unique strengths as well as limitations to be considered. When adolescents can accept their ADD disabilities, they become more willing to work on their problems and take credit for their successes.

Source: Reprinted with permission: Tribune Media Services.

HOME MANAGEMENT

PARENTING STYLES

Parents have different styles of raising children, and parenting styles do affect the behavior and personality development of children with ADD. The following variables in particular can affect parent-child interactions: consistency; democratic, autocratic and passive styles; conformity; self-esteem; and punishment (Goldstein & Goldstein, 1993).

Consistency is a significant variable in parent-child relationships. Research shows that children can deal with a variety of adult actions, as long as they know what to expect (Goldstein & Goldstein, 1993). Children whose parents are inconsistent in their child management have difficulty dealing effectively with other adults and their peers. Their own unpredictability makes children with ADD more likely than youngsters without ADD to encounter inconsistency from even the most knowledgeable parents. The combination of parental inconsistency and a child's ADD difficulties can lead to significant social problems.

Democratic, autocratic, and passive styles of parenting represent another important variable in parenting. How do parents handle their children? If their parenting style is democratic, the child is allowed to participate in making decisions. Parents who have an autocratic style tend to make decisions without the child's input. When parents are passive, youngsters will make their own decisions. Difficulties may arise for children with ADD when their parents are either autocratic or passive. When children cannot meet the demands of autocratic parents, the children can become oppositional, which leads to power struggles. When parents are passive and set too few limits, youngsters with ADD cannot learn responsibility. Democratic parents encourage cooperation when they work with their children to reach mutual decisions.

Conformity constitutes another parenting variable. Parents who overemphasize conformity may pressure their children to always fit in with the expectations of others. This could be difficult for youngsters with ADD, who have trouble obeying rules and following limits. The combination of rigidly conforming parents and a child with ADD may lead to conduct disorders in the youngster (Goldstein & Goldstein, 1993).

Consideration of self-esteem is another parenting variable. Children's feelings about themselves are influenced by the perceptions of other people. Without realizing it, some parents may undermine the self-esteem of their children with ADD through constant nagging and complaints about their children's behaviors.

The use of punishment distinguishes another parenting style. Punishment occurs when a parent administers an aversive consequence following a specific behavior by the child. Punishment should be used cautiously for children with ADD, who need to be shown what appropriate behaviors are and given opportunities to practice. Children need appropriate models to emulate and opportunities to observe specific examples of positive behavior.

GENERAL SUGGESTIONS FOR HOME MANAGEMENT

The following general suggestions are for parents to use in the home.

1. Parents can assist their sons or daughters with ADD by focusing on schedules, rules, instructions, and stimulus control (Barkley, 1990). Changes in schedule can be upsetting for these children because they need structure and predictability. A consistent routine for mealtimes, bedtime, play, homework, and so on, helps. If possible, changes in schedules should be explained ahead of time with an explicit description of the behavior expected of the child (Lerner & Lowenthal, 1993).

2. Instructions should be simple, clear, and given one at a time. Modeling and demonstration should accompany them. Rules need to be explained, with the appropriate consequences administered if they are broken (Silver, 1993b).

3. Stimulus control in the form of a nondistracting environment is helpful at home to help the child with time management. At playtime, the child should play with one or two friends at a time rather than competing in large groups.

DEALING WITH SPECIFIC PROBLEMS

Problems can occur at specific times during the daily routine, such as when getting dressed in the morning, at mealtime, at bedtime, and in public places. Getting dressed can become a power struggle when parents dictate to a child with ADD what he or she should wear. A solution can be to allow the child to choose between a couple of outfits. When allowed to make choices, these children feel more independent and are less oppositional (Friedman & Doyal, 1992).

Because of their short attention spans, youngsters with ADD should not be forced to sit for long periods during meals. They should be expected to come when called for meals. If they are late, the natural consequence of missing the meal should be applied. Dawdling at bedtime can be decreased by enforcing a strict time for the child to be in bed but allowing him or her to play quietly or read until falling asleep. Inappropriate behavior in public places can be decreased by applying the same behavior management techniques that are used at home. Even though using measures such as time-out in public can be embarrassing when the child makes a fuss, consistency in behavior management reduces the chances that the inappropriate behavior will occur again. Appropriate public behavior should be reinforced with rewards, praise, and privileges that have been agreed upon in advance (Friedman & Doyal, 1992; McCarney & Bauer, 1990).

SUMMARY

Parent training, counseling, parenting styles, and home management are important considerations for parents of children with ADD.

Guidelines for parent training include consistency in home management, practice in the home setting, improvement in parent-child relationships, and increasing compliance. A number of parent training programs are available.

Sometimes counseling is needed by the parents, family, and child. There are several stages of parental grief that can be expected. It is important to consider the feelings of parent, family, and child. There are benefits to family counseling, couple counseling, child counseling, and adolescent counseling.

Parents often need help in home management of children with ADD, and many welcome specific suggestions. Parents of children with ADD should be supplied with the information and supportive services they need to meet the challenges of raising children with attention deficit disorders.

DISCUSSION QUESTIONS

1. Discuss the special challenges parents may face in raising a child with attention deficit disorders. Name two ways that parents can help their children.

2. Describe parent training programs. Describe three ways in which parents can build self-esteem in their child.

3. Describe the five stages of parental grief. What are the implications of this concept for children with attention deficit disorders?

4. Describe parent counseling. What are three types of family counseling?

5. Suggest three strategies parents might use in home management of children with attention deficit disorders.

PART III

MEDICATION

AND

NEUROBIOLOGY

CHAPTER 8

MEDICAL
TREATMENT
OF ADD

Snapshot

Issues in Using Medications for ADD
Multimodal Treatment
Parent Concerns about Medications
School Responsibility
Considerations for the Physician
Types of Medications for ADD

Psychostimulant Medications
Ritalin and Dexedrine
Cylert
Psychostimulant Treatment for Adolescents
and Adults
Side Effects of Psychostimulant Medications
The Effectiveness of Psychostimulant
Medications
Evaluating the Effects of Psychostimulant
Medications

Other Medications
Antidepressants: Tofranil, Norpramin, and
Elavil
Antihypertension Medication: Clonidine

Controversial Therapies
The Feingold Diet and the Elimination of
Food Additives
Identifying and Avoiding Allergens
Megavitamin Therapy
Hypoglycemia Countermeasures
Anti–Motion Sickness Medication
Anticandida Regimens
Biofeedback

F rom the time Anita was in kindergarten, her teachers started to contact her parents to discuss Anita's disruptive behavior in school. Her teachers reported that Anita was bossy with other children, would not stay in her seat or at her desk, and constantly walked around the classroom. She seemed oblivious to the teacher's instructions, rarely finished her assignments, forgot her homework. Though she seemed bright, she was beginning to fail in academic subjects.

At age 9, when Anita was in the fourth grade, Anita's parents decided to discuss the problem with her pediatrician, Dr. Virginia Green. After a thorough examination and consulta-

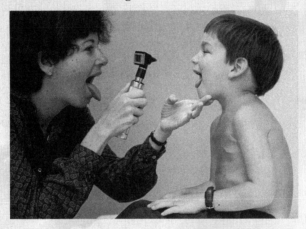

tion with a clinical psychologist, Dr. Green diagnosed Anita's problem as an attention deficit disorder. Dr. Green recommended trial use of the medication Ritalin to see whether the medication would improve her attention span and reduce her impulsive behavior and overactivity. Dr. Green asked the parents to watch for possible negative side effects.

To evaluate the effect of the medication, Dr. Green had Anita's teacher and parents complete behavior rating scales. She also asked Anita's parents and teacher to observe and report on Anita's behavior, and she talked to Anita about her own reactions and feelings. At first, Anita had minor symptoms of insomnia and a decrease in appetite, but these symptoms soon disappeared.

Anita's parents and her teacher observed an immediate change in Anita's behavior. Her teacher observed a marked improvement in her ability to stay at a task longer. She had fewer disruptive behaviors (such as blurting out comments in class, getting out of her seat, and breaking class rules) and was more cooperative and less domineering. In addition, she was beginning to develop friendships with two girls in the class. Her mother said she seemed happier with her family and was able to concentrate on her homework. Anita said she felt more relaxed and liked going to school.

The marked improvement led Dr. Green to recommend continuing the Ritalin during the school year. She suggested that lower doses be tried during nonschool times such as weekends and vacations. Dr. Green cautioned Anita's mother that close observation of Anita would be particularly important during periods of change in the dosage.

The subject of this chapter is the use of medication to treat attention deficit disorders. Because these medications affect the nervous system, they are called psychopharmacological agents. This chapter discusses issues involved in using medications for ADD, describes psychostimulant medications, discusses other types of medications, and reviews controversial therapies.

ISSUES IN USING MEDICATIONS FOR ADD

The use of medications to treat behavior and attention problems is not new. More than 50 years ago, a physician named Bradley (1937) reported on a study in which he treated children hospitalized for behavior problems with the psychostimulant medication Benzedrine. Bradley reported substantial improvements in behavior and attention in these children. However, the benefits of psychostimulant medications were not appreciated until the mid-1950s. Psychostimulant medications are thought to change the concentrations of chemicals within the brain. These neurotransmitter chemicals are associated with the control and regulation of arousal, attention, and activity (Parker, 1992).

Understandably, parents and teachers have many questions and concerns about using medication to treat attention deficit disorders. Some of the common questions about using medications are discussed in this section.

MULTIMODAL TREATMENT

It is important to stress that medication must be only one part of a broader treatment plan. A multimodal plan of treatment combines medication, effective instruction, behavior management strategies, family and child counseling or therapy, and good parenting and home management. Medication should not be considered a "silver bullet" or the single solution to the problems the child is facing. Rather, medical treatment should be recognized as one part of a total interdisciplinary management and intervention program. An individual's improvement is greatest when all components of the treatment are present and are working in conjunction (Accardo, Blondis, & Whitman, 1991; Barkley, 1990; Blondis, Clippard, Scroggs, & Peterson, 1991; Goldstein & Goldstein, 1993).

PARENT CONCERNS ABOUT MEDICATIONS

Deciding to try medication for their child is not easy for parents. Many reluctant parents agonize over the decision, often putting it off for years. It is up to the physician and the parents to decide whether a child will receive medical treatment. Parents should learn as much as they can about the effects of medication, and the physician must conscientiously prescribe and closely monitor all medical treatment. Often, the dosage and the type of medication must be adjusted, and sometimes a medication must be stopped altogether (Rief, 1993).

Monitoring the effects of any medical intervention is a vital part of the treatment, and for it, the physician needs accurate observations from parents and teachers, whose feedback provides the best evidence on a medication's effectiveness or ineffectiveness. Observations can be reported informally by telephone and during office visits or more formally by completing rating scales. Parents can observe changes in a child's peer relationships, family functioning, social skills, self-confidence, and self-esteem. Visits of sufficient frequency to the physician are also important in the monitoring process (DuPaul, Barkley, & McMurray, 1991; Greenberg & Horn, 1991).

Also important is that the child understand the reasons for the medication. The reasons should be explained in developmentally appropriate language. If the child is not a willing partner in the medication trial, he or she can sabotage the experiment by refusing to take the medication.

SCHOOL RESPONSIBILITY

Teachers become an integral part of the medical treatment, because they have the opportunity to observe the child's behavior on a daily basis, both on and off medication. Physicians need teachers' observations and completed rating scales to know how well a medication is working and whether the dosage or medication should be changed. Teachers can report on changes in the student's behavior, attention span, academic performance, and social and emotional adjustment.

Schools may also become involved if the child must take medication during school hours. Many of the medications used to treat ADD last only about four hours, and if the child does not go home for lunch, he or she will need a second dose during the school day. School policies must be developed to guide school personnel in giving medications to children. Sometimes the school nurse becomes involved in administering the medication at school (Slavin, 1983).

CONSIDERATIONS FOR THE PHYSICIAN

The goal of treatment with medication is to improve the symptoms of ADD (*not* to control behavior). Research shows that children who take medication for ADD symptoms attribute their successes to *themselves,* not to the medication (CH.A.D.D., 1993c). Medication should not be routinely recommended when a child is diagnosed as having ADD. Before being prescribed medication, the child should have a complete physical and psychological examination to establish the severity of the ADD symptoms, to rule out alternative explanations for the symptoms, and to identify any conditions that might rule out the use of certain medications. Any psychopharmacological agent affects various mental and physical functions, which need to be monitored periodically.

Individuals with ADD need a multimodal treatment approach, which includes all appropriate interventions that are necessary for children and adults with ADD to succeed. In addition to medical treatment, children with ADD need other forms of therapy, including educational and behavioral interventions, and individual and family counseling.

In prescribing medication for children with ADD, physicians should communicate the treatment plan to parents and seek feedback on the medication's effects from both parents and teachers. The following factors must be considered before medication is prescribed (Barkley, 1990; DuPaul, Barkley, & McMurray, 1991; Parker, 1992).

Medical trials.   The specific dose of medicine appropriate for each child must be determined individually. There is no consistent relationship between weight, height, or age and clinical response to medications, so a medication trial is often used to determine the most beneficial dosage. The trial usually begins with a low dose that is gradually increased until clinical benefits are observed. Often, the dosage must be raised several times. The child is monitored both on and off the medication. Observations from parents and teachers, and parent and teacher rating scales, are useful in determining the effects of the dosage (CH.A.D.D., 1993c)

The severity of the child's symptoms.   The more severe the behavioral symptoms such as hyperactivity and excessive impulsivity, the more likely a trial of medication will be necessary in addition to other interventions.

The child's age.   Generally, psychostimulants are not as effective for preschoolers as for older children and adolescents. In addition, the side effects could be more severe for very young children (Friedman & Doyal, 1992; Parker, 1992).

The presence of anxiety or depression.   Students who appear very anxious or depressed or who have frequent psychosomatic complaints (headaches, stomachaches, and so on) may react better to an antidepressant than to a psychostimulant.

Side effects.   Hundreds of studies on the effects of psychostimulants have been conducted on thousands of children. Overall, relatively few long-term side effects have been identified. Most side effects of psychostimulants are mild and of short term. The most common are a reduction in appetite and difficulty in sleeping. Less often, children experience "stimulant rebound," a decline in mood or an increase in activity when the medication is stopped or as it is wearing off. Studies show that height and weight are not affected in the long term. Often, when patients experience side effects from psychostimulants, other types of medications (such as antidepressants or antihypertensive medications) are prescribed instead (CH.A.D.D., 1993c).

A relatively rare but more serious potential side effect of psychostimulant medications is the unmasking of latent tics or involuntary motor movements, such as eye blinking, shrugging, and clearing of the throat. Usually, the tics will disappear when the medication is stopped. Tourette's syndrome is a chronic tic disorder that involves vocal and motor tics. Some authorities estimate that 1% of children with ADD have Tourette's syndrome. Caution is recommended when treating children with a family history of tics or Tourette's syndrome (CH.A.D.D., 1993c).

Politics

In 1993, the United States experienced a serious shortage of Ritalin. Users were unable to get Ritalin prescriptions filled, with even the generic medication, methylphenidate, in short supply. The shortage occurred because the Food and Drug Administration (FDA) sets a quota for the production of methylphenidate, and that year it was set too low. Attempts by the manufacturer of Ritalin (CIBA Pharmaceutical) failed to convince the FDA to raise its limits. The organization Children and Adults with Attention Deficit Disorders (CH.A.D.D.) urged its members to send letters to every member of Congress and the administrator of the FDA to increase the methylphenidate quota for the year. In October of 1993, the FDA increased the 1993 production quota, but the decision came too late to prevent shortages for the remainder of 1993 (Horn, 1993). The power of ADD advocacy groups is apparent; members of Congress responded to this issue by calling for an investigation into the FDA's policies.

TYPES OF MEDICATIONS FOR ADD

Various medications are used in treating ADD. The most commonly used by far are stimulants, though in some cases, other conditions preclude their use, and sometimes they are ineffective. Often, several types of medications used together prove the most effective.

The psychopharmacological agents used with individuals with ADD are classified as: psychostimulants, antidepressants, antipsychotics, antimanics, antianxiety agents, anticonvulsants, and miscellaneous medications, including propranolol and clonidine (Cantwell, 1990). An overview of the medications most commonly used for ADD is shown in Table 8.1.

PSYCHOSTIMULANT MEDICATIONS

The most common type of medication used in treating ADD is psychostimulant medication. It is estimated that 3% of elementary school students in the United States are currently being treated with psychostimulants (Safer, 1988).

As noted earlier, the effectiveness of psychostimulants in reducing hyperactivity was first reported more than 50 years ago (Bradley, 1937), when children taking the psychostimulant Benzedrine showed longer attention spans and an improved ability to concentrate, with a corresponding decrease in hyperactivity and oppositional behavior.

Current research on how psychostimulant medication affects the brain and central nervous system of individuals with ADD is discussed in greater detail in Chapter 9. In brief, psychostimulant medication appears to increase the arousal or alertness of the central nervous system in patients with ADD (DuPaul, Barkley, & McMurray, 1991). The psychostimulants are thought to stimulate the production of the chemical neurotransmitters needed to send information from the brain stem to the parts of the brain that deal with attending, inhibition, and activity (Busch, 1993; Goldstein & Goldstein, 1990).

Research also suggests that psychostimulants make children more sensitive to reinforcers in the environment, thereby increasing their attention spans and persistence in responding

TABLE 8.1 Overview of medications commonly used for ADD

Brand name	Generic name	Type of medication	Positives	Negatives	Comments
Ritalin (tablets)	Methylphenidate	Psychostimulant	Excellent safety record. Easy to use and evaluate. Works in 15–20 minutes.	Lasts only 4 hours. Must be administered frequently.	The most frequently prescribed medication. Watch for tics or Tourette's syndrome.
Ritalin SR20 (sustained release)	Methylphenidate	Psychostimulant	Excellent safety record. Easy to use and evaluate. Longer lasting (6–8 hours).	Does not work as well as Ritalin tablets.	Can be used along with regular Ritalin.
Dexedrine (tablets)	Dextroamphetamine	Psychostimulant	Excellent safety record. Rapid onset (20–30 minutes).	Lasts only 4 hours. Must be administered frequently.	Some patients do well on Dexedrine tablets.
Dexedrine (spansules)	Dextroamphetamine	Psychostimulant	Excellent safety record. Longer lasting (6–8 hours).	Slower onset (takes 1–2 hours).	Can be used along with Dexedrine tablets. Some patients do well.
Cylert (tablets)	Pemoline	Psychostimulant	Long lasting (6–8 hours).	Slower onset (several hours).	Not as safe as the other stimulants. Requires liver function blood test every 6 months.
Tofranil and Norpramin (tablets)	Imipramine & desipramine	Antidepressant	Long lasting (12–24 hours). Can be administered at night. Often works when stimulants do not.	Has possible side effects. May take 1–3 weeks for full effects. Should not be started and stopped abruptly.	High doses may improve depression symptoms and mood swings.
Catapress (patches or tablets)	Clonidine	Antihypertensive medication	Patches long lasting (5–6 days). Can be used with Tourette's syndrome.	Tablets are shorter lasting (4 hours). Patches are expensive.	Tablets cost less. Often has positive effect on defiant behavior.

Sources: Based on "Thoughts on the Medical Treatment of ADHD," May 1993, by T. D. Mandelkorn, in *The CH.A.D.D.er Box*, 6(3), 1, 7–9; and "Medical Management of Attention Deficit Disorders," in *CH.A.D.D. Facts 3*, 1993.

180

to environmental events (Haenlein & Caul, 1987; Lou et al., 1989).

The behavioral effects of these stimulants when administered to youngsters with ADD are not paradoxical, as is commonly thought. They have similar effects on children who do not have ADD (Rapoport et al., 1980). The benefits for children with ADD are that the medications appear to lengthen their attention spans, control impulsivity, decrease distractibility and motor activity, and improve visual-motor integration (Parker, 1992).

The brand names (and the generic names) of the psycho-stimulant medications most widely used for ADD are, in order of their popularity:

1. Ritalin (methylphenidate)
2. Dexedrine (dextroamphetamine)
3. Cylert (pemoline)

RITALIN AND DEXEDRINE

The dosage of Ritalin and Dexedrine that is prescribed depends on the child's body weight, severity of symptoms, and target symptoms. Once a child's optimal dose is decided, it is usually administered twice a day, at breakfast and at lunch. The behavioral effects of Ritalin and Dexedrine are most beneficial 1 to 2 hours after dosage and usually diminish within 4 to 5 hours (Donnelly & Rapoport, 1985).

Both Ritalin and Dexedrine are also available in longer-lasting, sustained-release forms. The advantage of sustained-release forms is that they do not have to be administered at lunchtime and therefore afford the student more confidentiality. However, some studies indicate that the sustained-release forms of Ritalin may be less effective than the standard preparation for elementary-age children (Pelham & Hoza, 1987; Pelham et al., 1987). For this reason, physicians usually prescribe the short-acting Ritalin. Taking the second Ritalin dose in school may be difficult if the school has no relevant policy or trained personnel available to administer the medication.

CYLERT

Cylert's longer-lasting effects continue for 7 to 8 hours after ingestion. The disadvantage of Cylert is that it takes up to 6

weeks for maximum effectiveness. Cylert is generally administered once a day, in the morning. Another disadvantage
of Cylert is that it impairs liver function in about 3% of children
taking this medication, so children given Cylert must have their
liver function periodically checked. The impairment may not
be completely reversed when the medication is discontinued
(Parker, Storm, Petti, & Anthony, 1991).

PSYCHOSTIMULANT TREATMENT
FOR ADOLESCENTS AND ADULTS

Until recently, experts believed that psychostimulant treatment was no longer needed from about age 13, or from the
onset of puberty. However, that belief is changing as recent
studies indicate that ADD does not typically disappear in
adolescence and adulthood (Barkley, Fischer, Edelbrook, &
Smallish, 1990; Weiss & Hechtman, 1986). Research results
have demonstrated the effectiveness of stimulant treatment for
ADD in adolescents and adults. The current thinking is that
psychostimulant treatment can be used as needed throughout early childhood, adolescence, and adulthood (Klorman,
Coon, & Borgstedt, 1987; Wender, 1987). Periodic trials off the
medication are recommended to determine continued need.
In many cases, the physician may prescribe lower doses of
medication at nonschool times such as on weekends or over
school vacations.

SIDE EFFECTS OF
PSYCHOSTIMULANT MEDICATIONS

Most side effects of psychostimulants are mild and temporary. The most common are insomnia and decreased appetite. Less common are irritability, headaches, stomach pain,
temporary growth retardation, increased heart rate, elevated
blood pressure, and depression. These side effects usually
diminish as the child becomes tolerant of the medication, as
the dosage is reduced, or both (Barkley, 1990).

If the child has a family history of tic disorders or Tourette's
syndrome, psychostimulants should not be prescribed, as they

CLOSE TO HOME   JOHN McPHERSON

"Tommy? He's upstairs in his room having 'time out.'"

Source: Reprinted by permission, Universal Press Syndicate.

can trigger the tics or the onset of Tourette's (Silver & Hagin, 1990).

A "rebound effect" sometimes occurs with children on stimulants. In such cases, the child's behavior significantly deteriorates in the late afternoon or evening following a daytime dose of the psychostimulant. This wearing off of the medication causes the child to temporarily exhibit more impulsivity, distractibility, and hyperactivity than was previously observed (Johnston, Pelham, Hoza, & Sturges, 1988; Parker, 1992). An additional low dose of medicine in the late afternoon or an increase in the noontime dose may alleviate this rebound effect.

THE EFFECTIVENESS OF PSYCHOSTIMULANT MEDICATIONS

About 75% of children with ADD show general improvement with psychostimulant medication (Barkley, 1990). However, 25% do not improve. For those children who do not improve with psychostimulants, other medications and other interventions will be needed.

A major study on the effects of psychostimulant medication on children with attention deficit disorders was conducted by Swanson et al. (1993). This study synthesized the findings of other research reviews, which analyzed research of the effects of using psychostimulant medication to treat children with ADD. Swanson et al. (1993) found in the research reviews a consensus about what can be expected of psychostimulant treatment for children with ADD, as well as what should not be expected.

The following benefits can be expected:

1. *Psychostimulation treatment leads to temporary management of diagnostic symptoms.* This includes the following:

■ A decrease in overactivity. Children improve in their ability to modulate motor behavior.
■ Improved attention. Children increase their concentration or effort on tasks.
■ A decrease in impulsivity. Children improve in their self-regulation behaviors.

2. *Psychostimulation treatment leads to improvement of associated features.* This includes the following:

■ Improvement in deportment. Children increase their compliance and effort.
■ Improvement in social interactions. Children decrease their negative behaviors.
■ Improvement in academic productivity. Children increase in the amount and accuracy of their work.

This study also showed what should not be expected from the use of psychostimulant medications:

■ Children with ADD do not respond paradoxically to psychostimulants. Children without ADD respond similarly.
■ A child's response cannot be predicted from neurological signs, physiological measures, or biochemical markers.
■ Side effects are infrequent.
■ Skills and higher-order processes show little effect.
■ There is no long-term improvement in adjustment.

Effects on Learning and Academic Achievement

Recent studies of the effects of stimulant medications on academic performance show that the classroom work of students with ADD improves with medication with regard to such tasks as completing math problems, studying spelling words, and reading short paragraphs (Douglas, Barr, O'Neill, & Britton, 1986; Tannock, Schachar, Carr, & Logan, 1989). The extent of the improvement was significant, ranging from 20% to 40%. Similar positive results were found in several other research studies (Pelham et al., 1985). The subjects not only increased the quantity of work they completed but also improved their rate and accuracy. These results confirm informal teacher and parent observations that students receiving psychostimulants improve in their schoolwork. Though short-term improvements in academic performance have been documented, however, whether these improvements will last is still unclear (Parker, 1992).

Some early studies reported adverse effects of stimulants on learning (Sprague & Gadow, 1976; Swanson & Kinsbourne, 1978). These studies described some students as appearing "zombie-like" on medication. Recent studies also show that very high doses appear to make some youngsters overly quiet and somber. These children tend not to interact socially with their peers and may become isolated (Pelham, 1989; Swanson, 1989). These results support the hypothesis that stimulants can produce overfocusing of attention that can impair learning rather than improve it.

Since the negative effects of stimulants appear to be dose-related, the optimal dose of psychostimulants for learning may be lower than is needed for improvements in behavior (Sprague & Sleator, 1976; Swanson, 1985). Stimulant medication must be monitored carefully for each child. Some children will show improvements in learning with low doses, whereas others may need a higher dosage to achieve the same results.

Effects on Behavior

Stimulant medications have been found to positively affect many behaviors of children with ADD. They can improve children's attention span for completing tasks (Douglas et al., 1986; Rapport et al., 1985), inhibit impulsivity (Rapport et al.,

1987), reduce aggression (Klorman et al., 1988), and reduce non-compliance with adult commands (Barkley, Karlsson, Strzelecki, & Murphy, 1984). When on medication, hyperactive children are more attentive and compliant with their parents, are better able to work and play independently, and appear less bossy and domineering with their peers (Cunningham, Siegel, & Offord, 1985). Youngsters on psychostimulant medication also communicate better and cooperate more when playing structured games with their peers (Whalen, Henker, & Granger, 1989). Behavior improvements extend to many settings, including school, playground, home, and community.

Effects on Social Relationships

A common problem for students with ADD is their unpopularity and negative interactions with both their peers and adults. These children are often demanding, annoying, and intrusive, all traits that discourage social acceptance. The best-documented effect of stimulant treatment is that it can increase the positive interactions of children with ADD (Pelham, Walker, Sturges, & Hoza, 1989). For example, Abikoff and Gittelman (1987) found that hyperactive students with ADD who were treated with Ritalin could not be distinguished from their nonhyperactive classmates by rates of compliance with teacher directions and numbers of disruptive behaviors in the classroom. In the home setting, there is evidence of better relationships with parents, less maternal criticism, and more positive interactions. A child's interactions with both parents and teachers seem to be normalized when the child receives medical treatment (Whalen & Henker, 1986). However, though medication can diminish the disruptive behaviors of children with ADD, it does not teach actual social skills such as cultivating and keeping friendships. Children with ADD often have difficulty in their social perceptions and may need direct training in social skills in addition to medication.

EVALUATING THE EFFECTS OF PSYCHOSTIMULANT MEDICATIONS

To measure the effects of psychostimulants, teacher rating scales, parent rating scales, and direct observations are used. These methods of assessment are discussed in Chapter 4.

OTHER MEDICATIONS

When an alternative to psychostimulant medications is needed for individuals with attention deficit disorders, several other medications can be used. Antidepressants and antihypertension medications are often used in treating ADD.

ANTIDEPRESSANTS: TOFRANIL, NORPRAMIN, AND ELAVIL

The medications Tofranil (imipramine), Norpramin (desipramine), and Elavil (amitriptyline) are tricyclic antidepressants that are effective in treating children with ADD under the following conditions: when stimulants have not been effective or have unacceptable side effects or when the youngster appears anxious or depressed or has a strong family history of these conditions (Pliszke, 1987). Antidepressants, which are used less often than stimulants, seem to have a different mechanism of action, and may be less effective than the psychostimulants in treating ADD (Parker et al., 1991). Antidepressants are usually administered in the morning, after school, or in the evening.

The effect of long-term use of these medications has not been well researched. Children with ADD who are anxious or depressed may do best with an initial trial of antidepressant followed, if necessary, by a psychostimulant for the more typical ADD symptoms. Possible side effects of tricyclics may include increased blood pressure and heart rate, constipation, confusion, and, rarely, seizures and maniclike behavior (Parker, 1992). The latter two side effects usually occur in vulnerable youngsters who can be identified during assessment.

ANTIHYPERTENSION MEDICATION: CLONIDINE

Clonidine, a monoamine oxidase inhibitor, is an antihypertensive medication that has been found to improve the behavior of students with ADD (Hunt, Mindera, & Cohen, 1985; Zametkin et al., 1985). Teacher and parent rating scales indicate that hyperactivity decreased and that conduct problems improved for youngsters with ADD who were administered clonidine (Hunt, Mindera, & Cohen, 1985). Usually, this medication is prescribed for severely overactive, aggressive youngsters, for children with motor tics, or for those who have responded unfavorably to psychostimulants (Conner, 1994). Clonidine may be taken orally or through a skin patch. It usually reduces ADD symptoms in about two weeks. Its major side effect is sedation, which occurs approximately 1 hour after dosage and lasts from 30 to 60 minutes. The sedative effect generally decreases as the child becomes tolerant of the medication (Hunt et al., 1985; Parker, 1992; Zametkin et al., 1985).

CONTROVERSIAL THERAPIES

Our knowledge of attention deficit disorders is not complete, but certain approaches to treatment are generally accepted and not controversial. These treatments are long term and multimodal, and require constant monitoring. Parents who are seeking help for their child may turn in desperation to therapies that are considered controversial. Unfortunately, many professionals and nonprofessionals use methods that are claimed to be useful but have not been carefully researched and have not met scientific standards of effectiveness (Silver, 1993a). Among the controversial remedies described in this section are: treatments involving special diets and the elimination of food additives, identifying and avoiding allergens, megavitamin therapy, regulation of blood sugar levels, anti–motion sickness medication, anticandida regimens, and biofeedback.

THE FEINGOLD DIET AND THE ELIMINATION OF FOOD ADDITIVES

One of the most controversial theories is that of Dr. Benjamin Feingold (1975), who proposed that food additives in the diet increase hyperactivity in children. Feingold believed that artificial flavors, preservatives, and food colorings should be eliminated from youngsters' diets. His original hypothesis related these food additives to overactivity, but he later generalized this theory to other behaviors including learning difficulties and inattention. His theory suggested that an additive-free diet would alleviate most of these problems, and individual cases were described in which such diets led to improvement in the behavior of hyperactive children. In the past 15 years, however, many well-controlled studies have consistently failed to support the Feingold theory. Though a few studies have reported limited success, at best this indicates that some children with ADD may respond somewhat to this diet (Friedman & Doyal, 1992; Goldstein & Ingersoll, 1992).

IDENTIFYING AND AVOIDING ALLERGENS

Another theory holds that allergies to a substance in one's diet or to the environment can induce symptoms of attention deficit disorders. The allergy theory suggests that specific children develop diet- and environmentally related allergies that adversely affect their behavior and learning. Proponents of this theory report cases in which children's activity levels, behaviors, and schoolwork improved when the causes of their allergies were removed. A one-week trial elimination diet is suggested to assess the effectiveness of the treatment. Among the food items thought to cause allergies that may adversely affect learning, behavior, and activity levels are sugar, milk, corn, eggs, wheat, chocolate, and citrus (Crook, 1983). Although a few studies indicate negative effects of sugar, a recent, well-designed study showed that sugar had few effects. This well-controlled study tested the effects of diets high in sugar (sucrose) and aspartame (artificial sweetener) on children's behavior and cognitive performance (Wolraich et al., 1994). In this double-blind study, two groups of children were tested: 25 normal preschool children (ages 3 to 5) and 23 school-age children (ages 6 to 10) who were described by their parents as sensitive to sugar. The researchers found no significant differences in measures of behavior and cognitive function resulting from an increase in the subjects' diets of sucrose or of aspartame.

At present, many authorities contend that the allergy theory has not been confirmed through adequate research and that avoidance of foods causing allergies is not a significant intervention for children with ADD (Friedman & Doyal, 1992).

MEGAVITAMIN THERAPY

The use of megavitamins as a treatment for ADD has been championed by some practitioners (Alder, 1979; Brenner, 1982). Treatment includes ingesting large amounts of vitamins in the form of capsules, pills, or liquids. The theory suggests that treating hyperactive children with high doses of vitamins will decrease their overactivity, improve their attention, and reduce their impulsivity. Another theory is that learning and behavior problems result from a lack of trace minerals, such as potassium, sodium, and copper, in children's diets. However, the megavitamin theory remains controversial because of a lack of well-controlled studies that support this claim. More rigorous research is needed to test this theory (Silver, 1993a).

HYPOGLYCEMIA COUNTERMEASURES

Another diet-related theory holds that children may have attention, behavior, and learning problems because of a deficiency in their blood sugar levels. Treatment consists of controlling the child's eating patterns. According to this theory, without diet control, the blood sugar level decreases about an hour after eating, and the youngster's behavior and learning deteriorate. Again, more well-controlled studies are needed to test this theory (Silver, 1993a).

ANTI-MOTION SICKNESS MEDICATION

Advocates of this remedy consider ADD to be caused by problems in the inner ear. They contend that ADD symptoms of inattention and impulsivity could be related to problems with balance and coordination caused by dysfunctioning of the inner ear. Treatment consists of anti-motion sickness medication and vitamins. However, this theory is inconsistent with existing knowledge about ADD. There is no known relationship between attention, impulsivity, and the functions of the inner ear. There are also no well-controlled studies that support the inner-ear-dysfunction hypothesis. Most authorities have discounted this theory (Goldstein & Ingersoll, 1992).

ANTICANDIDA REGIMENS

Candida is a yeastlike organism that lives in the human body. Normally, its growth is kept in check by a strong immune system and "friendly" bacteria. When these bacteria are killed by antibiotics or when the immune system is weakened, candida can overgrow. This may lead to vaginal infections and sometimes infections of the nails, skin, or mouth. Some contend that the toxins caused by this candida overgrowth can make a person susceptible to ADD and psychiatric problems. Treatment consists of antifungal medication and a low-sugar diet, as sugar is believed to stimulate candida growth. There is little evidence to support this hypothesis as a cause of ADD (Goldstein & Ingersoll, 1992).

BIOFEEDBACK

Advocates of this technique stress training students with ADD to increase the brain wave activity associated with attention and decrease the brain wave activity associated with distractibility. The result should be improved attention (Goldstein & Ingersoll, 1992). The most popular biofeedback method is to graph electrical activity as children learn to relax their bodies. However, biofeedback therapy has not been proved an effective treatment for ADD and should be used with caution (Suter, Fredrickson, & Portuesi, 1983) until it is supported by more rigorous studies.

SUMMARY

This chapter reviews the use of medication to treat attention deficit disorders.

Many issues must be considered when using medication to treat ADD. Medication should be only one part of a broader treatment plan. A multimodal treatment plan combines medication, effective instruction, behavior management strategies, family and child counseling or therapy, and good parenting and home management. In addition to medication, other interventions are needed to assist children who have behavioral, social, learning, and academic difficulties.

Many parents agonize over the decision to try medications. Teachers and schools, as well as parents, are an integral part of the medical treatment, offering important feedback to the physician about the effects of medication.

There are many considerations for the physician before prescribing medication and in carefully monitoring the effects of the medication.

Many different types of medications are used in treating attention deficit disorders. Psychostimulant medications are the most commonly used and include Ritalin, Dexedrine, and Cylert. Other commonly used medications include antidepressants (Tofranil, Norpramin, Elavil) and antihypertension medication (clonidine).

Medication can affect the child's social development, behavior, and academic achievement. It is important to know about and to watch for side effects.

There are several controversial therapies for treating ADD. Many lack acceptable research evidence. These alternative treatments include: the Feingold diet and the elimination of food additives, identifying and avoiding allergens, megavitamin therapy, hypoglycemia countermeasures, anti–motion sickness medication, anticandida regimens, and biofeedback.

DISCUSSION QUESTIONS

1. What is meant by a *multimodal* plan for the treatment of attention deficit disorders?

2. Describe two of the issues involved in using medication in the treatment of attention deficit disorders.

3. What are three of the psychostimulant medications widely used to treat individuals with attention deficit disorders? How effective are they? What are the benefits of psychostimulant medications? What are some possible side effects?

4. In addition to psychostimulants, what other types of medications are sometimes used to treat attention deficit disorders?

5. Name three of the controversial therapies used to treat attention deficit disorders. Why are they considered controversial?

BIOLOGICAL

BASES OF ADD

S ince Charles Bradley first described over 50 years ago that pharmacology is a potent medical intervention for children with Attention-Deficit Hyperactivity Disorder (ADHD), more than 20 medications have been used for the study and treatment of children with ADHD in an attempt to possibly elucidate the unknown pathophysiology of this disorder. These neuropharmacological investigations, along with other well-established findings in areas such as genetic studies, follow-up studies, associations with other neurological disorders, and biochemical marker studies, together increasingly point toward a neurobiological basis for ADHD. . . .

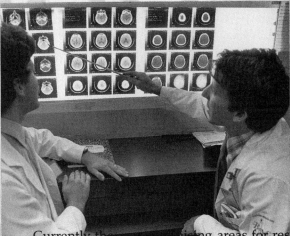

Currently the most promising areas for research appear to be in-depth studies of response to stimulants and further physiological studies using the brain imaging techniques. Although the results of these studies have been impressive and have vastly improved our understanding of normal and abnormal cerebral function, remarkably little is still known about the local biochemistry and physiology of human cerebral substructures.

Could it be that a dysfunction of the central nervous system is the key to our understanding of the etiology of Attention-Deficit Hyperactivity Disorder? Individually each finding is insufficient to prove that ADHD has a neurobiological basis. Indeed, it may still be a long time until the underlying

Source: From "The Neurobiology of Attention-Deficit Hyperactivity Disorder," by Alan Zametkin. In *CH.A.D.D.er, 1991,* 5(1), 10–11.

cause of ADHD is established. We must not rule out that various interacting biological and psychosocial variables may be implicated in the "cause" of ADHD. However, when data including family studies, drug response studies, biological marker studies, and ADHD's association with other neuro-psychiatric syndromes [are] combined, the picture of ADHD as a neurobiological disorder is increasingly convincing.

The quotation in the snapshot is from Alan Zametkin of the National Institute of Mental Health, in Bethesda, Maryland. Fascinated by the mystery of the human brain and its relation-ship to attention deficit disorders, Zametkin has been on the forefront of landmark brain research. Although this work represents a giant step toward establishing evidence of the neurological basis of attention deficit disorders, Zametkin acknowledges that there is much to be accomplished. The bits of evidence that exist about the cause of attention deficit disorders come from many different types of studies.

The questions guiding neuroscientists in their research on the neurobiology of ADD are: In what ways does the brain function differently in individuals with ADD? How do these differences affect the ability to attend, to control impulsivity, and to regulate motor activity? What are the neurochemical, neuroanatomical, and neurophysiological causes of ADD? How does medication mediate brain function? What role does gen-etics play in ADD? This chapter examines several major theories about the neurobiological causes of ADD and looks at the find-ings of research on the brain.

THE NEED TO KNOW: BIOLOGICAL BASES OF ADD

Those who are responsible for and involved with children, adolescents, and adults with attention deficit disorders (teach-ers, parents, psychologists, health professionals, and others) need to know basic facts about the relationship of the central nervous system to problems in attention, impulse control, and hyperactivity, as well as being familiar with current research. After all, behavior and learning cannot be separated from what happens within the brain, because they are themselves neuro-logical processes that originate within the brain. A dysfunction in the central nervous system can seriously impair the process of attending and the behavior required to learn.

Teachers, parents, and other professionals who work with individuals with ADD need to know something of the brain—its structure, its functions, and its dysfunctions. They should also know how medications—psychopharmacological agents—affect the brain and change behavior.

We noted in Chapter 8 that to work effectively with physicians, educators and parents need a working knowledge of medicine and neurology. In particular, since teachers and parents are often called upon to provide feedback to physicians about the effectiveness of a medication, they should know about the psychopharmacology used with ADD, including the different types of treatment, dosages, and side effects.

THE NEUROBIOLOGICAL BASES OF ADD

Neuroscientists—that is, researchers who study brain function and dysfunction—generally agree that the condition of attention deficit disorders is caused by a variation or malfunction within the neurobiological system. All human behavior is mediated by the brain or central nervous system, including the ability to attend to tasks, to control impulsivity, and to regulate one's activity. A subtle alteration in the complex organ of the brain can cause problems in inattention, impulsivity, and hyperactive behavior.

Since the turn of the century, the scientific community has presumed that a dysfunction in the brain or central nervous system was the cause of attention deficit disorders. In their attempts to understand how brain variations result in behavior associated with ADD, brain researchers have developed several different theories of brain dysfunction that they have tested through research.

Today, new technology is available to study the workings of the brain, as well as brain dysfunctions, enabling researchers to significantly expand our knowledge of the brain, and changing many of our concepts of ADD. There are at least a dozen different neurobiological explanations of the etiology of ADD, each of which adds an important piece to the puzzle (Riccio, Hynd, Cohen, & Gonzalez, 1993; Zametkin & Rapoport, 1986). In this section, we examine these theories and the research supporting them.

NEUROCHEMICAL THEORIES OF ADD

Currently, the most productive and promising research about the causes of attention deficit disorders is being done in the area of neurochemistry. Explanations of the brain chemistry associated with attention deficit disorders are complex and still in development.

THE NEUROCHEMICAL MODEL OF THE ATTENTION SYSTEM

The neurochemical model of ADD treats the condition as a dysfunction of the attentional system. It is thought that individuals with ADD do not release enough of the chemicals needed to send information from the brain stem to other parts of the brain (Goldstein & Goldstein, 1990). Deficits in attention occur when the central nervous system (or brain) is unable to produce enough of a family of neurotransmitters called the catecholamines. Of the more than 50 identified chemical neurotransmitters, the most important in the attentional system are norepinephrine and dopamine. These neurotransmitters are thought to affect a wide variety of behaviors, including the regulation of attention, inhibition, and motor responses. They may be involved in the transmission of such messages as: "ignore distractions," "stay focused," "don't fidget," "be efficient," "reflect," "don't overreact" (Busch, 1993).

A deficiency in the production of the neurotransmitters norepinephrine or dopamine results in decreased stimulation of the brain, and a consequent dysfunction of the neural circuits underlying attention (Hynd, Hern, Voeller, & Marshall, 1991; Riccio et al., 1993). These neurotransmitter deficiencies occur within an area of the brain called the brain stem, an elongated part of the brain that extends from the base of the cerebral hemispheres to the spinal cord.

These chemicals are then distributed from the brain stem to other areas of the brain through neurons—that is, nerve cells—passing from one nerve ending to another nerve ending and thereby transmitting messages (Goldstein & Goldstein, 1990). Figure 9.1 illustrates the brain stem center and its communication with other areas of the brain. Other areas of the brain thought to be implicated in attention deficit disorders are the prefrontal lobes, responsible for selective attention; the

FIGURE 9.1   The brain stem and its communication with other areas of the brain
Source: From *Managing Attention Disorders in Children: A Guide for Practitioners,* p. 45, by S. Goldstein and M. Goldstein. Copyright © 1990 by John Wiley and Sons, Inc. Reprinted by permission.

motor strip area, responsible for fidgetiness and overactive behavior; and the subcortical/limbic areas, thought to be responsible for poor pencil control, disinhibition, and emotional overresponsiveness. These abnormalities appear to be reversed by stimulant medication (Busch, 1993).

In the nervous system, information is transmitted as follows: The brain is a complex information network made up of millions of nerve cells called neurons. Information moves through the brain as nerve impulses that are transmitted from cell to cell by neurotransmitters. An impulse travels along the cell body of a *sending* nerve cell. Between the sending nerve cell and the *receiving* nerve cell is a small space, called a *synapse.* The impulse causes the sending cell to release chemicals—neurotransmitters—from tiny sacs located at the synapse between the sending cell and the receiving cell. The chemicals are taken up by receptors in the receiving nerve cell, causing that cell to fire and thus pass the impulse along to the next cell. After the cell fires, the chemical is deactivated and taken up again for storage in the sacs in the original sending cell. The chemicals that are activated in this process regulate attention, activity, mood, and behavior (Hynd et al., 1991; Parker, 1992). A diagram of the neurotransmitter process is shown in Figure 9.2. A malfunction could occur anywhere in the system—in the

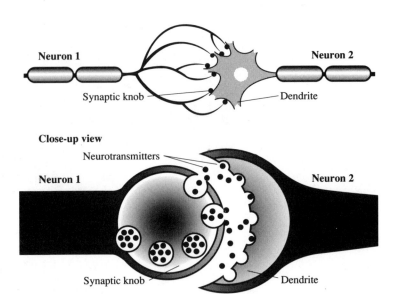

FIGURE 9.2   The neurotransmitter system
   Source: From *The ADD Hyperactivity Handbook for Schools*, p. 15, by H. C. Parker. Copyright © 1992 by Specialty Press, Inc. Reprinted by permission.

production of the chemicals in the brain stem or in the distribution to other parts of the brain through the neurotransmitter system.

THE EFFECTS OF PSYCHOSTIMULANT MEDICATION

The neurochemical theory also explains how the psychostimulant medications that are used to treat ADD work. The neurochemical theory proposes that individuals with ADD have an insufficiency in the neurotransmitter activity within the brain stem. The psychostimulant medications increase the production of norepinephrine, leading to a decrease (when the neurotransmitter level approaches normal), in the behaviors associated with ADD—inattention impulsivity, and hyperactivity. In this way, the medication, through its action on the neurotransmitters, improves the child's attention, motivation, motor responses, activity level, restlessness, and responsivity (Hynd et al., 1991).

Clinical and research observations confirm that ADD is associated with a deficiency of norepinephrine. The level of norepinephrine can be measured through laboratory tests of the blood, urine, and cerebrospinal fluid. Studies show that before taking medication individuals with ADD have a deficiency of norepinephrine in the brain stem area; after taking psychostimulant medications their norepinephrine levels are normal.

RESISTANCE TO THYROID HORMONE AND ADHD

A recent report (Hauser et al., 1993) identified a linkage between ADHD and a resistance to thyroid hormone. In this study, 104 members of 18 families were studied for behavioral abnormalities, using criterion-based structured interviews. Forty-nine subjects exhibited generalized resistance to thyroid hormone and 55 did not. A significantly higher percentage of adults and children with generalized resistance to thyroid hormone also had attention-deficit hyperactivity disorder. The likelihood of having the disorder was 15 times higher for adults with generalized resistance to thyroid hormone than for other adult family members and 10 times higher for children with generalized resistance than for other children. They also found that males were three times as likely as females to have attention-deficit hyperactivity disorder. Weiss, Stein, Trommer, and Refetoff (1993) also found that children with ADHD are more likely to have thyroid abnormalities. Only a small percentage of individuals with ADHD have a generalized resistance to thyroid hormone, however. More study is needed to determine whether thyroid hormone might be useful in treating ADD.

Source: Reprinted with permission: Tribune Media Services.

BRAIN RESEARCH AND ADD

Advanced brain research suggests that individuals with attention deficit disorders exhibit differences in brain function or structure. Areas of the brain that may be involved include the frontal lobe, brain stem, reticular activating system, thalamus, hypothalamus, and basal ganglia (Riccio et al., 1993).

TECHNOLOGICAL ADVANCES IN STUDYING THE BRAIN

Several new technological innovations allow scientists to study the active, living brain, and studies using these technological advances are promising. The new technologies include magnetic resonance imaging (MRI), brain electrical activity mapping (BEAM), and positron emission tomography (PET).

Magnetic resonance imaging (MRI) uses an advanced neuroimaging device that converts signals into a sharp image on a video screen. The MRI device generates images of multiple sections of the brain, revealing the shape and location of various brain structures. Promising research with the MRI has been conducted on individuals with dyslexia. This research shows that the frontal region of the brain of dyslexic and ADHD individuals is symmetrical and smaller than that of normal individuals (Hynd, 1992; Hynd & Semrud-Clickman, 1989).

Brain electrical activity mapping (BEAM) monitors brain wave activity. BEAM technology is a major advancement over the earlier electroencephalograph (EEG) system. The BEAM process uses computers to convert and map electrical brain waves produced by subjects in response to sounds, signs, and words. Research with BEAM has shown that the electrical activity of brains of individuals with dyslexia differs significantly from that of normal brains. Differences were found in the left hemisphere, the medial front lobe, and the occipital lobe, which is the brain's visual center (Duffy, 1988; Duffy & McAnulty, 1985).

Positron emission tomography (PET) has proved the most successful research approach in regard to ADD. PET is a device that permits the measurement of metabolism within the brain. Dr. Alan Zametkin and his colleagues at the National Institute of Mental Health used PET imaging to demonstrate that the metabolism of individuals with attention deficit disorders is uniquely different from that of normal individuals, in that individuals with ADD metabolize less glucose in the brain (Zametkin et al., 1990).

RESEARCH ON CEREBRAL GLUCOSE METABOLISM IN INDIVIDUALS WITH ADD

The research of Zametkin and his colleagues (1990), which used PET technology, has been heralded as the most compelling scientific evidence to date of the biological basis of attention deficit disorders. This study demonstrated that cerebral glucose metabolism in the brains of subjects with ADD differs significantly from that in control subjects.

Using positron emission tomography, a scientist can inject glucose that has been "tagged" with a radioactive chemical into a patient's veins. Glucose is the basic fuel of human cells, so when it is taken up by the cells of the brain, the PET scanner can measure the role of metabolism by determining how much glucose the brain is using in a specified amount of time (Friedman & Doyal, 1992).

Zametkin and his colleagues collected data over several years on the metabolic activity in the brains of adults who had been diagnosed as hyperactive as children and who still displayed many of the symptoms of hyperactivity. The research team compared the brain activity of the hyperactive subjects with that of normal subjects, and discovered that the rate of metabolism was significantly slower in the hyperactive subjects. The ADD subjects used less glucose overall, particularly in the right frontal area, and specifically in the posterior-medial orbital areas.

The photo on page 204 is from a breakthrough study by Zametkin et al. (1990). It compares the brains of normal subjects with those of adult subjects with ADHD, using the technology of PET. The photograph shows substantial differences between the ADHD and the non-ADHD brains.

The research team also succeeded in mapping the areas of the brain most affected. They found a relationship between the areas of the brain that were affected in the hyperactive subjects and the nature of the symptoms of hyperactivity. For example, areas in the premotor strip that helps control purposeful

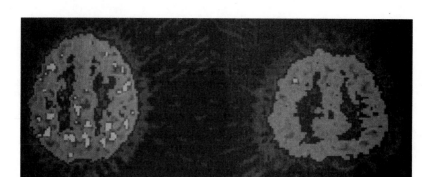

PET image of brains of a non-ADHD adult (left) and an adult with ADHD (right)

movements were affected, as were areas in the frontal lobes known to be involved in impulse control.

The study also analyzed the effects of medication. They found that when the hyperactive subjects with ADD were treated with medication such as Ritalin, the chemical activity in the affected areas of their brains changed and resembled that of the normal subjects. The researchers caution that this is only preliminary information and much research remains to be done. A critical analysis of this study was made by Reid, Maag, and Vasa (1994).

PET IMAGES OF LANGUAGE PATHWAYS IN THE BRAIN

Another intriguing research study using PET images shows that separate processing locations exist in the brain for words that are read and words that are heard (Bower, 1988; Kotulak, 1988). The PET images reveal anatomical specificity— that is, the brain processes language information along different pathways for different cognitive activities. (This is called *parallel processing*.) As shown in the photo on page 205, the activities of *hearing* a word, *seeing* a word, *saying* a word, and *thinking* a word are located in different areas of the brain. Neuroscientists believe that PET technology is very promising and will usher in a new era of human brain research.

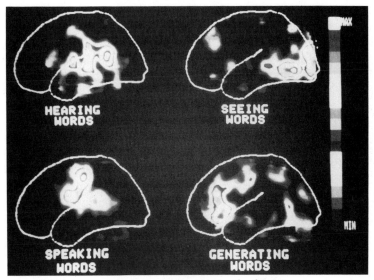

PET images of language processing pathways in the brain

DIFFERENCES IN BRAIN DYSFUNCTION BETWEEN ATTENTION DEFICIT DISORDERS AND LEARNING DISABILITIES

The condition of learning disabilities is also defined as a neurological disorder. Goldstein and Goldstein (1990) note that the neurological disorder of learning disabilities differs from that of attention deficit disorders. Learning disabilities are associated with a dysfunction in the cerebral cortex, as opposed to the brain-stem regulatory centers, as for ADD. Psychostimulant medication that would improve the attentional system would not improve the function of cortical neurons. For example, the attentional system regulates a child's ability to concentrate on reading, whereas the cerebral cortex determines the child's reading comprehension. Psychostimulant medications that improve attention skills may have little direct affect on learning (Goldstein & Goldstein, 1990).

Both children with attention deficit disorders and children with learning disabilities may have academic difficulties, but the causes of their academic problems differ. Stanford and

Hynd (1994) studied the behavioral profiles of three types of children: (a) children with attention deficit disorders with hyperactivity, (b) children with attention deficit disorders without hyperactivity, and (c) children with learning disabilities. Measures of behavior for all three groups were obtained through parent and teacher rating scales. The researchers found that the behavior profile for each type of child was distinct. Children with attention deficit disorders with hyperactivity were more disruptive, shifted tasks more frequently, displayed acting-out behavior, called out in class, and had difficulty taking turns. Children with attention deficit disorders without hyperactivity were more withdrawn, prone to daydream, underactive, and shy. Children with learning disabilities more closely resembled the ADD without hyperactivity group, yet many of their behavioral symptoms were different.

GENETIC FACTORS AND ADD

The neurobiological theories suggest that genetic factors are involved in ADD. Indeed, heredity is thought to be the most common cause of ADD (Parker, 1992). The problem tends to run in families and to be associated with other problems of impulse control.

FAMILY HISTORY STUDIES

When family histories of patients with ADD are taken, a common finding is that other close family members also have symptoms of attentional problems. The father or an uncle, for example, may have displayed similar behaviors in childhood. In one research study, hyperactivity was noted in the parents of hyperactive children four times as often as in those of control subjects (Cantwell, 1972). In another study, 59 hyperactive children were compared with 41 children who were not hyperactive. The researchers found that 12 parents of the 59 hyperactive children were retrospectively diagnosed as hyperactive based on descriptions of behavior and old school records (Friedman & Doyal, 1992). Still another study shows that 20% to 32% of the parents of children with ADD also have symptoms of ADD (Barkley, 1990). Cumulatively, these studies demonstrate a genetic predisposition for attention deficit disorders.

ADOPTED CHILDREN

The genetic theory of ADD is supported by the finding that the incidence of ADD in adopted children is higher than for biological children. In fact, the incidence of ADD among adopted children and adolescents in the United States is about five times higher than would be expected in the general population (Silver, 1992). The speculation is that the biological parents of the adopted children probably had attention deficit disorders.

TWIN STUDIES

Twin studies also support the genetic theory of ADD. Researchers at the University of Minnesota conducted a large-scale longitudinal study of twins who were reared apart. They studied the characteristics of twins to sort out which qualities of mind and body are shaped by genetics and which are shaped by environment. The study compared the characteristics of identical twins, who have identical genes (since both originate from the same fertilized egg), with those of fraternal twins, who are not genetically identical.

The study found that even when identical twins were reared apart, they had similar characteristics in terms of hyperactivity. If one identical twin was hyperactive, so was the other. For the fraternal twins, the likelihood of having the same hyperactive characteristics was the same as for normal siblings. The researchers concluded that genetics or heritability plays a significant role in the characteristic of hyperactivity (Goodman & Stevenson, 1989). The implication of the twin studies is that there is a genetic predisposition to attention deficit disorders.

PSYCHOMEDICAL DISORDERS THAT RESEMBLE ADD

Several psychomedical or medical disorders have symptoms similar to those of ADD. Although the behaviors stemming from these disorders mimic ADD, they are completely different problems. They should be distinguished from ADD through thorough evaluation, because these disorders require different diagnostic procedures and a distinctive plan of treatment. A variety of disorders can be mistaken for ADD. Popper (1991) identifies the following "ADD look-alike" disorders:

1. *Depression.* Some inattentive children with impulsive and hyperactive behavior may be suffering from depression. The depression may be temporary (feeling blue or demoralized) or more persistent (dysthymic disorder) or severe enough to warrant a psychiatric diagnosis of depression. These individuals require treatment for depression, not for ADD.

2. *Stress-induced anxiety states.* Environmental stress caused by a home, school, academic, or social situation may result in a state of anxiety. Though the symptoms may look like ADD, the source of the problem lies in the environment, and treatment must focus on helping the individual change the environment or cope with it more successfully.

3. *Biologically based anxiety.* Individuals with disorders such as separation anxiety or obsessive-compulsive disorders may also have symptoms similar to those of ADD. However, stimulant medication may only worsen the symptoms of such disorders, for which other approaches and medications are needed.

4. *Child abuse or neglect.* Sometimes children respond to sexual abuse, physical abuse, or neglect with behaviors that resemble those of children with ADD. These problems, too, must be distinguished from ADD, because they require vastly different treatment.

5. *Bipolar disorders.* Bipolar disorders include a group of biomedical conditions, of which manic-depressive illness in adults is one of the most severe. Symptoms of bipolar disorders in children and adolescents include impulsivity, inattention, overly strong feelings, an overbearing manner, irritability, unprovoked hostility, and difficulty in getting going in the morning. Children and adolescents with severe bipolar disorders may display lengthy temper tantrums, grossly distorted views of the world, and dangerous destructiveness during their rages. Stimulant medication may worsen their symptoms and can be quite risky. Individuals with bipolar disorders may do better with other medications, such as lithium.

6. *Schizophrenia.* A few children with ADD symptoms may have the serious biomedical disorder of schizophrenia. Stimulant medications can be risky for these children, too, who need other treatments and medication therapy.

7. *Other medical disorders.* A number of other medical disorders can mimic ADD. These include disorders of sleep (or arousal), malfunctions of the thyroid gland, and excessive ingestion of lead. Again, a thorough diagnosis is needed to distinguish these problems from ADD.

SUMMARY

Teachers, parents, and other professionals who work with children with ADD should be knowledgeable about the brain and how variations in brain function affect behavior. Parents and teachers are often called upon to provide feedback to physicians about the effectiveness of medication.

Neuroscientists generally agree that attention deficit disorders are neurobiologically based. There are several theories about the neurobiological origins of ADD, many of which involve neurochemical dysfunctions. Neurochemical models of ADD view attention deficit disorders as due to a malfunction of the area of the brain called the brain stem and deficiencies in the levels of neurotransmitters necessary for sending information from the brain stem to other parts of the brain.

New technologies for examining the brain include magnetic resonance imaging (MRI), brain electrical activity mapping (BEAM), and positron emission tomography (PET). It is the PET research conducted by Zametkin and his colleagues that has been most productive, showing that the brains of individuals with ADD metabolize glucose at a significantly slower rate.

There is much evidence that ADD is genetic. Family members of children with ADD commonly have symptoms of ADD. Twin studies also demonstrate the heritability of ADD.

There are several psychomedical disorders with symptoms similar to ADD's. They include depression, stress-induced anxiety states, biologically based anxiety, child abuse or neglect, bipolar disorders, and schizophrenia, among others.

DISCUSSION QUESTIONS

1. The neurochemical theory of attention deficit disorders posits that ADD is related to a malfunction of the chemical system within the brain. Does the neurochemical theory suggest an overproduction of chemicals within the brain, or an insufficiency of chemicals?

2. What are neurotransmitters?

3. Individuals with ADD who take psychostimulant medication often improve in attention. Explain how this fact either supports or contradicts the theory of a neurobiological basis of ADD.

4. What is the relationship between heredity and attention deficit disorders?

5. What evidence is there to support the genetic theory of ADD?

6. Describe two conditions with symptoms that are similar to those of attention deficit disorders.

U.S. DEPARTMENT OF EDUCATION: CLARIFICATION OF POLICY TO ADDRESS THE NEEDS OF CHILDREN WITH ATTENTION DEFICIT DISORDERS WITHIN GENERAL AND/OR SPECIAL EDUCATION

I. *Introduction*

There is a growing awareness in the education community that attention deficit disorder (ADD) and attention-deficit hyperactive disorder (ADHD) can result in significant learning problems for children with those conditions.[1] While estimates of the prevalence of ADD vary widely, we believe that three to five percent of school-aged children may have significant educational problems related to this disorder. Because ADD has broad implications for education as a whole, the Department believes it should clarify State and local responsibility under Federal law for addressing the needs of children with ADD in the schools. Ensuring that these students are able to reach their fullest potential is an inherent part of the National education goals and AMERICA 2000. The National goals, and the strategy for achieving them, are based on the assumptions that: (1) all children can learn and benefit from their education; and (2) the educational community must work to improve the learning opportunities for all children.

---

[1]While we recognize that the disorders ADD and ADHD vary, the term ADD is being used to encompass children with both disorders.

This memorandum clarifies the circumstances under which children with ADD are eligible for special education services under Part B of the Individuals with Disabilities Education Act (Part B), as well as the Part B requirements for evaluation of such children's unique educational needs. This memorandum will also clarify the responsibility of State and local educational agencies (SEAs and LEAs) to provide special education and related services to eligible children with ADD under Part B. Finally, this memorandum clarifies the responsibilities of LEAs to provide regular or special education and related aids and services to those children with ADD who are not eligible under Part B, but who fall within the definition of "handicapped person" under Section 504 of the Rehabilitation Act of 1973. Because of the overall educational responsibility to provide services for these children, it is important that general and special education coordinate their efforts.

II. *Eligibility for Special Education and Related Services under Part B*
Last year during the reauthorization of the Education of the Handicapped Act [now the Individuals with Disabilities Education Act], Congress gave serious consideration to including ADD in the definition of "children with disabilities" in the statute. The Department took the position that ADD does not need to be added as a separate disability category in the statutory definition since children with ADD who require special education and related services can meet the eligibility criteria for services under Part B. This continues to be the Department's position.

No change with respect to ADD was made by Congress in the statutory definition of "children with disabilities"; however, language was included in Section 102(a) of the Education of the Handicapped Act Amendments of 1990 that required the Secretary to issue a Notice of Inquiry (NOI) soliciting public comment on special education for children with ADD under Part B. In response to the NOI (published November 29, 1990 in the *Federal Register*), the Department received over 2000 written comments, which have been transmitted to the Congress. Our review of these written comments indicates that there is confusion in the field regarding the extent to which children with ADD may be served in special education programs conducted under Part B.

A. *Description of Part B*

Part B requires SEAs and LEAs to make a free appropriate public education (FAPE) available to all eligible children with disabilities and to ensure that the rights and protections of Part B are extended to those children and their parents. 20 U.S.C. 1412(2); 34 CFR §§300.121 and 300.2. Under Part B, FAPE, among other elements, includes the provision of special education and related services, at no cost to parents, in conformity with an individualized education program (IEP). 34 CFR §300.4.

In order to be eligible under Part B, a child must be evaluated in accordance with 34 CFR §§300.530-300.534 as having one or more specified physical or mental impairments, and must be found to require special education and related services by reason of one or more of these impairments.[2] 20 U.S.C. 1401(a) (1); 34 CFR §300.5. SEAs and LEAs must ensure that children with ADD who are determined eligible for services under Part B receive special education and related services designed to meet their unique needs, including special education and related services needs arising from the ADD. A full continuum of placement alternatives, including the regular classroom, must be available for providing special education and related services required in the IEP.

B. *Eligibility for Part B Services under the "Other Health Impaired" Category*

The list of chronic or acute health problems included within the definition of "other health impaired" in the Part B regulations is not exhaustive. The term "other health impaired" includes chronic or acute impairments that result in limited alertness, which adversely affects educational performance. Thus, children with ADD should be classified as eligible for services under the "other health impaired" category in instances where the ADD is a chronic or acute health problem that results in limited alertness, which adversely affects educational

[2]The Part B regulations define 11 specified disabilities. 34 CFR §300.5(b) (1)–(11). The Education of the Handicapped Act Amendments of 1990 amended the Individuals with Disabilities Education Act [formerly the Education of the Handicapped Act] to specify that autism and traumatic brain injury are separate disability categories. *See* section 602(a)(1) of the Act, to be codified at 20 U.S.C. 1401(a)(1).

performance. In other words, children with ADD, where the ADD is a chronic or acute health problem resulting in limited alertness, may be considered disabled under Part B solely on the basis of this disorder within the "other health impaired" category in situations where special education and related services are needed because of the ADD.

C. *Eligibility for Part B services under Other Disability Categories*

Children with ADD are also eligible for services under Part B if the children satisfy the criteria applicable to other disability categories. For example, children with ADD are also eligible for services under the "specific learning disability" category of Part B if they meet the criteria stated in §§300.5(b) (9) and 300.541 or under the "seriously emotionally disturbed" category of Part B if they meet the criteria stated in §300.5(b) (8).

III. *Evaluations under Part B*

A. *Requirements*

SEAs and LEAs have an affirmative obligation to evaluate a child who is suspected of having a disability to determine the child's need for special education and related services. Under Part B, SEAs and LEAs are required to have procedures for locating, identifying and evaluating all children who have a disability or are suspected of having a disability and are in need of special education and related services. 34 CFR §§300.128 and 300.220. This responsibility, known as "child find," is applicable to all children from birth through 21, regardless of the severity of their disability.

Consistent with this responsibility and the obligation to make FAPE available to all eligible children with disabilities, SEAs and LEAs must ensure that evaluations of children who are suspected of needing special education and related services are conducted without undue delay. 20 U.S.C. 1412(2). Because of its responsibility resulting from the FAPE and child find requirements of Part B, an LEA may not refuse to evaluate the possible need for special education and related services of a child with a prior medical diagnosis of ADD solely by reason of that medical diagnosis. However, a medical diagnosis of ADD alone is not sufficient to render a child eligible for services under Part B.

Under Part B, before any action is taken with respect to the initial placement of a child with a disability in a program providing special education and related services, "a full and individual evaluation of the child's educational needs must be conducted in accordance with requirements of §300.532." 34 CFR §300.531. Section 300.532(a) requires that a child's evaluation must be conducted by a multidisciplinary team, including at least one teacher or other specialist with knowledge in the area of suspected disability.

B. *Disagreements over Evaluations*

Any proposal or refusal of an agency to initiate or change the identification, evaluation, or educational placement of the child, or the provision of FAPE to the child is subject to the written prior notice requirements of 34 CFR §§300.504-300.505.[3] If a parent disagrees with the LEA's refusal to evaluate a child or the LEA's evaluation and determination that a child does not have a disability for which the child is eligible for services under Part B, the parent may request a due process hearing pursuant to 34 CFR §§300.506-300.513 of the Part B regulations.

IV. *Obligations under Section 504 of SEAs and LEAs to Children with ADD Found Not to Require Special Education and Related Services under Part B*

Even if a child with ADD is found not to be eligible for services under Part B, the requirements of Section 504 of the Rehabilitation Act of 1973 (Section 504) and its implementing regulation at 34 CFR Part 104 may be applicable. Section 504 prohibits discrimination on the basis of handicap by recipients of Federal funds. Since Section 504 is a civil rights law, rather than a funding law, its requirements

[3]Section 300.505 of the Part B regulations sets out the elements that must be contained in the prior written notice to parents:

(1) A full explanation of all of the procedural safeguards available to the parents under Subpart E;

(2) A description of the action proposed or refused by the agency, an explanation of why the agency proposes or refuses to take the action, and a description of any options the agency considered and the reasons why those options were rejected;

(3) A description of each evaluation procedure, test, record, or report the agency uses as a basis for the proposal or refusal; and

(4) A description of any other factors which are relevant to the agency's proposal or refusal.

are framed in different terms than those of Part B. While the Section 504 regulation was written with an eye to consistency with Part B, it is more general, and there are some differences arising from the differing natures of the two laws. For instance, the protections of Section 504 extend to some children who do not fall within the disability categories specified in Part B.

A. *Definition*

Section 504 requires every recipient that operates a public elementary or secondary education program to address the needs of children who are considered "handicapped persons" under Section 504 as adequately as the needs of nonhandicapped persons are met. "Handicapped person" is defined in the Section 504 regulation as any person who has a physical or mental impairment which substantially limits a major life activity (*e.g.,* learning). 34 CFR §104.3(j). Thus, depending on the severity of their condition, children with ADD *may* fit within that definition.

B. *Programs and Services under Section 504*

Under Section 504, an LEA must provide a free appropriate public education to each qualified handicapped child. A free appropriate public education, under Section 504, consists of regular or special education and related aids and services that are designed to meet the individual student's needs and based on adherence to the regulatory requirements on educational setting, evaluation, placement, and procedural safeguards. 34 CFR §§104.33, 104.34, 104.35, and 104.36. A student may be handicapped within the meaning of Section 504, and therefore entitled to regular or special education and related aids and services under the Section 504 regulation, even though the student may not be eligible for special education and related services under Part B.

Under Section 504, if parents believe that their child is handicapped by ADD, the LEA must evaluate the child to determine whether he or she is handicapped as defined by Section 504. If an LEA determines that a child is not handicapped under Section 504, the parent has the right to contest that determination. If the child is determined to be handicapped under Section 504, the LEA must make an individualized determination of the child's educational needs for regular or special education or related aids and services. 34 CFR

§104.35. For children determined to be handicapped under Section 504, implementation of an individualized education program developed in accordance with Part B, although not required, is one means of meeting the free appropriate public education requirements of Section 504.[4] The child's education must be provided in the regular education classroom unless it is demonstrated that education in the regular environment with the use of supplementary aids and services cannot be achieved satisfactorily. 34 CFR §104.34.

Should it be determined that the child with ADD is handicapped for purposes of Section 504 and needs only adjustments in the regular classroom, rather than special education, those adjustments are required by Section 504. A range of strategies is available to meet the educational needs of children with ADD.

Regular classroom teachers are important in identifying the appropriate educational adaptations and interventions for many children with ADD.

SEAs and LEAs should take the necessary steps to promote coordination between special and regular education programs. Steps also should be taken to train regular education teachers and other personnel to develop their awareness about ADD and its manifestations and the adaptations that can be implemented in regular education programs to address the instructional needs of these children. Examples of adaptations in regular education programs could include the following:

> providing a structured learning environment; repeating and simplifying instructions about in-class and homework assignments; supplementing verbal instructions with visual instructions; using behavioral management techniques; adjusting class schedules; modifying test delivery; using tape recorders, computer-aided instruction, and other audio-visual equipment; selecting modified textbooks or workbooks; and tailoring homework assignments.

Other provisions range from consultation to special resources and may include reducing class size; use of one-on-one tutorials; classroom aides and note takers;

---

[4]Many LEAs use the same process for determining the needs of students under Section 504 that they use for implementing Part B.

involvement of a "services coordinator" to oversee implementation of special programs and services, and possible modification of nonacademic times such as lunchroom, recess, and physical education.

Through the use of appropriate adaptations and interventions in regular classes, many of which may be required by Section 504, the Department believes that LEAs will be able to effectively address the instructional needs of many children with ADD.

C. *Procedural Safeguards under Section 504*

Procedural safeguards under the Section 504 regulation are stated more generally than in Part B. The Section 504 regulation requires the LEA to make available a system of procedural safeguards that permits parents to challenge actions regarding the identification, evaluation, or educational placement of their handicapped child whom they believe needs special education or related services. 34 CFR §104.36. The Section 504 regulation requires that the system of procedural safeguards include notice, an opportunity for the parents or guardian to examine relevant records, an impartial hearing with opportunity for participation by the parents or guardian and representation by counsel, and a review procedure. Compliance with procedural safeguards of Part B is one means of fulfilling the Section 504 requirement.[5] However, in an impartial due process hearing raising issues under the Section 504 regulation, the impartial hearing officer must make a determination based upon that regulation.

V. *Conclusion*

Congress and the Department have recognized the need to provide information and assistance to teachers, administrators, parents and other interested persons regarding the identification, evaluation, and instructional needs of children with ADD. The Department has formed a work group to explore strategies across principal offices to address this issue. The work group also plans to identify some ways that the Department can work with the education associations to cooperatively consider the programs and services needed by children with ADD across special and regular education.

---

[5]Again, many LEAs and some SEAs are conserving time and resources by using the same due process procedures for resolving disputes under both laws.

In fiscal year 1991, the Congress appropriated funds for the Department to synthesize and disseminate current knowledge related to ADD. Four centers will be established in Fall 1991 to analyze and synthesize the current research literature on ADD relating to identification, assessment, and interventions. Research syntheses will be prepared in formats suitable for educators, parents and researchers. Existing clearinghouses and networks, as well as Federal, State and local organizations will be utilized to disseminate these research syntheses to parents, educators and administrators, and other interested persons.

In addition, the Federal Resource Center will work with SEAs and the six regional resource centers authorized under the Individuals with Disabilities Education Act to identify effective identification and assessment procedures, as well as intervention strategies being implemented across the country for children with ADD. A document describing current practice will be developed and disseminated to parents, educators and administrators, and other interested persons through the regional resource centers network, as well as by parent training centers, other parent and consumer organizations, and professional organizations. Also, the Office for Civil Rights' ten regional offices stand ready to provide technical assistance to parents and educators.

It is our hope that the above information will be of assistance to your State as you plan for the needs of children with ADD who require special education and related services under Part B, as well as for the needs of the broader group of children with ADD who do not qualify for special education and related services under Part B, but for whom special education or adaptations in regular education programs are needed. If you have any questions, please contact Jean Peelen, Office for Civil Rights; (Phone: 202/732-1635); Judy Schrag, Office of Special Education Programs (Phone: 202/732-1007); or Dan Bonner, Office of Elementary and Secondary Education (Phone: 202/401-0984).

ORGANIZATIONS

The following organizations are useful support groups for children with attention deficit disorders. Many of them have local and state chapters. They hold informative meetings for parents and teachers. Call the national offices to obtain information about local chapters.

Attention Deficit Disorder Association (ADDA)
8091 South Ireland Way
Aurora, CO 80016
(800) 487-2282

ADDA (mailing address)
P.O. Box 488
West Newbury, MA 01895

Children and Adults with Attention Deficit Disorders
(CH.A.D.D.)
499 N.W. 70th Avenue, Suite 308
Plantation, FL 33317
(305) 587-4599

Council for Exceptional Children
1920 Association Drive
Reston, VA 22091
(703) 620-3660

Learning Disabilities Association of American (LDA)
4156 Library Road
Pittsburgh, PA 15234

National Center for Learning Disabilities
99 Park Avenue
New York, NY 10016
(212) 687-7211

National Information Center for Handicapped Children and Youth
P.O. Box 1492
Washington, DC 20013
(800) 999-5599

Orton Dyslexia Society
724 York Road
Baltimore, MD 21204
(301) 296-0232

APPENDIX C

RESOURCES

This appendix contains general information for teachers and parents. It includes listings of videotapes about ADD, videotapes about learning disabilities, teaching materials, and training materials. It also includes information on publishers, distributors, and test publishers.

VIDEOTAPES ON ATTENTION DEFICIT DISORDERS

ADD: Stepping Out of the Dark
A.D.D. Video
P.O. Box 622
New Palz, NY 12561 An award-winning video for parents, educators, and health professionals. This documentary features perspectives from families, a doctor, adults with ADD, and an educator. $32.95 (+ $1.50 and $2.39 tax for NYS residents only).

ADHD in the Classroom: Strategies for Teachers
by Russell A. Barkley
ADD Warehouse
Informs teachers of practical ways to provide a better learning atmosphere for students with ADD.
About 30 minutes. $95.

ADHD: What Do We Know?
Narrated by a well-known ADHD expert, Russell A. Barkley. Discusses what is known about the condition of attention-deficit hyperactivity disorders and assessment methods.
35 minutes. $75.
Source: Guilford Publications, Dept. 8A, 72 Spring St., New York, NY 10012. 800/365-7006. Also available from ADD Warehouse.

ADHD: What Can We Do?
Narrated by Russell A. Barkley, an expert on ADHD. Discusses management techniques and actual experiences of parents, teachers, and children with ADHD.
35 minutes. $75.

Source: Guilford Publications, Dept. 8A, 72 Spring St., New York, NY 10012. 800/365-7006. Also available from ADD Warehouse.

It's Just Attention Disorder
Dr. Sam Goldstein
For use by professionals to help ADHD children and adolescents become active participants in their treatment.
30 minutes. $89.95.
Childswork/Childsplay. Center for Applied Psychology, Inc., P.O. Box 1586, King of Prussia, PA 19406. (800) 962-1141.

Why Won't My Child Pay Attention?
Neurology, Learning and Behavior Center
230 South 500 East, Suite 100
Salt Lake City, Utah 84102
Also available from ADD Warehouse.
Features Sam Goldstein, Ph.D., and presents information on attention deficit disorders for parents. About 76 minutes. $30.

1-2-3 Magic: Training Your Preschooler and Preteens to Do What You Want
Child Management Press
Glen Ellyn, Illinois
Also available from ADD Warehouse
Features Thomas Phelan, Ph.D., and presents a method for parents to manage their hyperactive children at home. About 2 hours. $40.

VIDEOTAPES ON LEARNING DISABILITIES

A Child's First Words
Shows how speech and language development in children under age 4 can affect the child's ability to learn. Alerts parents to the milestones of good speech and language acquisition in children under age 4 and tells them how to get help if they need it.
Price: $21
Time: 18 minutes
Source: LDA

All Children Learn Differently

Narrated by Steve Allen. Shows interviews with twelve specialists in the fields of medicine, perception, language, and education. Takes a nutritional and educational approach to the remediation of learning disabilities and stresses the need for the "right professional team" for each child.

Price: $42

Time: 30 minutes

Source: LDA

Dyslexia: The Hidden Disability

Documentary that examines the history, symptoms, possible causes, and successful techniques for dealing with this severe reading disability. Designed for teachers who feel unprepared to recognize or help dyslexic students, for parents who suspect dyslexia in their child, and for individuals who work in the field.

Price: $85

Time: 60 minutes

Source: Grand Rapids Community College, Media Services, 143 Bostwick NE, Grand Rapids, MI 49503. 616-771-3830.

Effective Methods for Using Computers with Children with Special Needs

Discusses and demonstrates effective methods for using computers with children who have disabilities, including learning disabilities.

Price: $50

Time: 30 minutes

Source: LDA or National Lekotek Center, 2100 Ridge Avenue, Evanston, IL 60201. 708-328-0001.

Homework and Learning Disabilities: A Commonsense Approach

Shows ways of helping children with learning disabilities do their homework. Positive, practical techniques offer a solution to many homework problems. This video helps to clarify responsibilities of teachers, parents, and students; establish structure and routine to encourage better study habits; develop abilities and study techniques to maximize learning; and assist children in making the most of their strengths and abilities.

This video stresses cooperation between home and school, while working for the ultimate benefit of the child.
Price: $99
Time: 34 minutes
Source: Menninger Clinic and Center for Learning Disabilities. 800/345-6036.

How Difficult Can This Be? Understanding Learning Disabilities. The F.A.T. City Workshop Video

Features a unique workshop wherein adults have the opportunity to experience learning disabilities firsthand. The frustration, anxiety, and tension that children with learning disabilities face daily is demonstrated through a series of simulations. The participants are professionals (teachers, social workers, psychologists) and parents of children with learning disabilities. Following the workshop, the participants reflect on their reactions to the experience and how it will change the way that they deal with LD children at home and in the classroom. Presented by Richard Lavoie.
Price: $39.95
Time: 45 minutes
Source: LDA or PBS Video. 800/344-3337.

I'm Not Stupid

A highly recommended video that depicts the constant battle of the child with learning disabilities within the school setting. Points out how the child with learning disabilities is often misdiagnosed as slow, retarded, emotionally disturbed, or even just lazy. This video is for parents, teachers, administrators, students, or anyone who wants to learn what it is like to live with learning disabilities.
Price: $22
Time: 53 minutes
Source: LDA

Learning Disability: A Family Crisis

When a child's learning disability is discovered, the family may experience an emotional crisis. This videotape dramatizes what happens in the family of an 8-year-old boy when his learning disability is diagnosed by the school staff. The multifaceted process of identification and treatment is complicated by the emotional reaction of the parents, who must struggle to come to terms with their child's disability. Parental support is a key factor in the successful treatment of learning disabilities. The video

describes strategies that teachers, special educators, school psychologists, counselors, and other mental health professionals can employ to reduce stress and enhance the family's ability to cope effectively. Professional commentary is provided by a range of recognized national experts.
Price: $165
Time: 45 minutes
Source: Menninger Clinic and Center for Learning Disabilities. 800/345-6036.

Reach for the Stars
An inspiring story for people with learning disabilities. Each year the Lab School of Washington presents awards to selected entertainers, athletes, scholars, and so forth, who have accomplished great success in their fields—in spite of learning disabilities. This presentation focuses on G. Chris Andersen, Cher, Tom Cruise, Bruce Jenner, Robert Rauschenberg, and Richard Strauss.
Price: $22
Time: 22 minutes
Source: LDA

Strengths and Weaknesses: College Students with Learning Disabilities
Four students share their experiences and feelings, and four professionals explore possible adjustment and compensation relative to learning disabilities. The students' emphasis on what they can do provides optimistic prognoses for their academic survival.
Time: 28 minutes
Source: Altschuyl Group, 930 Pitner Avenue, Evanston, IL 60202. 708/325-6700.

TEACHING MATERIALS

Educators Manual
by Mary Fowler in collaboration with R. Barkley, R. Reeve, and S. Zentall.
Case Associates
3927 Old Lee Highway
Fairfax, VA 22030 (800) 545-5583

An in-depth look at ADD from an educational perspective.
Price: $10

The Educators Inservice Program on Attention Deficit Disorders

Reviewed by R. Barkley, R. Reeve, and S. Zentall.
Case Associates (see above)
A comprehensive multimedia presentation designed to inform educators about attention deficit disorders. Each program includes a complete script, 47 full-color transparencies, and CH.A.D.D.'s *Educators Manual*.
Price: $100

TRAINING MATERIALS

ADAPT: Attention Deficit Accommodation Plan for Teaching

by Harvey Parker.
Helps teachers identify ways to adjust their teaching style to fit elementary and middle school students' style of learning and performance.
ADAPT Kit: $20
ADAPT Teacher Planbooks: $6
ADAPT Student Planbooks: $14
Source: ADD Warehouse

I Can Problem Solve (ICPS) Preschool, Kindergarten-Primary, Intermediate Elementary

by Myrna Shure.
Helps children learn to resolve and prevent interpersonal problems. Takes a cognitive approach that teaches children how to think. Teaches that there is more than one way to solve a problem. Useful for children who are impulsive or inhibited. Three different levels:
Preschool: $47
Kindergarten & primary: $47
Intermediate elementary: $47
Source: ADD Warehouse

Home Token Economy

by Jack Alvord.
Uses a token system for rewards and lost rewards. Designed for parents to use in the home.
Price: $11
Source: ADD Warehouse

Listen, Look, and Think: A Self-Regulation Program for Children
by Harvey Parker.
Helps children learn to pay attention in school or when doing homework.
Price: $20
Source: ADD Warehouse

Social Skills Activities
by Darlene Mannix
Ready-to-use lessons and reproducible activity sheets to help children become aware of acceptable social behavior and acquire basic social skills.
Price: $30
Source: ADD Warehouse

PUBLISHERS, DISTRIBUTORS, AND TEST PUBLISHERS

T. M. Achenbach
University Associates in Psychiatry
Department of Psychiatry
University of Vermont
One South Prospect St.
Burlington, VT 05401

ADD Warehouse
300 N.W. 70th Avenue, Suite 102
Plantation, FL 33317
(800) 233-9273
This source distributes a catalog of books, videotapes, and other resources on attention deficit disorders.

Learning Disabilities Association (LDA)
4156 Library Road
Pittsburgh, PA 15234
(412) 341-1515

Hawthorne Educational Services, Inc.
800 Gray Oak Drive
Columbia, MO 65201

MetriTech, Inc.
Champaign, IL

Multi-Health Systems, Inc.
908 Niagara Falls Blvd.
North Tonawanda, NY 14120-2060

Psychological Assessment Resources
Odessa, FL

REFERENCES

ABIKOFF, H. (1987). An evaluation of cognitive-behavioral therapy for hyperactive children. In B. Lahey & A. Kazdin (Eds.), *Advances in clinical child psychology* (Vol. 10, pp. 171–216). New York: Plenum.

ABIKOFF, H., & GITTLEMAN, R. (1987). The normalizing effects of methylphenidate on the classroom behavior of ADHD children. *Journal of Abnormal Child Psychology, 13,* 33–44.

ABRAMOWITZ, A. J., & O'LEARY, S. G. (1991). Behavior interventions for the classroom: Implications for children with ADHD. *School Psychology Review, 20,* 221–235.

ACCARDO, P., BLONDIS, T., & WHITMAN, B. (Eds.). (1991). *Attentional deficit disorders and hyperactivity in children.* New York: Marcel Dekker.

ACHENBACH, T. M. (1991). *Child behavior checklist for ages 4–18.* Burlington: University of Vermont.

ACHENBACH, T. M., & EDELBROOK, C. (1983). *Manual for the Child Behavior Checklist and Revised Child Behavior Profile.* Burlington: University of Vermont, Department of Psychiatry.

ALDER, S. (1979). Megavitamin treatment for behaviorally disturbed and learning disabled children. *Journal of Learning Disabilities, 12,* 678–681.

AMERICAN PSYCHIATRIC ASSOCIATION. (1968). *Diagnostic and statistical manual of mental disorders* (2nd ed.). Washington, DC: Author.

AMERICAN PSYCHIATRIC ASSOCIATION. (1980). *Diagnostic and statistical manual of mental disorders* (3rd ed.). Washington, DC: Author.

AMERICAN PSYCHIATRIC ASSOCIATION. (1987). *Diagnostic and statistical manual of mental disorders* (3rd ed., rev.). Washington, DC: Author.

AMERICAN PSYCHIATRIC ASSOCIATION. (1993). *DSM-IV draft criteria.* Washington, DC: Author.

AMERICAN PSYCHIATRIC ASSOCIATION. (1994). *Diagnostic and statistical manual of mental disorders* (4th ed.). Washington, DC: Author.

ARONOFSKY, D. (1992). ADD: A brief summary of school district legal obligations and children's education rights. In M. Fowler (Ed.), *CH.A.D.D. educators manual* (pp. 57–60). Plantation, FL: CH.A.D.D.

BARKLEY, R. A. (1987). *Defiant children: A clinician's manual for parent training.* New York: Guilford Press.

BARKLEY, R. A. (1990). *Attention deficit hyperactivity disorder: A handbook for diagnosis and treatment.* New York: Guilford Press.

BARKLEY, R. A. (1993). A new theory of ADHD. *The ADHD Report, 1*(5), 1–4.

BARKLEY, R. A., DuPAUL, G., & McMURRAY, M. (1991). Attention deficit disorder with and without hyperactivity: Clinical response to three dose levels of methylphenidate. *Pediatrics, 87*(4), 519–531.

BARKLEY, R. A., FISCHER, M., EDELBROOK, C. S., & SMALLISH, L. (1990). The adolescent outcome of hyperactive children diagnosed by research criteria: An 8-year prospective follow-up study.

Journal of the American Academy of Child and Adolescent Psychiatry,
29(4), 546–557.

BARKLEY, R. A., KARLSSON, J., STRZELECKI, E., & MURPHY, J.
(1984). Effects of age and Ritalin dosage on the mother-child interactions of hyperactive children. *Journal of Consulting and Clinical
Psychology, 52,* 750–753.

BARKLEY, R. A., & MURPHY, K. (1993). Guidelines for written clinical
reports concerning ADHD adults. *ADHD Report, 1*(5), 8–9.

BERLINER, D. C. (1984). The half-full glass: A review of research on
teaching. In P. L. Hosford (Ed.), *Using what we know about teaching*
(pp. 51–77). Alexandria, VA: Association for Supervision and Curriculum Development.

BICKEL, W., & BICKEL, D. (1986). Effective schools, classrooms, and
instruction: Implications for special education. *Exceptional Children,
20*(6), 489–519.

BLONDIS, T. A., CLIPPARD, D. S., SCROGGS, D. J., & PETERSON,
L. (1991). Multidisciplinary habilitative prescriptions for the attentional deficit hyperactivity disorder child. In P. Accardo, T. Blondis,
& B. Whitman (Eds.), *Attention deficit disorders and hyperactivity in
children* (pp. 223–247). New York: Marcel Dekker.

BOWER, B. (1988). Lighting language lanes in the brain. *Science News,
133*(18), 28.

BRADLEY, C. (1937). The behavior of children receiving benzedrine.
American Journal of Psychiatry, 94, 577–585.

BRENNER, A. (1982). The effects of megadoses of selected B-complex
vitamins on children with hyperkinesis: Controlled studies with
long-term follow-up. *Journal of Learning Disabilities, 15,* 258–264.

BROOKS, R. B. (1992). Fostering self-esteem in children with ADD:
The search for islands of competence. *CH.A.D.D.er, 6*(3), 14–16.

BROPHY, J. E., & GOOD, T. L. (1986). Teacher behavior and student
achievement. In M. C. Wittrock (Ed.), *Handbook of research on teaching*
(3rd ed., pp. 328–375). New York: Macmillan.

BRONOWSKI, J. (1967). Human and animal languages. *To honor Roman
Jakobson* (Vol. 1). The Hague, Netherlands: Mouton.

BRONOWSKI, J. (1977). Human and animal languages. *A sense of the
future* (pp. 103–131). Cambridge, MA: MIT Press.

BUSCH, B. (1993). Attention deficits: Current concepts, controversies,
management, and approaches to classroom instruction. *Annals of
Dyslexia, 43,* 5–25.

CAMP, B. W. (1980). Two psychoeducational treatment programs for
young aggressive boys. In C. Whalen & B. Henker (Eds.), *Hyperactive children: The social ecology of identification and treatment* (pp. 191–
200). New York: Academic Press.

CANTWELL, D. (1972). Psychiatric illness in the families of hyperactive
children. *Archives of General Psychiatry, 27,* 414–417.

CANTWELL, D. (1990). Pediatric psychopharmacology: Part II. *Directions in Psychiatry, 32,* 2–7.

CANTWELL, D., & BAKER, L. (1991). Association between attention
deficit hyperactivity disorder and learning disorders. *Journal of Learning Disabilities, 24,* 88–95.

CH.A.D.D. (1988). *Attention deficit disorders: A guide for teachers.* Plantation, FL: Author.

CH.A.D.D. (1992). Testimony to the Senate and U.S. House of Representatives Subcommittee on Appropriations. *CH.A.D.D.ER, 6*(2), 24.

CH.A.D.D. (1993a). CH.A.D.D. position on inclusion. *CH.A.D.D.er Box, 6*(4), 11.

CH.A.D.D. (1993b). *Medical management of attention deficit disorder* (CH.A.D.D. Facts 3). Plantation, FL: Author.

CH.A.D.D. (1993c). *Parenting a child with attention deficit disorder* (CH.A.D.D. Facts 2). Plantation, FL: Author.

CH.A.D.D. (1993d). *A teacher's guide: Attention deficit hyperactivity disorder in children.* Plantation, FL: ADD Warehouse.

CH.A.D.D. NATIONAL BOARD OF DIRECTORS. (1993). Attention deficit disorder: Not just a children's problem anymore. *CH.A.D.D.er Box, 7*(2), 19–21.

CHERKES-JUKOWSKI, M., STOLZENBERG, J., & SEGAL, L. (1991). Prompted cognitive testing as a diagnostic compensation for attentional deficits: The Raven Standard Progressive Matrices and attention deficit disorder. *Learning Disabilities: A Multidisciplinary Journal, 2*(1), 1–7.

CLEMENTS, S. (1966). *Task Force One: Minimal brain dysfunction in children* (NINDS Monograph No. 3). Rockville, MD: Department of Health, Education, and Welfare.

CLEMENTS, S., & PETERS, J. (1962). *Minimal brain dysfunction in children: Terminology and justification* (Public Health Service Publication No. 1415). Washington, DC: Department of Health, Education, and Welfare.

COHEN, M. D. (1993, December). The advocate: Planning for IEP meetings: A pound of anticipation is worth two pounds of cure. *CH.A.D.D.er,* pp. 6–7.

CONNER, D. (1994). Current status of clonidine in ADHD. *The ADHD Report, 2*(1), 5–6.

CONNERS, C. K. (1969). A teacher rating scale for use in drug studies with children. *American Journal of psychiatry, 125,* 884–888.

CONNERS, C. K. (1973). Rating scales for use in drug studies with children. *Psychopharmacology Bulletin* [Special issue: Pharmacology with children], *9,* 24–84.

CONNERS, C. K. (1989). *Conners Teachers Rating Scale-28 (CTRS-28).* Tonawanda, NY: Multi-Health Systems.

COUNCIL FOR EXCEPTIONAL CHILDREN. (1992). *Children with ADD: A shared responsibility.* Reston, VA: Author.

COUNCIL OF ADMINISTRATORS OF SPECIAL EDUCATION. (1992). *Student access: A resource guide for educators.* Albuquerque, NM: Author.

COWLEY, G., & RAMO, J. (1993, July 26). The not-young and the restless. *Newsweek,* pp. 48–49.

CROOK, W. (1983). Let's look at what they eat. *Academic Therapy, 18,* 629–631.

CUNNINGHAM, C. E., SIEGEL, L. S., & OFFORD, D. R. (1985). A developmental dose-response analysis of the effects of methylphenidate on the peer interactions of attention deficit disordered boys. *Journal of Child Psychology and Psychiatry, 26,* 955–971.

Doctors not needed to diagnose attention deficit disorder, Ed says. (1992). *Education of the Handicapped, 18*(11), 5.

DONNELLY, M., & RAPOPORT, J. L. (1985). Attention deficit disorders. In J. M. Wiener (Ed.), *Diagnosis and psychopharmacology of childhood and adolescent disorders* (pp. 179–197). New York: Wiley.

DOUGLAS, V. I., BARR, R. G., O'NEILL, M. E., & BRITTON, B. G. (1986). Short-term effects of methylphenidate on the cognitive, learning, and academic performance of children with attention deficit disorder. *Journal of Child Psychology and Psychiatry, 27,* 191–212.

DUFFY, F. (1988). Neurophysiological studies in dyslexia. In D. Plum (Ed.), *Language, communication, and the brain.* New York: Raven Press.

DUFFY, F., & McANULTY, G. (1985). Brain electrical activity mapping (BEAM): The search for a physiological signature in dyslexia. In F. Duffy & N. Geschwind (Eds.), *Dyslexia: A neuroscientific approach to clinical evaluation* (pp. 105–122). Boston: Little, Brown.

DuPAUL, G. J. (1991). Parent and teacher ratings of ADHD symptoms: Psychometric properties in a community-based sample. *Journal of Clinical Child Psychology, 20*(3), 245–253.

DuPAUL, G. J., BARKLEY, R. A., & McMURRAY, M. B. (1991). Therapeutic effects of medication on ADHD: Implications for school psychologists. *School Psychology Review, 20,* 203–219.

DuPAUL, G., GUEVREMONT, D., & BARKLEY, R. (1992). Behavior treatment of attention-deficit hyperactivity disorder in the classroom: The use of the Attention Training System. *Behavior Modification, 16,* 204–225.

DuPAUL, G., RAPPORT, M., & PERRIELLO, L. (1991). Teacher ratings of academic skills: The developing of the Academic Performance Rating Scale. *School Psychology Review, 29*(2), 284–300.

EDELBROOK, C. S., & ACHENBACH, T. M. (1984). The teacher version of the Child Behavior Profile: I. Boys aged 6–11. *Journal of Consulting and Clinical Psychology, 52,* 207–217.

EISERMAN, W. D., & OSGUTHORPE, R. T. (1985, April). *Increasing social acceptance: Mentally retarded students tutoring regular class peers.* Paper presented at the annual meeting of the Council for Exceptional Children, Anaheim, CA.

ELLIS, E., DESHLER, D., LENZ, B., CLARK, F., & SCHUMACHER, J. (1991). An instructional model for teaching learning strategies. *Focus on Exceptional Children, 23*(6), 1–16.

EPSTEIN, M., SHAYWITZ, S., SHAYWITZ, B., & WOOLSTON, J. (1991). The boundaries of attention deficit disorder. *Journal of Learning Disabilities, 24,* 78–86.

FEINGOLD, B. (1975). *Why your child is hyperactive.* New York: Random House.

FIORE, T. A., BECKER, E. A., & NERO, R. C. (1993). Educational interventions for students with attention deficit disorder. *Exceptional Children, 60*(2), 163–173.

FOREHAND, R. L., & McMAHON, R. J. (1981). *Helping the noncompliant child: A clinician's guide to parent training.* New York: Guilford Press.

FOWLER, M. (1992). *CH.A.D.D. educators manual: An in-depth look at attention deficit disorders from an educational perspective.* Plantation, FL: CH.A.D.D.

FOWLER, S. A., DOUGHERTY, B. S., KIRBY, K., & KOHLER, F. W. (1986). Role reversals: An analysis of therapeutic effects with disruptive boys during their appointments as peer monitors. *Journal of Applied Behavior Analysis, 19,* 437–444.

FRICK, P., & LAHEY, E. (1991). Nature and characteristics of attention-deficit hyperactivity disorder. *School Psychology Review, 20*(2), 163–173.

FRIEDMAN, R. J., & DOYAL, G. T. (1992). *Management of children and adolescents with attention deficit-hyperactivity disorder.* Austin, TX: Pro-Ed.

FRIEND, M., & COOK, L. (1992). *Interactions: Collaborative skills for school professionals.* White Plains, NY: Longman.

FUCHS, D., & FUCHS, L. (1994). Inclusive schools of movement and the radicalization of special education reform. *Exceptional Children, 60*(4), 294–309.

GADDES, W. H. (1985). *Learning disabilities and brain function: A neuropsychological approach.* New York: Springer-Verlag.

GALLAGHER, J. (1993). What is special about special education integrated with regular education? In K. Waldron, A. Riester, & J. Moore (Eds.), *Special education: The challenge of the future* (p. 210). San Francisco: EMText.

GOLDSTEIN, K. (1936). Modification of behavior subsequent to cerebral lesion. *Psychiatric Quarterly, 10,* 539–610.

GOLDSTEIN, S. (1993). ADHD in the adolescent years. *CH.A.D.D.er Box, 6*(4), 1, 7–9.

GOLDSTEIN, S., & GOLDSTEIN, M. (1990). *Managing attention disorders in children.* New York: Wiley.

GOLDSTEIN, S., & GOLDSTEIN, M. (1993). *Managing attention disorders in children: A guide for practitioners.* New York: Wiley.

GOLDSTEIN, S., & INGERSOLL, B. (1992). Controversial treatments for children with attention deficit disorder. *CH.A.D.D.er, 6*(2), 19–23.

GOODMAN, R., & STEVENSON, J. (1989). A twin study of hyperactivity: II. The aetiological role of genes, family relationships, and perinatal adversity. *Journal of Child Psychology and Psychiatry, 30,* 691–709.

GORDON, M., THOMASON, D., COOPER, S., & IVERS, C. (1991). Nonmedical treatment of ADHD/hyperactivity: The Attention Training System. *Journal of School Psychology, 29,* 151–159.

GOYETTE, C. H., CONNERS, C. K., & ULRICH, R. F. (1978). Normative data on revised Conners Parent and Teacher Rating Scales. *Journal of Abnormal Child Psychology, 6,* 211–236.

GRANT, D., & BERG, E. (1948). *The Wisconsin Card Sort Test.* Odessa, FL: Psychological Assessment Resources.

GREENBERG, G. S., & HORN, W. F. (1991). *Attention deficit hyperactivity disorder.* Champaign, IL: Research Press.

GUALTIERI, C. T. (1988). Psychopharmacology and the neurobehavioral sequence of traumatic brain injury. *Brain Injury, 2,* 101–129.

HAAKE, C. A. (1991). Behavioral markers and intervention strategies for regular and special education teachers. In P. Accardo, T. Blondis, & B. Whitman (Eds.), *Attentional deficit disorders and hyperactivity in children* (pp. 251–285). New York: Marcel Dekker.

HAENLEIN, M., & CAUL, W. F. (1987). Attention deficit disorder with hyperactivity: A specific hypothesis of reward dysfunction. *Journal of the American Academy of Child and Adolescent Psychiatry, 26,* 356–362.

HAUSER, P., ZAMETKIN, A. J., MARTINEZ, P., VITRELLO, B., MATOCHIK, J. A., Mixsen, A. J., & Weintraub, B. D. (1993). Attention deficit-hyperactivity disorder in people with generalized resistance to thyroid hormone. *New England Journal of Medicine, 328*(14), 997–1001.

HOCUTT, A., McKINNEY, J., & MONTAGUE, M. (1993). Issues in the education of students with attention deficit disorder: Introduction to special issues. *Exceptional Children, 60*(2), 103–107.

HORN, W. F. (1993, December). Report from the National Executive Director. *CH.A.D.D.er,* pp. 3, 15.

HUBBARD, K. (1993, December). A Wisconsin school district responds to ADD. *CH.A.D.D.er,* pp. 8–9.

HUNSUCKER, G. (1993). *Attention deficit disorder.* Fort Worth, TX: Forrest Publishing.

HUNT, R. D., MINDERA, R. B., & COHEN, D. J. (1985). Clonidine benefits children with attention deficit disorder and hyperactivity: Report of a double-blind placebo-crossover therapeutic trial. *Journal of the American Academy of Child and Adolescent Psychiatry, 6,* 47–59.

HYND, G. W. (1992). Neurological aspects of dyslexia: Comments on the balance model. *Journal of Learning Disabilities, 25,* 110–113.

HYND, G. W., HERN, L., VOELLER, K., & MARSHALL, R. (1991). Neurobiological basis of attention deficit hyperactivity disorder (ADHD). *School Psychology, 20*(2), 174–186.

HYND, G., & SEMRUD-CLICKMAN, M. (1989). Dyslexia and brain morphology. *Psychological Bulletin, 106,* 447–882.

IDOL, L. (1989). The resource/consulting teacher: An integrated model of service delivery. *Remedial and Special Education, 10*(6), 38–48.

IDOL, L., PAOLUCCI-WHITCOMB, P., & NEVIN, A. (1986). *Collaborative consultation.* Austin, TX: Pro-Ed.

IGNORING IEP COSTS TEACHER $15,000! (1994, February). *CH.A.D.D.er Box,* pp. 1, 7.

INGERSOLL, B. D. (1990). The ADHD child in the family. *CH.A.D.D.er, 4,* 8–9.

JASTAK, S., & WILKERSON, G. (1993). *Wide Range Achievement Test-III (WRAT-III).* Wilmington, DE: Jastak Assessment Systems.

JEFFERSON COUNTY PUBLIC SCHOOLS. (1993). ADHD assessment packet. Photocopied materials. (Available from Federal Resource Center for Special Education, University of Kentucky, 314 Mineral Industries Bldg., Lexington, KY 40506.

JOHNSON, D. W., & JOHNSON, R. (1983). The socialization and achievement crisis: Are cooperative learning experiences the solution? In L. Bickman (Ed.), *Applied social psychology annual 4.* Beverly Hills, CA: Sage.

JOHNSON, D. W., & JOHNSON, R. T. (1984). Building acceptance of differences between handicapped and nonhandicapped students: The effects of cooperative and individualistic problems. *Journal of Social Psychology, 122,* 257–267.

JOHNSON, D. W., & JOHNSON, R. (1985). Motivational processes in cooperative, competitive, and individualistic learning situations. In C. Ames & R. Ames (Eds.), *Attitudes and attitude changes in special education: Its theory and practice.* New York: Academic Press.

JOHNSON, D. W., & JOHNSON, R. T. (1986). Mainstreaming and cooperative learning strategies. *Exceptional Children, 52,* 553–561.

JOHNSON, D. W., JOHNSON, R., & MARUYAMA, G. (1983). Interdependence and interpersonal attraction among heterogeneous and homogeneous individuals: A theoretical formulation and meta-analysis of the research. *Review of Educational Research, 53,* 5–54.

JOHNSTON, C., PELHAM, W. E., HOZA, J., & STURGES, J. (1988). Psychostimulant rebound in attention deficit disordered boys. *Journal of the American Academy of Child and Adolescent Psychiatry, 27,* 806–810.

JONES, C. (1993). The young and the restless: Helping the preschool child with attention deficit hyperactivity disorder. *CH.A.D.D.er, 7*(2), 13–18.

KAGAN, J. (1966). Reflection-impulsivity: The generality and dynamics of conceptual tempo. *Journal of Abnormal Psychology, 71,* 17–24.

KAUFMAN, A. S., & KAUFMAN, N. L. (1983). *Kaufman Assessment Battery for Children.* Circle Pines, MN: American Guidance Service.

KAUFFMAN, J. (1993). How we might achieve the radical reform of special education. *Exceptional Children, 60,* 6–16.

KAUFFMAN, J., & TRENT, S. (1991). Issues in services delivery for students with learning disabilities. In B. Wong (Ed.), *Learning about learning disabilities* (pp. 466–485). San Diego: Academic Press.

KELLEY, M. L., & CARPER, L. B. (1988). Home-based reinforcement procedures. In J. C. Witt, S. N. Elliot, & F. M. Gresham (Eds.), *Handbook of behavior therapy in education* (pp. 419–438). New York: Plenum.

KENDALL, P., & BRASWELL, L. (1984). *Cognitive-behavioral therapy for impulsive children.* New York: Guilford Press.

KIRK, S., & CHALFONT, J. (1984). *Development and academic learning disabilities.* Denver: Love Publishing.

KLAUSS, M. H., & KENNEL, J. H. (1981). *Parent-infant bonding.* St. Louis: C. V. Mosby.

KLORMAN, R., BRUMAGHIM, J. T., SALZMAN, L. F., STRAUSS, J., BORGSTED, A. D., McBRIDE, M. C., & LOEB, S. (1988). Effects of methylphenidate on attention-deficit hyperactivity disorder with and without aggressive/noncompliant features. *Journal of Abnormal Psychology, 97,* 413–422.

KLORMAN, R., COON, H. W., & BORGSTEDT, A.D. (1987). Effects of methylphenidate on adolescents with a childhood history of attention deficit disorder: Clinical findings. *Journal of the American Academy of Child and Adolescent Psychiatry, 26,* 363–367.

KOTULAK, R. (1988, May 8). Mapping the learning and memory pathways of the brain. *Chicago Tribune,* Sec. 5, p. 6.

KOUTNIK, G. (1992). Identifying attention deficits: Hawthorne's Attention Deficit Disorders Evaluation Scale (ADDES). *The School Psychologist, 4,* 16–17.

KÜBLER-ROSS, E. (1969). *On death and dying.* New York: Macmillan.

LAHEY, B., & CARLSON, C. (1991). Validity of the diagnostic category of attention deficit disorder without hyperactivity: A review of the literature. *Journal of Learning Disabilities, 24,* 110–120.

LANDAW, S., & MOORE, L. (1991). Social skills deficits in children with attention deficit hyperactivity disorder. *School Psychology Review, 20*(2), 235–251.

LAUFER, M., & DENHOFF, E. (1957). Hyperkinetic behavior syndrome in children. *Journal of Pediatrics, 50,* 463–474.

LEARNING DISABILITIES ASSOCIATION OF AMERICA. (1993). Position paper on full inclusion of students with learning disabilities in the regular education classroom. *Journal of Learning Disabilities, 26*(9), 594.

LERNER, J. W. (1993). *Learning disabilities: Theories, diagnosis, and teaching strategies.* Boston: Houghton Mifflin.

LERNER, J. W., DAWSON, D. K., & HORVATH, L. J. (1980). *Cases in learning and behavior problems: A guide to individualized education programs.* Boston: Houghton Mifflin.

LERNER, J. W., & LERNER, S. R. (1991). Attention deficit disorder: Issues and questions. *Focus on Exceptional Children, 24*(3), 1–17.

LERNER, J. W., & LERNER, S. R. (1993). Attention deficit disorder: Issues and questions. In E. Meyen, G. Vergason, & R. Whelan (Eds.), *Challenges facing special education* (pp. 241–266). Denver: Love.

LERNER, J. W., & LOWENTHAL, B. (1993). Attention deficit disorders: New responsibilities for the special educator. *Learning Disabilities: A Multidisciplinary Journal, 4*(1), 1–7.

LIND, S. (1993). Are we mislabeling overexcitable children? *Understanding Our Gifted, 5* (Issue 5A), 1, 8–10.

LLOYD, J. W., CROWLEY, P., KOHLER, F. W., & STRAIN, P. (1988). Redefining the applied research agenda: Cooperative learning, prereferral, teacher consultation, and peer-mediated interventions. *Journal of Learning Disabilities, 21*(1), 43–52.

LONEY, J., & MILICH, R. (1982). Hyperactivity, inattention, and aggression in clinical practice. In D. Routh & M. Wolraich (Eds.), *Advances in developmental and behavioral pediatrics* (Vol. 3, pp. 113–147). Greenwich, CT: JAI Press.

LOU, H., HENRIKSEN, L., & BRUHN, P. (1984). Focal cerebral hyperfusion in children with dysphasia and/or attention deficit disorder. *Archives of Neurology, 41,* 825–829.

LOU, H., HENRIKSEN, L., BRUHN, P., BORNER, H., & NIELSON, J. (1989). Striatal dysfunction in attention deficit and hyperkinetic disorder. *Archives of Neurology, 46,* 48–52.

MADSON, C. (1990, January-February). ADD/ADHD recognized as handicapping conditions under Section 504, Rehabilitation Act of 1973. *HAAD Enough,* pp. 10–11.

MANDELKORN, T. D. (1993). Thoughts on the medical treatment of ADHD. *CH.A.D.D.er Box, 6*(3), 1, 7–9.

MANGANELLO, R. (1994). Time management instruction for students with learning disabilities. *Teaching Exceptional Children, 26*(2), 61.

MANNUZZA, S., KLEIN, R., & BESSLER, A. (1993). Adult outcomes of hyperactive boys: Educational achievement, occupational rank, and psychiatric status. *Archives of General Psychiatry, 50*(7), 566–577.

MARION, M. (1991). *Guidance of young children.* Columbus, OH: Charles E. Merrill.

MATHER, N., & JAFFE, L. E. (1992). *Woodcock-Johnson Psycho-Educational Battery–Revised: Recommendations and reports.* Brandon, VT: Clinical Psychology.

McBURNETT, K., LAHEY, B., & PFIFFNER, L. (1993). Diagnosis of attention deficit disorders in DSM-IV: Scientific basis and implications for education. *Exceptional Children, 60*(2), 108–177.

McCARNEY, S. B. (1989). *Attention deficit disorders intervention manual.* Columbia, MO: Hawthorne.

McCARNEY, S. B., & BAUER, A. M. (1990). *The parent's guide to attention deficit disorders.* Columbia, MO: Hawthorne.

McKINNEY, J., MONTAGUE, M., & HOCUTT, A. (1993). Educational assessment of students with attention deficit disorder. *Exceptional Children, 60,* 125–131.

MEISGEIER, C. (no date). *Synergistic education.* Houston, TX: University of Houston.

MEYER, A. (1904). The anatomical facts and clinical varieties of traumatic insanity. *American Journal of Insanity, 60,* 373–431.

NEWBY, R., FISCHER, M., & ROMAN, M. (1991). Parent training for families of children with ADHD. *School Psychology Review, 20*(2), 252–265.

OFFICE OF CIVIL RIGHTS. (1994). *OCR facts: Section 504 coverage of children with ADD.* Washington, DC: Office of Civil Rights, Department of Education.

OFFICE OF CIVIL RIGHTS ISSUES CLARIFICATION ON 504 COVERAGE. (1994, March). *CH.A.D.D.er Box,* pp. 8–9.

OFFICE OF SPECIAL EDUCATION AND REHABILITATION. (1992). A clarification of state and local responsibility under federal law to address the needs of children with attention deficit disorder. *OSERS News in Print, 4*(3), 27–29.

O'LEARY, K. D., & O'LEARY, S. G. (1977). *Classroom management: The successful use of behavior modification.* New York: Pergamon Press.

ORTIZ, A. A. (1991, November). Testimony before the CEC Task Force on children with attention deficit disorders, New Orleans.

OSGUTHORPE, R. T., & SCRUGGS, T. E. (1986). Special education students as tutors: A review and analysis. *Remedial and Special Education, 7*(4), 15–25.

OSTRANDER, R., & SILVER, L. B. (1993). Psychological interventions and therapies for children and adolescents with learning disabilities. In L. B. Silver (Ed.), *Child and adolescent psychiatric clinics of North America: Vol. 2. Learning disabilities* (pp. 323–336). Philadelphia: Saunders.

PALINSCAR, H., & KLENK, I. (1991). Fostering literacy learning in supportive contexts. *Journal of Learning Disabilities, 25,* 211–225.

PARKER, C., STORM, G., PETTI, T. A., & ANTHONY, V. Q. (1991). Medical management of children with attention deficit disorders. *CH.A.D.D.er, 5*(2), 17–19.

PARKER, H. C. (1992). *The ADD hyperactivity handbook for schools.* Plantation, FL: Impact.

PATTERSON, G., & FLEISCHMAN, M. (1979). Maintenance of treatment effects: Some considerations concerning family systems and follow-up data. *Behavior Therapy, 10,* 168–185.

PATTERSON, G. R. (1982). *A social learning approach to family intervention: Vol. 3. Coercive family process.* Eugene, OR: Castalia.

PELHAM, W. E. (1989). Behavior therapy, behavioral assessment, and psychostimulant medication in the treatment of attention deficit disorders: An interactive approach. In L. M. Bloomingdale & J. M. Swanson (Eds.), *Attention deficit disorder: IV. Emerging trends in attentional and behavioral disorders of childhood* (pp. 169–202). New York: Pergamon Press.

PELHAM, W. E., BENDER, M. E., CADDELL, J. M., BOOTH, S., & MOORER, S. (1985). The dose-response effects of methylphenidate on classroom academic and social behavior in children with attention deficit disorder. *Archives of General Psychiatry, 42,* 948–952.

PELHAM, W. E., & HOZA, J. (1987). Behavioral assessment of psychostimulant effects on ADD children in a summer day treatment program. In R. Prinz (Ed.), *Advances in behavioral assessment of children and families* (Vol. 3, pp. 3–33). Greenwich, CT: JAI Press.

PELHAM, W. E., STURGES, J., HOZA, J., SCHMIDT, C., BIYISMA, J. J., MILICH, R., & MOORER, S. (1987). Sustained release and standard methylphenidate effects on cognitive and social behavior in children with attention deficit disorder. *Pediatrics, 80,* 491–501.

PELHAM, W. E., Jr., WALKER, J. L., STURGES, J., & HOZA, J. (1989). Comparative effects of methylphenidate on ADD girls and ADD boys. *Journal of the American Academy of Child and Adolescent Psychiatry, 28,* 773–776.

PFIFFNER, L., & O'LEARY, S. (1987). The efficacy of all positive behavior management as a function of prior use of negative consequences. *Journal of Applied Behavior Analysis, 20,* 265–271.

PHELAN, T. W. (1990). *1-2-3 magic: Training your preschooler and preteen to do what you want them to do.* Plantation, FL: ADD Warehouse.

PIAGET, J. (1970). *The science of education and the psychology of the child.* New York: Grossman.

PIECHOWSKI, M. M. (1991). Emotional development and emotional giftedness. In N. Colangelo & G. Davis (Eds.), *A handbook of gifted education* (pp. 285–306). Boston: Allyn & Bacon.

PISTERMAN, S., McGRATH, P., FIRESTONE, P., GOODMAN, J., WEBSTER, L., & MALLORY, R. (1989). Outcome of parent-mediated treatment of preschoolers with attention deficit disorder with hyperactivity. *Journal of Consulting and Clinical Psychology, 57,* 628–654.

PLISZKE, S. R. (1987). Tricyclic antidepressants in the treatment of children with attention deficit disorder. *Journal of the American Academy of Child and Adolescent Psychiatry, 26,* 127–132.

POPPER, C. W. (1991). ADD look-alikes. *CH.A.D.D.er, 5*(2), 16.

PROFESSIONAL GROUP FOR ATTENTION AND RELATED DISORDERS (PGARD). (1991). *Response from PGARD to the Congressional Notice of Inquiry on ADD.* Unpublished manuscript.

QUAY, H. C., & PETERSON, D. R. (1987). *Manual for the revised Behavior Manual Checklist.* Unpublished manuscript, University of Miami, Coral Gables, FL.

RALEY, T. (1993, November). *The basics of ADD: Guidelines for parents and teachers.* Presentation at the Learning Disabilities Association of Texas Conference, Austin, TX.

RAPOPORT, J., BUCHSBAUM, M., WEINGARTNER, H., ZAHN, T., LUDLOW, C., BARTKO, J., MIKKELSON, E., LANGER, D., & BUNNEY, W. (1980). Dextroamphetamine: Cognitive and behavioral effects in normal and hyperactive boys and normal adult males. *Archives of General Psychiatry, 37,* 933–946.

RAPPORT, M. D., JONES, J. T., DUPAUL, G. J., KELLY, K., GARDNER, M. J., TUCKER, S. B., & SHEA, M. S. (1987). Attention deficit disorder and methylphenidate: Group and single-subject analyses of dose effects on attention in clinic and classroom settings. *Journal of Clinical Child Psychology, 16,* 329–338.

RAPPORT, M. D., STONER, G., DUPAUL, G. J., BIRMINGHAM, B. K., & TUCKER, S. (1985). Methylphenidate in hyperactive children: Differential effects of dose-response effects on children's impulsivity across settings. *Journal of the American Academy of Child and Adolescent Psychiatry, 27,* 60–69.

REED, M. (1991). *Extraordinary children: Ordinary lives.* Champaign, IL: Research Press.

REEVE, R. (1991). Parents' role in helping their child in school. *CH.A.D.D.er, 5*(2), 11.

REEVE, R. E. (1990). ADHD: Facts and fallacies. *Intervention in Schools and Clinic, 26*(2), 70–78.

REID, R., MAAG, J., & VASA, S. (1994). Attention deficit hyperactivity disorder as a disability category: A critique. *Exceptional Children, 60*(3), 198–214.

RESNICK, L., & KLOPFER, L. (1989). *Toward the thinking curriculum: Current cognitive research.* Alexandria, VA: Association for Supervision and Curriculum Development.

RICCIO, C., HYND, G., COHEN, M., & GONZALEZ, J. (1993). Neurological basis of attention deficit hyperactivity disorder. *Exceptional Children, 60*(2), 118–124.

RICHARD, M. (1993, December). Ask CH.A.D.D. *CH.A.D.D.er,* p. 10.

RIEF, S. F. (1993). *How to reach and teach ADD/ADHD children.* West Nyack, NY: Center for Applied Research in Education.

ROBBINS, P., & WOLFE, P. (1987). Reflections on a Hunter-based staff development project. *Educational Leadership, 44,* 50–61.

ROBIN, A. L., & FOSTER, S. L. (1989). *Negotiating parent-adolescent conflict: A behavioral family systems approach.* New York: Guilford Press.

ROSEN, L., O'LEARY, S., JOYCE, S., CONWAY, G., & PFIFFNER, L. (1984). The importance of prudent and negative consequences for maintaining the appropriate behavior of hyperactive students. *Journal of Abnormal Child Psychology, 12,* 581–604.

ROSENSHINE, B., STEVENS, R. (1986). Teaching functions. In M. Wittock (Ed.), *Handbook of research on teaching* (3rd ed., pp. 376–391). New York: Macmillan.

ROTHSTEIN, L. (1993). Legal issues. In S. Vogel & P. Adelman (Eds.), *Success for college students with learning disabilities* (pp. 21–36). New York: Springer-Verlag.

SAFER, O. J. (1988). A survey of medication treatment for hyperactive/inattentive students. *Journal of the American Medical Association, 260,* 2256–2258.

SCHAUGHENCY, E., & ROTHLIND, J. (1991). Assessment and classification of attention-deficit hyperactivity disorders. *School Psychology Review, 20,* 187–202.

SCHILLER, E., & HAUSER, J. (1992). OSERS' initiative for meeting the needs of children with attention deficit disorders. *OSERS News in Print, 4*(3), 30–31.

SCHMIDT, T. (1992). Isn't ADHD wonderful!! *CH.A.D.D.er Box, 5,* 3.

SCRUGGS, T., & MASTROPIERI, M. (1991). *Teaching students to remember: Strategies for learning mnemonically.* Cambridge, MA: Brookline Books.

SCRUGGS, T. E., & OSGUTHORPE, R. T. (1986). Tutoring interventions within special education settings: A comparison of cross-age and peer tutoring. *Psychology in the Schools, 23,* 187–193.

SHAFFER, D., FISHER, P., PIACENTINI, J., SCHWAB-STONE, M., & WICKS, J. (1992). *Diagnostic interview schedule for children* (Version 2, 3). New York: Columbia University Press.

SHARP, K. B. (1993). *Comparing the technical aspect of attention deficit disorders rating scales.* Columbia, MO: Educational Services.

SHAYWITZ, B. (1987). Hyperactivity/attention deficit disorder. *Learning disabilities: A report to the U.S. Congress.* Washington, DC: Interagency Committee on Learning Disabilities.

SHAYWITZ, S., & SHAYWITZ, B. (1988). Attention deficit disorder: Current perspectives. In J. Kavanagh & J. Truss (Eds.), *Learning disabilities: Proceedings of the national conference* (pp. 369–567). Parkton, MD: York Press.

SHAYWITZ, S., & SHAYWITZ, B. (1991). Introduction to the special series on attention deficit disorder. *Journal of Learning Disabilities, 24,* 68–71.

SHORES, R., GUNTER, P., DENNY, K., & JACK, S. (1993). Classroom influences on aggressive and disruptive behaviors of students with emotional and behavioral disorders. *Focus on Exceptional Children, 26*(2), 1–12.

SILVER, A., & HAGIN, R. (1990). *Disorders of learning in childhood.* New York: Wiley.

SILVER, L. (1990). Attention-deficit hyperactivity disorder: Is it a learning disability or a related disorder? *Journal of Learning Disabilities, 23,* 394–397.

SILVER, L. B. (1989). Psychological and family problems associated with learning disabilities: Assessment and intervention. *Journal of the American Academy of Child and Adolescent Psychiatry, 38,* 319–325.

SILVER, L. B. (1992). *The misunderstood child: A guide for parents of children with learning disabilities.* Blue Ridge Summit, PA: Tab Books.

SILVER, L. B. (1993a). The controversial therapies for treating learning disabilities. In L. B. Silver (Ed.), *Child and adolescent psychiatric clinics of North America: Vol 2. Learning disabilities* (pp. 339–350). Philadelphia: Saunders.

SILVER, L. B. (1993b). *Dr. Larry Silver's advice to parents on attention-deficit hyperactivity disorder.* Washington, DC: American Psychiatric Press.

SLAVIN, R. E. (1983). *Cooperative learning.* New York: Longman.

SLAVIN, R. E. (1991). *Educational psychology.* Englewood Cliffs, NJ: Prentice-Hall.

SLAVIN, R. E., MADDEN, N. A., & LEAVEY, M. (1984). Effects of cooperative learning and individualized instruction on mainstreamed students. *Exceptional Children, 50,* 434–443.

SPRAGUE, R. L., & GADOW, K. D. (1976). The role of the teacher in drug treatment. *School Review, 85,* 109–140.

SPRAGUE, R. L., & SLEATOR, E. K. (1976). Drugs and dosages: Implications for learning disabilities. In R. M. Knight & D. J. Bakker (Eds.), *The neuropsychology of learning disorders* (pp. 351–366). Baltimore: University Park Press.

STANFORD, L., & HYND, G. (1994). Congruence of behavioral symptomatology in children with ADD/H, ADD/WO, and learning disabilities. *Journal of Learning Disabilities, 27*(4), 243–253.

STILL, G. F. (1902). Some abnormal psychial conditions in children. *Lancet, i,* 1008–1012, 1077–1082, 1163–1168.

STRAIN, P. S., KERR, M. M., & RAGLAND, E. U. (1981). The use of peer social initiations in the treatment of social withdrawl. In P. S. Strain (Ed.), *The utilization of classroom peers as behavior change agents* (pp. 101–128). New York: Plenum.

STRAUSS, A., & LEHTINEN, L. (1947). *Psychopathology and education of the brain-injured child.* New York: Grune & Stratton.

STROOP, J. R. (1935). Studies of interference in serial verbal reactions. *Journal of Experimental Psychology, 18,* 643–662.

SUGAI, G., & TINDALL, G. (1993). *Effective school collaboration.* Pacific Grove, CA: Brooks/Cole.

SUPREME COURT RULES PUBLIC SCHOOLS MAY HAVE TO PAY PARENTS FOR PRIVATE SCHOOL COSTS. (1993, December). *CH.A.D.D.er,* pp. 1–12.

SUTER, S., FREDRICKSON, M., & PORTUESI, L. (1983). Mediation of skin temperature biofeedback effects in children. *Biofeedback and Self-Regulation, 8,* 567–584.

SWANSON, J. M. (1985). Measures of cognitive functioning appropriate for use in pediatric psychopharmacological research studies. *Psychopharmacological Bulletin, 21,* 887–890.

SWANSON, J. M. (1989). Paired associate learning in the assessment of ADD-H children. In L. M. Bloomingdale & J. M. Swanson (Eds.), *Attention deficit disorder: V. Emerging trends in attentional and behavioral disorders of childhood* (pp. 87–124). New York: Pergamon Press.

SWANSON, J. M., & KINSBOURNE, M. (1978). Should you use stimulants to treat the hyperactive child? *Modern Medicine, 46,* 71–80.

SWANSON, M., McBURNETT, K., WIGAL, T., PFIFFNER, L., LERNER, M., WILLIAMS, L., CHRISTIAN, D., TAMM, L., WILLCUTT, E., CROWLEY, K., CLEVENGER, W., KHOUZAM, N., WOO, C., CRINELLA, F., & FISHER, T. (1993). Effect of stimulant medication on children with attention deficit disorder: A "review of reviews." *Exceptional Children, 60*(2), 154–162.

TANNOCK, R., SCHACHAR, R. J., CARR, R. P., & LOGAN, G. D. (1989). Dose-response of methylphenidate on academic performance and overt behavior in hyperactive children. *Pediatrics, 84,* 648–657.

TEETER, P. (1991). Attention-deficit hyperactivity disorder: A psychoeducational paradigm. *School Psychology Review, 20,* 266–280.

TORGESEN, J., KISTNER, J., & MORGAN, S. (1987). Component processes in working memory. In J. G. Borkowski & J. D. Day (Eds.), *Cognition in special children: Comparative approaches to retardation, learning disability, and giftedness* (pp. 49–86). Norwood, NJ: Ablex.

TRENNERY, M., CROSSON, B., DeBOE, J., & LEBER, W. (1989). *The Stroop Neuropsychological Screening Test.* Odessa, FL: Psychological Assessment Resources.

TURNBULL, H. R. (1993). *Free appropriate public education: The law and children with disabilities.* Denver: Love Publishing.

U.S. DEPARTMENT OF EDUCATION. (1991, September 16). Clarification of policy to address the needs of children with attention deficit disorders within the general and/or special education. Memorandum.

VANDERCOOK, T., YORK, J., & SULLIVAN, B. (1993, Winter). True or false? Truly collaborative relationships can exist between university and public school personnel. *OSERS News in Print*, pp. 31–37.

VOGEL, S., & ADELMAN, P. (1993). *Success for college students with learning disabilities.* NY: Springer-Verlag.

WEBB, J., & LATIMER, D. (1993). ADHD and children who are gifted. *Exceptional Children, 60*(2), 183–184.

WECHSLER, D. (1981). *Wechsler Intelligence Scale for Children–Revised (WISC-R).* San Antonio, TX: Psychological Corporation.

WECHSLER, D. (1989). *Wechsler Preschool and Primary Scale of Intelligence–Revised (WPPSI-R).* San Antonio, TX: Psychological Corporation.

WECHSLER, D. (1991). *Wechsler Intelligence Scale for Children–Third Edition (WISC-III).* San Antonio, TX: Psychology Corporation.

WEISS, G., & HECHTMAN, L. (1986). *Hyperactive children grown up.* New York: Guilford Press.

WEISS, R., STEIN, M., TROMMER, B., & REFETOFF, S. (1993). Attention-deficit hyperactivity disorder and thyroid function. *Journal of Pediatrics, 123*(4), 539–545.

WENDER, P. (1987). *The hyperactive child, adolescent, and adult.* New York: Oxford Press.

WERNER, H., & STRAUSS, A. (1941). Pathology of the figure-background relation in the child. *Journal of Abnormal and Social Psychology, 36,* 234–248.

WEST, J. F., & CANNON, G. (1988). Essential collaborative consultation competencies for regular and special education. *Journal of Learning Disabilities, 21*(1), 56–63.

WEST, J. F., & IDOL, L. (1990). Collaborative consultation in the education of mildly handicapped and at-risk students. *Remedial and Special Education, 11*(1), 22–31.

WEST, J. F., IDOL, L., & CANNON, G. (1989). *Collaboration in the schools: Communicating, interacting, and problem solving.* Austin, TX: Pro-Ed.

WHALEN, C. K., & HENKER, B. (1986). Cognitive behavior therapy for hyperactive children: What do we know? *Journal of Children in Contemporary Society, 19,* 123–141.

WHALEN, C. K., HENKER, B., & GRANGER, D. A. (1989). Ratings of medication effects in hyperactive children: Viable or vulnerable? *Behavioral Assessment, 11,* 179–199.

WHITMAN, B. Y., & SMITH, C. (1991). Living with a hyperactive child: Principles of families, family therapy, and behavior management. In P. Accardo, T. Blondis, & B. Whitman (Eds.), *Attentional deficit disorders and hyperactivity in children,* (pp. 176–221). New York: Marcel Dekker.

WINOGRAD, P., & HARE, V. (1988). Direct instruction of reading comprehension strategies: The nature of teacher explanation. In C. Weinstein, E. Goetz, & P. Alexander (Eds.), *Learning and study strategies: Issues in assessment, instruction and evaluation* (pp. 121–140). San Diego: Academic Press.

WOLF, D. P. (1989). Portfolio assessment: Sampling student work. *Educational Leadership, 46*(7), 35–39.

WOLRAICH, M., LINDGREN, S., STUMBO, P., STEGINK, L., APPLEBAUM, M., & KIRITSKY, M. (1994). Effects of diets high in sucrose or aspartame on the behavior and cognitive performance of children. *New England Journal of Medicine, 330*(5), 301–306.

WONG, B. (1991). The relevance of metacognition to learning disabilities. In B. Wong (Ed.), *Learning about learning disabilities* (pp. 232–261). San Diego: Academic Press.

WONG, B. (1992). On cognitive process-based instruction: An introduction. *Journal of Learning Disabilities, 25,* 150–155.

WOODCOCK, R., & JOHNSON, M. (1989). *Woodcock-Johnson Achievement Tests–Revised.* Chicago: Riverside.

ZAMETKIN, A. J. (1991). The neurobiology of attention-deficit hyperactivity disorder. *CH.A.D.D.er, 5*(1), 10–11.

ZAMETKIN, A. J., NORDAHL, T. E., GROSS, M., KING, A. C., SEMPLE, W. E., RUMSEY, J., HAMBURGER, S., & COHEN, R. M. (1990, November 15). Cerebral glucose metabolism of adults with hyperactivity of childhood onset. *New England Journal of Medicine, 323,* 1361–1364.

ZAMETKIN, A. J., & RAPOPORT, J. L. (1986). The pathophysiology of attention deficit disorder with hyperactivity: A review. In B. Lahey & A. Kazdin (Eds.), *Advances in clinical child psychology* (Vol. 9, pp. 177–216). New York: Plenum.

ZAMETKIN, A., RAPOPORT, J. L., MURPHY, D. L., LINNOILA, M., & ISMOND, D. (1985). Treatment of hyperactive children with monoamine oxidase inhibitors: Clinical efficacy. *Archives of General Psychiatry, 42,* 962–966.

ZENTALL, S. S. (1985). Stimulus-control factors in search performance of hyperactive children. *Journal of Learning Disabilities, 18,* 480–485.

ZENTALL, S. S. (1989). Attentional cueing in spelling tasks for hyperactive and comparison regular classroom children. *Journal of Special Education, 23,* 83–93.

ZENTALL, S. S. (1991a, September). *School and family factors that improve outcomes for ADHD youth.* Paper presented at the Third Annual Children with Attention Disorders Conference, Washington, DC.

ZENTALL, S. S. (1991b, November). Testimony to CEC Task Force on Children with Attention Deficit Disorder, New Orleans.

ZENTALL, S. S. (1992). Outcomes of ADD: Academic and social performance and their related school and home treatments. *Proceedings of the CH.A.D.D. Fourth Annual Convention,* 17–27.

ZENTALL, S. S. (1993). Research on the educational implications of attention deficit hyperactivity disorder. *Exceptional Children, 60*(2), 143–153.

ZENTALL, S. S., & DWYER, A. M. (1989). Color effects on the impulsivity and activity of hyperactive children. *Journal of School Psychology, 27,* 165–173.

ZENTALL, S. S., FALKINBERG, S. D., & SMITH, L. B. (1985). Effects of color stimulation and information on the copying performance of attention-problem adolescents. *Journal of Abnormal Child Psychology, 13,* 501–511.

PHOTO CREDITS

TO THE OWNER OF THIS BOOK:

We hope that you have found *Attention Deficit Disorders: Assessment and Teaching* useful. So that this book can be improved in a future edition, would you take the time to complete this sheet and return it? Thank you.

School and address: ——————————————————————————

Department: ————————————————————————————

Instructor's name: ——————————————————————————

1. What I like most about this book is: ————————————————

——————————————————————————————————

——————————————————————————————————

2. What I like least about this book is: ————————————————

——————————————————————————————————

——————————————————————————————————

3. My general reaction to this book is: ————————————————

——————————————————————————————————

4. The name of the course in which I used this book is: ——————————

——————————————————————————————————

5. Were all of the chapters of the book assigned for you to read? ——————

    If not, which ones weren't? ———————————————————

6. In the space below, or on a separate sheet of paper, please write specific suggestions for improving this book and anything else you'd care to share about your experience in using the book.

——————————————————————————————————

——————————————————————————————————

——————————————————————————————————

——————————————————————————————————

——————————————————————————————————

Optional:

Your name: _____ Date: _____

May Brooks/Cole quote you, either in promotion for *Attention Deficit Disorders: Assessment and Teaching* or in future publishing ventures?

Yes: _____ No: _____

Sincerely,

Janet W. Lerner
Barbara Lowenthal
Sue R. Lerner

FOLD HERE

BUSINESS REPLY MAIL

FIRST CLASS   PERMIT NO. 358   PACIFIC GROVE, CA

POSTAGE WILL BE PAID BY ADDRESSEE

ATT: *Janet W. Lerner, Barbara Lowenthal, Sue R. Lerner*

Brooks/Cole Publishing Company
511 Forest Lodge Road
Pacific Grove, California 93950-9968

FOLD HERE

Brooks/Cole is dedicated to publishing quality publications for education in the special education field. If you are interested in learning more about our publications, please fill in your name and address and request our latest special education catalogue, using this prepaid mailer.

Name: _____

Street Address: _____

City, State, and Zip: _____

FOLD HERE

FOLD HERE